THE CASE FOR THE CORPORATE DEATH PENALTY

The Case for the Corporate Death Penalty

Restoring Law and Order on Wall Street

Mary Kreiner Ramirez *and* Steven A. Ramirez

NEW YORK UNIVERSITY PRESS
New York

NEW YORK UNIVERSITY PRESS
New York
www.nyupress.org

References to Internet websites (URLs) were accurate at the time of writing. Neither the author nor New York University Press is responsible for URLs that may have expired or changed since the manuscript was prepared.

ISBN: 978-1-4798-8157-4

For Library of Congress Cataloging-in-Publication data, please contact the Library of Congress.

New York University Press books are printed on acid-free paper, and their binding materials are chosen for strength and durability. We strive to use environmentally responsible suppliers and materials to the greatest extent possible in publishing our books.

Manufactured in the United States of America

10 9 8 7 6 5 4 3 2 1

Also available as an ebook

For our parents, who taught us.

For our family, who supports us.

And, for Ferdinand Pecora, the Hellhound of Wall Street, who inspires us.

CONTENTS

ACKNOWLEDGMENTS

This book benefited from comments made by participants at faculty workshops at Case Western Reserve University School of Law, Indiana Tech Law School, Florida A&M University College of Law, and Loyola University of Chicago School of Law, at its Norman Amaker Public Interest Law & Social Justice Retreat. The book also benefited from excellent legal research by Kevin Dan, Raymond James, Jessica Backus, and Jose Lebron. Nicholas Flatley, CPA, assisted with accounting issues. Two anonymous reviewers provided excellent feedback and insights. Loyola University of Chicago supported this project through summer research stipends.

In defiance of any notion of the rule of law, our government failed to prosecute any senior bankers or large banks at any of the major financial firms at the center of the financial crisis of 2007 to 2009. This book demonstrates that the US government failed to pursue criminal misconduct that justified charges against the financiers at the center of the subprime crisis, and that justified dismantling Wall Street's most powerful megabanks under current law. At the outset, however, we must highlight that this book of necessity must proceed upon an inadequate factual foundation specifically because the government failed to adequately investigate and prosecute the enormous crimes underlying the financial crisis.

Criminal prosecutions entail the most thorough and reliable government investigations because they require proof beyond a reasonable doubt and other protections under our Constitution. Most notably, the defendant must be accorded the right to counsel and the right to confront witnesses through cross-examination. The rules of evidence further ensure that only relevant and reliable evidence is admitted in a criminal trial. Thus, the American people essentially were deprived of the most accurate and reliable instrument for learning the truth behind the financial crisis of 2007 to 2009.

Congress conducted many hearings on the financial crisis, and the firms we discuss appeared at the center of that maelstrom. The Securities and Exchange Commission (SEC) and the Department of Justice (DOJ) conducted many investigations and pursued civil fines and enforcement actions against many of the key wrongdoers during the crisis. Lawmakers directed the Financial Crisis Inquiry Commission (FCIC) to investigate the causes of the crisis, and the commission produced a voluminous report that is available for free online. Victims of securities fraud can and have pursued private litigation under the federal securities laws against virtually all of the firms we highlight. Massive settlements and some degree of judicial fact-finding occurred in connection with these civil actions. The media conducted some important investigations into the wrongdoing that occurred and reported extensively on whistleblowers. These sources, however, are necessarily inferior options for learning the truth behind the financial crisis.

The best source of truth is in the context of adversarial criminal trials with all the due process protections that defendants in our nation enjoy. Cross-examination of witnesses, in particular, is rightly termed "the greatest legal engine for the discovery of truth ever devised." There are many negative consequences to the federal government's failures to enforce the law, and we discuss them in great detail. Yet, one profoundly unpleasant consequence is that the American people must settle for lesser sources to learn the truth of what precipitated the financial collapse of 2008, and whether incentives and disincentives have been adjusted in the aftermath of the crisis. Massive fraud and other crimes caused the crisis, and the government let the perpetrators get away with billions in loot while the global economy suffered trillions in losses that we all paid.

Any book that seeks to examine and critique the government's wholesale failure to pursue appropriate criminal prosecutions must by necessity rely upon sources other than criminal findings of a jury after a full-blown government investigation and public trial. Our sources are therefore suboptimal. Nevertheless, in composing this book we endeavored to rely upon the best primary sources available whenever possible. We sought the government's own findings and investigatory activity whenever possible. We utilized the most reliable news sources for reports of witness accounts and important facts as a backup to sworn testimony or factual government findings. Furthermore, because we think that our ultimate conclusion—that an unprecedented breakdown in the rule of law occurred in our nation after the greatest financial collapse in history—is something that every citizen must reflect upon, we have strived to make the basis of our conclusion as transparent as possible. Therefore, whenever possible we employed Internet-based sources that are easily accessible to as many citizens as possible.

Another important reality that every reader should explicitly understand is that we cannot and do not find any particular individual or firm guilty of criminal misconduct. Only a jury after a full criminal trial could do so. A book cannot convict a suspect, and this book should not be read or understood to accuse anyone of criminal misconduct. On the other hand, we do take the federal government to task on the much more specific issue of whether sufficient evidence exists to show that an individual or firm should stand trial for criminal charges—or, stated otherwise, should face federal indictment. Even on this more narrow point, more caution regarding our conclusions is in order.

The government by definition may access sources unavailable to us as authors. The government may subpoena documents and compel sworn testimony. Under threat of indictment, the government may obtain more information from putative defendants not available to us. Government attorneys no doubt could access whistleblowers and informants to a much greater degree than us. In every case discussed in this book the government necessarily knows more than us. The most we can say as a result of this reality is that it appears or it seems that there is sufficient or strong evidence for any particular person or firm to suffer a criminal indictment.

Nor has the government been particularly forthcoming about its efforts and findings regarding the massive mortgage-related fraud that we chronicle in this book. For example, on October 9, 2012, the Financial Fraud Enforcement Task Force held a press conference to report on the DOJ-led interagency success in combating mortgage fraud launched a year earlier in October 2011. At the press conference, Attorney General Eric Holder was eager to demonstrate the government's pursuit of justice for Main Street, making the following statements regarding criminal prosecutions pursuant to the Distressed Homeowner Initiative: "[I]t's been a model of success. Over the past 12 months, it has enabled the Justice Department and its partners to file 285 federal criminal indictments . . . against 530 defendants for allegedly victimizing more than 73,000 American homeowners—and inflicting losses in excess of $1 billion" (DOJ 2012e). The DOJ has repeatedly stressed its priority of investigating and prosecuting mortgage fraud in numerous public statements.

Shortly after the press conference the DOJ's Office of the Inspector General (OIG) requested documentation to support the statistics provided, and in November 2012 DOJ officials admitted the statistics might not be accurate. Despite repeated requests for the corrected information, the DOJ waited 10 months, until August 2013, to release more accurate figures to the public. The press release dated October 9, 2012, has been modified on the DOJ's website to present supportable statistics and the faulty numbers have been corrected, but the true numbers paint a far less robust response: 107 criminal defendants have been charged (80 percent fewer defendants that the professed claim of 530); 17,185 criminal victims were involved (a 76 percent decline from the 73,000 victims claimed in the press conference); and, most strikingly, $95 million in criminal losses were addressed (down 91 percent from the claimed $1 billion). Moreover, the DOJ never offered accurate information regarding the number of executives charged, and thus this statistic does not appear in the modified press release. The OIG audit report added that for 10 months after DOJ acknowledged to OIG the statistics were inaccurate, those "seriously flawed" figures were repeatedly disseminated in various mortgage-fraud-related DOJ press releases (DOJ 2014a). The DOJ therefore does not always accurately disclose its findings and actions, compounding all the difficulties identified above with assessing the government's response to the criminality driving the financial crisis. Finally, the DOJ does not routinely explain its decisions to decline prosecution of any individual or firm.

Any focus on any particular individual or firm, however, misses the point of this book. We do not address the criminality of any particular person or firm but rather critique the conduct of the US government and the Department of Justice based upon an apparent pattern of unjustified decisions to decline criminal prosecutions (and administrative remedies such as ordering asset sales or spin-offs of subsidiaries to shareholders) of powerful financial institutions and powerful financiers. It is the decision that our government made that zero prosecutions of any megabank or Wall Street banker would proceed since the collapse of 2008 that we argue constitutes the historic breakdown in the rule of law. This book must be read in light of the above limitations and that particular purpose.

At base, this book confronts the historic breakdown in the rule of law and addresses the underlying lack of justification for the government's failure to enforce laws now on the books, promulgated well before the crisis. Furthermore, this book proposes attainable measures to restore the rule of law in the financial sector.

Introduction

I am concerned that the size of some of these institutions becomes so large that it does become difficult for us to prosecute them when we are hit with indications . . . it will have a negative impact on the . . . economy.
—Attorney General Eric Holder, March 6, 2013

One of the biggest problems about the . . . financial crisis and the whole subprime lending fiasco is that a lot of that stuff wasn't necessarily illegal, it was just immoral or inappropriate or reckless. That's exactly why we needed to pass Dodd-Frank, to prohibit some of these practices.
—President Barack Obama, October 6, 2011

A New Criminal Immunity for a New Economic Royalty

Former Federal Reserve Chairman Ben Bernanke made a stunning admission in late 2015: more Wall Street financiers at the center of the subprime crisis belong in jail. According to Bernanke no corporation can commit a crime except through acts of real individuals, and he would have preferred "to have more investigation of individual action, since obviously everything that went wrong or was illegal was done by some individual, not by an abstract firm" (Bernanke 2015). Earlier, another senior Federal Reserve official made a similar admission. He stated that the government refrained from criminal charges against Wall Street bankers because they could have destabilized the financial system (Carter & Nasiripour 2014). Certainly, these Federal Reserve leaders hold the ultimate backstage pass to the entire financial crisis and therefore can best explain that, yes, crimes occurred at the megabanks and, no, the government would not file criminal charges.

Yet, nothing can destabilize the nation's financial system more than fraud and similar financial crimes. A policy of declining to pursue financial crimes creates positive incentives for more fraud and eliminates disincentives. Inevitably, such a policy means more fraud and more financial crises ahead, as a direct result of perverse incentives. Indeed, fraud caused the greatest financial instability in modern history in 2008 and 2009.

For example, on August 21, 2014, the US Department of Justice (DOJ) entered into a $16.65 billion settlement with Bank of America Corporation for fraud in connection with the subprime mortgage debacle. DOJ trumpeted the settlement as "the largest civil settlement with a single entity in American history." Of course, fraud also constitutes a crime, and fraud involving a bank, or the sale of securities, constitutes a federal felony. This settlement surely arose from massive fraud. As DOJ itself stated, "the bank has acknowledged that it sold billions of dollars of [residential mortgage-backed securities] without disclosing to investors key facts about the quality of the securitized loans." Furthermore, "[t]he bank has also conceded that it originated risky mortgage loans and made misrepresentations about the quality of those loans to Fannie Mae, Freddie Mac and the Federal Housing Administration." The mortgages led to billions in losses for the duped investors (DOJ 2014b). This multibillion-dollar fraud occurred because some person or persons within the bank must have intended it.

Yet, the bank faced no criminal charges, and no individual employees faced criminal fraud charges. As former Fed Chairman Bernanke explained, however, a corporation cannot commit fraud (or any act, criminal or otherwise) except through its agents—real human beings—so some person or persons actually committed the massive frauds the DOJ found. The DOJ simply declined to enforce the criminal law and settled instead for a massive civil payment of innocent shareholder wealth (the ultimate source of the funds to pay the settlement) rather than a criminal sentence for any particular Bank of America banker or Bank of America itself as a corporate entity.

The Bank of America fraud settlement hardly stands as an isolated case. In late 2013, JPMorgan paid the government $13 billion in shareholder wealth to settle very similar claims that it misled investors about the risks of defaults in mortgage-backed securities that it sold. As part of the settlement, JPMorgan admitted it made "serious misrepresentations" to the investing public about the mortgages it sold in mortgage-backed securities pools (DOJ 2013a). Citigroup paid the government $7 billion in mid-2014 for failing to disclose the true risks of the loans it was securitizing and selling to investors worldwide (DOJ 2014d). These are just the largest civil settlements to date. The SEC also settled securities fraud claims with large banks ranging from Goldman Sachs to Royal Bank of Scotland for failing to disclose the risks of pools of mortgages sold to the investing public (SEC 2010b and 2013a).

Credit rating agencies typically rate debt securities such as mortgage-backed securities for risk. The banks could not have peddled high-risk mortgages as higher quality mortgages if the rating agencies did not acquiesce to their claimed valuation. Unfortunately, the rating agencies did and compromised the reliability of their ratings in order to enhance their revenues. For example, Standard & Poor's agreed to pay $1.4 billion to resolve claims of fraud (DOJ 2015c). Yet, again, no individual at any of these firms faced criminal charges for the frauds that occurred during the years immediately prior to the financial crisis.

These fraud settlements highlight that the Great Financial Crisis of 2008—a crisis that threatened the viability of capitalism itself—finds its roots in massive financial frauds of unprecedented proportions. Every step of the mortgage pipeline from the origination of home mortgages to the packaging of those mortgages into mortgage-backed securities to the rating and sale of those securities worldwide was ultimately corrupted by fraud. Without the frauds we discuss in this book the capital flows that fed the subprime bubble would not have endured so long or grown so massive. The bubble would not have become so dangerously inflated without the capital flows induced by fraud. While the economic toll of this massive financial fraud continued to mount into the 2016 elections, it certainly now exceeds $15 trillion in lost economic output and total wealth (including lost human capital) (Atkinson et al. 2013). The crisis continues to reverberate across the world and may yet erupt again because the perverse incentives feeding the financial fraud fundamentally remain in place and the lack of criminal accountability emerging from the crisis now amplifies them.

The lack of criminal accountability for this horrific economic crisis highlights a disturbing fact. By the end of 2015, a new and unprecedented lawlessness emerged at the apex of American capitalism. Specifically, the most economically and politically powerful financiers attained a broad criminal immunity for financial crimes. Crimes committed by this new economic royalty are not deterred but instead affirmed by the government's new unspoken policy of indulgences for those most likely to shower government agents and political leaders with various forms of largesse and patronage. This previously inconceivable affirmation of criminality promises to unleash future racketeering and mischief at the center of the US economy that will directly lead to massive costs for our entire society as distorted incentives for profit through crime take hold. Indeed, a recent study concluded that the megabanks at the center of global capitalism operate in an increasingly lawless manner, leading to ever increasing fines and penalties from shareholder wealth (McLannahan 2015). Beyond the direct costs of pervasive financial crime lay massive indirect costs ranging from a general loss of confidence in American financial markets to a general loss of confidence in the rule of law (*New York Times* 2012b). Ordinary citizens will hold the law in lower esteem if it looks rigged in favor of the wealthiest in society, and they too will fall prey to incentives to skirt legal prohibitions.

Unless reversed, this recent development risks the end of American economic superiority. No economy can prosper without a sturdy rule of law applicable to all economic actors, and granting indulgences to the most powerful in no way serves economic growth and stability. On the contrary, when a lawless class holds sway over massive resources, greater distortions will result as more capital flows into more financial crime. This invites financial instability and a dysfunctional financial sector that fails to appropriately fuel economic growth. If financial crimes pay, then we should not expect our financial sector to allocate capital to those with new ideas or profitable business plans. Such legitimate capital projects will instead need to compete with the more profitable allure of financial fraud, money laundering, and other larcenous behavior (S. Ramirez 2013a). Financial fraud causes financial crises with all of their ruinous macroeconomic consequences, as the Great Financial Crisis proves.

The government fails to appreciate the losses associated with this new lawlessness. Former US Attorney General Eric Holder claimed that bringing the most powerful economic criminals to justice would harm the economy—with little supporting explanation and in defiance of common sense. President Obama claims that while much of the misconduct that occurred during and before the crisis of 2008 was reprehensible, it was not necessarily illegal (White House 2011). These claims are false and can be the product only of an effort to deceive or a grand delusion regarding the nature and costs of financial lawlessness (*New York Times* 2012c).

Fraud is always criminal. Federal law criminalized bank fraud, mail fraud, wire fraud, and securities fraud long ago. Any violation of banking, securities, and commodities regulations also defies federal criminal law. Money laundering, lying to federal agents, perjury, market manipulation, and bid rigging all constitute federal crimes. This book amply shows that all of these crimes unquestionably occurred in the run-up to the crash of 2008 and continued in its aftermath. Simply put, the misconduct was *both* morally reprehensible and criminally punishable. All of these criminal prohibitions preceded the Dodd-Frank Act by many decades.

Furthermore, allowing criminals to run our financial sector is a surefire way to destroy modern finance—not save it. Who among us wishes to entrust our savings to crooks? Foreign investors will similarly avoid business in America if its most powerful financial leaders exist above the law. Indicting any individual cannot logically threaten the viability of any financial institution. Thus, claims that those committing crimes while employed at megabanks cannot be criminally prosecuted because doing so would harm big finance and thus the general economy simply defy logic and reason. Modern finance, as capitalism generally, is built upon the trust and confidence of our citizens and investors around the world. As those who promulgated the New Deal recognized long ago, during another financial collapse, as a capitalist economy grows more sophisticated the law must grow in a way that secures trust and transparency (S. Ramirez 2003).

The essential purpose of law is to curb and channel the exercise of power as productively as possible for the benefit of society as a whole. If law permits reprehensible and costly misconduct to crash an economy without accountability for individual wrongdoers, it has failed in this essential purpose. Criminal sanctions must penalize reprehensible misconduct that imposes staggering costs upon society generally. If the Obama administration really believes that reprehensible and costly misconduct escapes the scope of criminal law, then it should have proposed new legislation imposing more criminal sanctions for a wider array of misconduct. It did nothing of the sort. The Dodd-Frank Act imposed no significant new criminal liabilities at all and stands as the primary response of our government to the Great Financial Crisis of 2008. We will show probable cause exists to criminally investigate violations of federal laws that long predate the Dodd-Frank Act.

As of this writing, the government offers only weak excuses for failing to seek criminal sanctions against even a single senior officer or director of any of the megabanks at the center of the subprime debacle. A historic pattern of fraud and recklessness at the height of American finance resulted in no criminal indictments, much less convictions. While our nation fills its jails with petty drug offenders, no banker at the megabanks at the center of the crisis has faced criminal accountability. Yet, the misconduct of these individuals inflicted costs amounting to tens of trillions of dollars in the United States alone. Only raw economic and political power can account for this gross injustice.

In fact, the injustice may be even more alarming. There is reason to conclude that the federal government failed to even investigate potential criminality to the full extent of its tools. When the DOJ suspects criminality it is empowered to open a grand jury investigation. A grand jury may issue subpoenas to obtain documents and to require individuals to testify secretly under oath. The DOJ also may conduct wiretaps or inspire cooperating witnesses to wear a wire to record conversations with suspected criminals. There is little or no evidence that these tools were used to investigate wrongdoing in connection with the financial collapse of 2008. Instead, as we demonstrate, the government ignored willing whistleblowers. Although they exposed themselves to retaliation, as all whistleblowers must, the government too often failed to make use of these witnesses to investigate potential criminality (Cohan 2015).

Although the government must observe secrecy in the conduct of a grand jury investigation, witnesses face no secrecy mandate. Consequently high-profile grand jury investigations frequently leak out to the media. Any federal grand jury investigation of any individual senior manager of a megabank would necessarily be newsworthy. Either such leaks did not occur (unlikely) or the government simply pursued few grand jury inquiries. It simply defies history to think that major grand jury inquiries could occur without some press reports of grand jury activity.

In early 2013, *Frontline* investigated the reasons for government inaction in the face of the financial crisis. *Frontline* reporters interviewed former DOJ personnel who apparently stated that "when it came to Wall Street, there were no investigations going on; there were no subpoenas, no document reviews, no wiretaps" (PBS 2013b). This too suggests that no serious grand jury investigation occurred. The lack of investigative activity highlights the spread and acceleration of lawlessness. The chair of the FCIC, Phillip Angelides, notes that the FCIC gave the DOJ a "roadmap" to widespread wrongdoing, and referred individuals to the DOJ for criminal investigation. "Stunningly" no full and fair investigation followed these criminal referrals (Angelides 2016b). Apparently our government finds it unnecessary to even investigate the possibility of criminal prosecutions in the financial sector (PBS 2013a).

A typical white-collar crime investigation seeks to reveal the most culpable actors in a given criminal scheme. Consequently, investigations typically start with interviews and testimony of lower level employees. These individuals likely will not wish to serve time to protect their supervisors. They will face incentives, therefore, to cooperate with criminal investigators. That, in turn, exposes higher-ups to criminal sanctions. Thus, criminal immunity for high-ups necessarily implies that lower level employees working within the same organization and involved in the same criminal scheme also enjoy immunity from prosecution and even investigation. The perverse incentives of immunity from prosecution thereby spread throughout the megabanks.

Thus, for example, during 2013 and 2014, the megabanks (such as JPMorgan Chase and Citigroup) agreed to pay billions to the government for the fraudulent sale of toxic mortgages. The megabanks admitted they made "serious misrepresentations" to investors regarding the quality of mortgages sold. Furthermore, the government found powerful evidence that underlings disclosed these vast frauds to the highest managerial levels of the megabanks. Yet, rather than identify and prosecute those responsible for the misrepresentations, the government simply accepted fines that essentially punished innocent shareholders instead of senior leaders at the megabanks. Again, a corporation, including the megabanks, cannot commit fraud except through human beings working at and managing the firm. The corporation exists only as a matter of its legal charter—its articles of incorporation. All of its activities—lawful or otherwise—must be conducted through humans who act as the agents of the corporation (Black 2013a). Consequently, the government in these cases, allowed the real wrongdoers to walk away from criminal responsibility. Indeed, the government seemed completely uninterested in identifying any wrongdoer who could provide evidence leading to higher-ups.

Immunity from prosecution also fuels ever more criminal behavior. In the aftermath of the crisis, the megabanks filed thousands of fraudulent affidavits resulting in massive numbers of wrongful foreclosures. Often, the banks foreclosed wrongfully based upon the false affidavits that they generated in a robotic fashion that had little regard for truth. Millions of people lost their homes. Yet no criminal sanctions addressed this wide-ranging massive criminality (Weise 2013). One commentator stated that "it's difficult to find a fraud of this size on the court system in U.S. History" (Paltrow 2012).

As could be expected, since the Great Financial Crisis of 2008 the lawlessness in our financial sector has escalated. Beginning at least as early as 2007, the largest banks in the nation and the world—the megabanks—engaged in a wide-ranging international conspiracy to rig a key interest rate in the global financial system, the London Interbank Offered Rate, known as LIBOR (DOJ 2015a). According to the DOJ, the megabanks brazenly manipulated financial trading, including global currency markets. Despite the attention on the banks in 2008 and 2009, the conspiracy did not abate (DOJ 2015a). The DOJ specifically allowed the involved banks to continue their core operations and the bankers to face no personal criminal charges or financial penalties (Viswanatha 2015; DOJ 2015a). Even blatant lawlessness did not motivate DOJ to mete out the full arsenal of its legal weaponry to combat fraud in finance, as we document. As discussed in chapter 7, the DOJ would later accept guilty pleas from five banks for foreign currency exchange market manipulation, but again the banks were allowed to continue core operations (DOJ 2015b). At this writing, no bank executive has been charged in connection with these offenses.

Further examples of revelations of financial skullduggery have emerged. Specifically, in late 2012 the government declined to prosecute HSBC in the face of revelations of money laundering for drug cartels and rogue states such as Iran. Instead, the government deferred prosecution, exacting from HSBC a large fine—ultimately borne by the bank's innocent shareholders rather than its employees and officers who engaged in the criminal acts (Barrett & Perez 2012). Similarly, the government declined to prosecute the former Democratic Senator and Governor Jon Corzine who led MF Global into bankruptcy through speculation in Eurozone bonds with customer funds. Prosecution of individuals participating in these crimes could not conceivably threaten financial stability. MF Global did in fact enter bankruptcy with little impact on the global financial system (Patterson et al. 2013). Logically, the loss of confidence in the financial system results not from criminal prosecution (which repairs confidence) but from the crime itself. Yet, no criminal proceedings ensued.

The tepid response regarding the criminality of rigging LIBOR and criminal money laundering at HSBC and the lack of any criminal response to the MF Global conversion of customer funds are particularly revealing in light of historically high contributions to political campaigns. Because it is difficult to prosecute an underling without the disclosure of criminality up the chain of command, prosecution of any lower or midlevel financier at those firms would risk the disclosure of criminality among the firm's senior managers. If evidence of crimes by higher-ups should be presented in open court, the pressure to bring criminal charges would increase dramatically. It is the senior managers, however, who hold the power to give or withhold patronage. Therefore even pursuing lower level employees risks the loss of lobbying largesse, campaign contributions, job opportunities, and speaking fees for government officials from powerful senior managers.

The new realty is this: immunity from criminal prosecutions attaches if one engages in white-collar crime such as financial fraud, looting customer cash, or money laundering, so long as one works at a megabank or a financial firm managed by individuals with powerful political connections. Indeed, the government will probably not even investigate. The government may seek fines from the firm, effectively punishing shareholders. Or the government may seek relatively light monetary payments (in the form of civil or regulatory fines) from individuals. But criminal charges involving the largest banks and the most politically connected individuals appear out of the question.

The Corporate Death Penalty and Career Death Penalty in Finance?

Former Attorney General Eric Holder himself raised the prospect that some firms can be too big to prosecute in his testimony to Congress on March 6, 2013, as quoted in the epigraph to this chapter. In fact, criminal prosecutions could serve as a first step toward an orderly breakup of the megabanks under current law. In the financial sector, regulators hold the power to order spin-offs of regulated banks and brokerage firms to current megabank shareholders and to dismiss managers who allowed criminality to fester. Only the dismissed managers of the criminally managed megabanks need to suffer under this approach. We will show that historically shareholders have actually benefited from legally ordered breakups. For now the key point is that current law gives DOJ and financial regulators the power to effectively end the Too-Big-to-Fail problem insofar as criminal megabanks are concerned.

Shareholders can end up owning shares in a smaller, more efficient bank that does not use shareholder wealth to fund fines and settlements paid to the government. Noncriminal employees can continue to work in honest financial institutions. Virtually every megabank must be qualified (either directly or through affiliates) to operate as a federally insured depository institution, a bank holding company, or a securities or commodities broker. Financial firms and individuals that commit financial crimes face disqualification from the financial services sector for such violations, and this process can open the door to the orderly breakup of megabanks.

This means that the government would have held tremendous leverage had it pursued criminal conduct against Wall Street firms and managers. In terms of risk of loss, the loss of the right to participate in the financial sector makes the prospect of proceeding to a jury trial an intolerable gamble for senior managers. This can level the playing field against the resources the megabanks can field in defense. If the size of some financial institutions creates problems with applying the rule of law to the Wall Street megabanks, this power of disqualification could have operated to fragment the financial services industry through spin-offs to shareholders with little or no harm to the economy. Furthermore, senior managers who tolerate criminality could face severe sanctions—including a permanent bar from the banking or securities business—even if they themselves did not commit crimes. Attorney General Holder failed to address this regulatory and legal reality when he told Congress some firms are too big to jail. As such, he has it precisely backward: DOJ, along with other regulators, holds the power to restructure and fragment megabanks engaging in misconduct that violates the law, and need not suspend the rule of law based upon fears of a disorderly bankruptcy.

Despite substantial deregulation beginning in 1980, the financial services industry remains a highly regulated industry under law. In particular, lawmakers long ago demanded that all financial institutions and their managers adhere to the law and provided regulators with broad powers to oversee banks, bank holding companies, and broker-dealers that violate the law or suffer criminal convictions, including the power to effectively terminate the current corporate structure of such outlaw firms—essentially a corporate death penalty for megabanks managed in a criminal manner. The regulators also may expel lawbreaking individuals from the financial sector. This can effectively transfer control of viable businesses to new managers with better incentives to follow the law.

For example, all federally insured depository institutions (banks and thrifts) must comply with the Federal Deposit Insurance Act, under which the Federal Deposit Insurance Corporation (FDIC) Board of Directors may terminate the deposit insurance of any insured depository institution that violates any law. A bank that suffers a criminal conviction can lose its FDIC deposit insurance. Indeed, subject to the usual due process requirements of notice and hearing, the FDIC may terminate deposit insurance of any bank upon a civil determination of a legal or regulatory violation. The FDIC must notify depositors of a bank in advance of the termination of deposit insurance at a given bank. Of course, the FDIC may always seek or negotiate for less drastic measures such as a cease and desist order, divestment of assets, ouster of management, or "any other action [the FDIC] determines to be appropriate" (12 USC § 1818).

Another alternative under the Federal Deposit Insurance Act permits the FDIC to put any bank or thrift in receivership if it violates any law that harms its financial stability. In receivership, the FDIC seizes control of the institution, terminates management, and realizes upon the value of its assets while protecting depositors. Unsecured creditors and shareholders typically bear losses only if the bank ultimately proves to be insolvent. The FDIC as receiver holds the power to transfer the bank to new owners. Congress also gave the FDIC power to order less drastic remedies including limitations upon activities or functions of any insured bank found in violation of law. These less drastic measures could include spinning off the banks to megabank shareholders or otherwise forcing divestiture. The megabank's business would immediately suffer and contract if it lost the ability to access an insured bank subsidiary. The FDIC as receiver also may sue management for losses caused by unsafe and unsound banking practices or gross negligence, and terminate their banking careers (12 USC § 1821). The FDIC thus holds ample power to dismantle a bank that commits significant financial crimes, either by seizing control or terminating insurance, causing depositors to flee. These actions would amount to the corporate death penalty for an insured depository institution.

The Office of the Comptroller of the Currency (OCC) holds additional powers with respect to national banks. Specifically, under 12 USC section 93, the OCC may revoke the charter of any national bank based upon specified federal crimes, including money laundering. Money laundering is broadly defined in 18 USC section 1956 to include the promotion or concealment of illegal activities (such as wire fraud, mail fraud, bank fraud, and securities fraud) through financial transactions. The comptroller holds discretion to invoke this seldom-used power depending on a litany of factors including the degree to which the bank cooperated with law enforcement, the degree to which current management participated in the criminal acts, and the degree to which the bank has imposed preventative measures against potential future violations. This power gives the comptroller broad power to restructure banks found guilty of money laundering.

Similarly, under the Bank Holding Company Act, the Federal Reserve Board may examine any bank holding company (a firm that owns or controls at least one bank) to monitor legal compliance. If it finds any legal violations that (1) pose a "serious risk to the financial stability" of the bank holding company or any bank it owns and (2) are "inconsistent with sound banking principles," the Fed may order the divestiture of the bank subsidiary (or any other affiliate) by sale or spin-off of stock shares to the shareholders of the bank holding company (12 USC § 1844). Massive securities fraud and related crimes certainly suffice as inconsistent with sound banking principles and manifestly destabilize banks and bank holding companies. Consequently, this provision authorizes the Fed to fragment all megabanks doing business as bank holding companies that commit serious crimes. Again, this sanction applies mainly to bank managers who tolerated criminality, not to shareholders or innocent employees.

All securities broker-dealers must register with the SEC and submit to periodic examinations. If the SEC finds that any broker-dealer has willfully violated any provision of federal securities laws, any provision of the Commodity Exchange Act, or any regulation promulgated thereunder, it may limit the activities of the broker-dealer or revoke its registration. The SEC holds this same power with respect to any felonies committed in the course of the broker-dealer's business. The only limitation on the SEC's ability to levy sanctions for such financial crimes is that it find that the sanction is "in the public interest" (15 USC § 78o). The Commodity Exchange Act gives the Commodity Futures Trading Commission (CFTC) the same powers with respect to registered commodities brokers (7 USC § 12a). Like the FDIC, the SEC and CFTC also may disqualify individuals from the financial sector. Virtually every megabank has a subsidiary registered with the SEC or the CFTC, as we highlight in coming chapters. These subsidiaries give the megabanks crucial access to both the securities and derivatives markets. A megabank could not function in the manner it does today if it could not operate a securities broker-dealer and a commodities business.

Through these statutory provisions Congress consistently decided that criminals have no business in the financial sector. No financial firm can operate with much size or scale without a bank, securities, commodities, or bank holding company as part of its corporate structure. Consequently, the powers the government holds currently over all financial firms constitute nothing less than the corporate death penalty against financial firms that commit serious frauds or otherwise behave in a pervasively lawless manner. The problem, in other words, is not that the United States needs more or amended laws to stem the lawlessness of the financial sector revealed during the crisis of 2008 but that the government refuses to enforce the laws passed by Congress over a period of decades prior to 2008, reaching back to the New Deal.

These long-standing congressional acts demonstrate a democratic determination that the US government should take a zero-tolerance approach to lawlessness in finance. This value weighs heavily enough in these statutory statements that no financial firm can attain the privilege of operating for profit at the heart of our capitalist system without adhering to the law. This reflects a hard lesson learned from US financial history earlier in the 20th century when lawlessness in the financial sector led directly to the Great Depression. Notably, these congressional determinations applied to all firms in the entire financial sector regardless of size.

Indeed, the powers given to financial regulators throughout these various statutory schemes indicate that large financial firms of any size must adhere to the law or face fragmentation or restructuring. Granting the power of divestiture and revocation of registration to regulators for lawless financial firms necessarily means that successive Congresses contemplated breaking up large megabanks and continuously came to the conclusion that if they broke the law they should cease to exist. The acts discussed above reveal great clarity regarding the congressional approach to financial firms—of any size—that violate law and regulations.

The executive lacks the power to alter this well-embedded approach to lawlessness in the financial sector, as do the regulatory agencies the executive branch supervises. Yet, the story recounted herein leads to the conclusion that these protections legislated to safeguard financial markets were circumvented in the aftermath of the financial crisis—the government not only tolerated illegal behavior on an unprecedented scale in the financial sector but acted affirmatively to protect the megabanks and the financiers who run them from the consequences of their misconduct. The administration fumbled a clean opportunity to end Too-Big-to-Fail under current law for pervasive illegality, and acted contrary to democratically negotiated due process to save the Too-Big-to-Fail banks at the cost of the rule of law.

Too-Big-to-Fail stands in the United States today as testament to the power of financial elites to subvert sound regulation for profit, at the expense of the economy generally. The megabanks are larger than ever and still enjoy a capital advantage. Specifically, due to the perception that large banks enjoy the backing of the US Treasury, they can raise capital easier than their competitors and enjoy a lower cost of funds. Recent estimates assess the value of government subsidies to US megabanks at $70 billion a year (International Monetary Fund 2014). That means every man, woman, and child in the United States expends more than $200 per annum to keep these criminally inclined megabanks afloat.

The megabanks offer no offsetting economic benefit. Their operations are far-flung and complex, making them too big to manage. They also suffer from perverse incentives regarding risk because their government backing means they do not bear the full consequences of excessive risk (Zardkoohi et al. 2016). Without the massive government subsidy, only small, if any, operating efficiencies would remain, and there would be no benefit to shareholders since banks would tend toward instability. These distorted incentives also mean the megabanks are far more inclined toward criminality and other misbehavior (Federal Reserve Bank of St. Louis 2012). The increasing criminality associated with megabanks' business model leads to ever higher legal expenses, as shown in a recent study. Based upon regulatory findings, the CCP Research Foundation found that legal costs at the largest 16 megabanks around the world soared 20 percent in 2014 in a rolling five-year analysis (CCP Research Foundation 2015). In sum, the huge subsidy these megabanks enjoy is a total waste of taxpayer funds that serves only to entrench financial elites and encourage further criminality.

Rather than indulging the megabanks, breaking up criminal megabanks would not harm either the economy or the shareholders of the megabanks. Instead, forcing spin-offs of regulated subsidiaries to the shareholders of the megabanks would give shareholders ownership in smaller, more competitive businesses. The businesses would also enjoy the benefit of superior, well-incentivized management that would follow the law instead of using shareholder money to buy off the government for managerial immunity. So the corporate death penalty in the financial sector harms only the managers of the criminal megabanks. Job losses for other than criminal managers are not a necessary result of businesses that are spun off intact (Ramirez 2005).

The DOJ, in conjunction with regulatory agencies, could have negotiated asset dispositions and spin-offs that could have effectively curtailed the continuation of the Too-Big-to-Fail banks. While this type of "corporate death penalty" is controversial (and generally not available today for nonfinancial firms), Congress has decided that criminal enterprises are not entitled to participate in the nation's financial sector. This congressional policy enjoys strong support from both history and economics. Specifically, a financial sector pervaded by crime and fraud can lead to massive financial instability and economic depression or recession. In such circumstances the economic costs of financial crime quickly sum to trillions in lost economic output. That bitter economic history and experience is why Congress barred criminal organizations from the financial sector. Twice in the past 100 years, the United States reaped the economic plague of a fraud-ridden financial sector: the Great Depression and the subprime mortgage debacle (Ramirez 2014). The DOJ's policy today regarding Wall Street crimes can be termed only as in defiance of this congressional action. DOJ and other financial regulators now give the largest, most wealthy financiers and financial institutions a pass on financial crimes.

Never was this clearer than with respect to the government's approach to brazen currency manipulation at certain megabanks. In the spring of 2015, five global megabanks pled guilty to criminal charges arising from a conspiracy to manipulate and fix exchange rates. Traders at these firms communicated and coordinated trading almost daily in an online chat room and referred to themselves and their activities as "The Cartel" or "The Mafia." Furthermore, the traders lied to customers in order to collect undisclosed markups and commissions in certain currency-related transactions. This criminal conspiracy lasted for years. Yet, instead of using these traders' guilty pleas to break up the banks, the government did the opposite. Specifically the SEC granted the crooks waivers from certain automatic disqualifications in order to permit the guilty criminals to continue their core businesses unencumbered by legal disqualifications. The SEC granted these same five institutions no fewer than 23 similar waivers over a nine-year period.

SEC Commissioner Kara Stein dissented from the official SEC position, stating, "I am troubled by repeated instances of noncompliance at these global financial institutions, which may be indicative of a continuing culture that does not adequately support legal and ethical behavior. Further, I am concerned that the latest series of actions has effectively rendered criminal convictions of financial institutions largely symbolic.

Firms and institutions increasingly rely on the Commission's repeated issuance of waivers to remove the consequences of a criminal conviction, consequences that may actually positively contribute to a firm's compliance and conduct going forward." The cost of this criminality may not always include historic market crashes such as that seen in 2008. Still, this criminality takes a constant toll on investor confidence in our financial system and slowly saps capital formation. As commissioner Stein stated, "Allowing these institutions to continue business as usual, after multiple and serious regulatory and criminal violations, poses risks to investors and the American public that are being ignored" (Stein 2015). The government's efforts to remove the sting of criminal convictions "render the plea deals, at least in part, an exercise in stagecraft" (Protess & Corkery 2015).

In other words, even in those rare circumstances where the government obtained criminal convictions (against firms only and not the managers overseeing the criminal conduct), the government bent over backward to remove the sting of the conviction and allow the core business of the firms to continue. Usually, this core business involves more criminal misconduct. Due to the dominance of the megabanks and their manifest criminal inclinations, our financial system teeters toward a giant racketeering enterprise. Government complicity plays a key role in this pseudo-capitalistic nightmare. Bill Black concludes that regulators lack "moral courage" (Black 2013b). Indeed, these manifest efforts of the government to assure the megabanks that all of their business lines will remain undisturbed by government enforcement reek of cronyism.

Corrupted Justice and the Rule of Law

This reality is at odds with American history. In the past, administrations took great care not to use criminal prosecution to achieve political goals. President Richard Nixon nearly faced impeachment based in part on interference with DOJ law enforcement lawsuits. The Bush administration pursued charges against Enron's top officers despite their close political alliance, as will be discussed in chapter 1. A systematic failure to prosecute or investigate criminality of the most powerful stands without precedent in US history.

The perverse and distorted incentives created as a result of this new policy should disturb every American. The financial crisis of 2008 shook the foundations of capitalism in the United States and the world. Governments around the world expended trillions in taxpayer money to stabilize the financial system and repair the damage. The economy still has not fully recovered. Economists at the Federal Reserve Bank of Dallas estimate output and wealth losses at $15 trillion and rising in the United States alone. The crisis will cost every working-age American citizen (other than a few dozen financial titans) hundreds of thousands of dollars.

Furthermore, because only the most economically powerful enjoy this criminal immunity, they necessarily hold the greatest destructive capability. These financial chieftains literally direct trillions in credit and investments, the lifeblood of any capitalist economy. If they can profit from criminality and enjoy criminal immunity, we should expect much of our precious capital as a society to end up in shady dealings and outright antisocial activities. For example, HSBC invested its banking resources in drug cartels and rogue nations. MF Global lost customer funds speculating on distressed Eurozone bonds. Instead of expecting financial titans to fund productive and sustainable growth, we should expect a financial sector that has learned that crime does in fact pay.

This operates to diminish investment. If plunder for profit is permitted, then no investors can rest assured that their investment monies are applied as agreed. Investors will naturally avoid financial markets dominated by crooks. Foreigners will naturally invest in economies that uphold the rule of law with no exemptions based upon power. A less law-abiding America means less investment here. The cost of capital will increase in tandem with the perception of lawlessness, stifling growth and employment. We will show that foreign media outlets now question the rule of law in the US financial sector.

The damage does not end there. If the most powerful act above the law, then social incentives to skirt the law increase across our population. Soon competitors will strive to achieve the same immunity. The temptation to profit however one may achieve it becomes more powerful if people believe the law has no moral authority. Selective enforcement based upon political and economic power necessarily corrodes the rule of law generally (M. Ramirez 2013).

The US Constitution specifically ensures that no politician is above the law. As Thomas Jefferson stated long ago, "The most sacred of the duties of a government [is] to do equal and impartial justice to all its citizens" (Looney 2012, 633–34). The same sentiment underlies Chief Justice John Marshall's long-standing maxim, "The government of the United States [is] a government of laws, and not of men" (*Marbury v. Madison* 1803). The United States is founded on the principle that no person may act above the law. America needs to apply to the financial sector this heritage of imposing the rule of law on all. The first step is to ensure that no economic actor enjoys criminal immunity. Allowing bankers and banks to operate above the law is both economically and morally unjustifiable.

In the final analysis we simply posit that the rule of law in the financial sector should apply to all—including the megabanks—in accordance with congressional commands. No valid counterargument to this point exists. The fact that following the law would greatly diminish the Too-Big-to-Fail problem adds policy weight to our proposal that lawmakers and regulators follow the law. To the extent some may argue that Too-Big-to-Fail megabanks and megabankers should not face the same criminal penalties as all others, they essentially argue that rule of law itself should take a back seat to the interests of the megabanks. That, in turn, means that Too-Big-to-Fail is irreconcilable with the very heart of the American legal system. Criminal indulgences for the most powerful financial institutions and financiers enjoy no legal, historical, or other basis. Instead, they exist as a result of too much economic power and wealth in too few hands. Such concentrated economic power leads directly to the lawlessness we identify in this book.

The Obligation to Tell the Truth, the Whole Truth, and Nothing but the Truth

Congress also directly prohibited all forms of fraud in the financial sector and backed this legal prohibition up with stiff criminal penalties and an extended statute of limitations of 10 years. A wide array of federal laws mandate that all financial sector agents fully disclose material facts for securities, investments, and other products. We will discuss such laws in depth in coming chapters in specific contexts where the government enforced these legal requirements and in more recent contexts where the government should have enforced these laws and regulations. For now, the key point is that whether viewed under federal statutes related to bank, mail, securities, or wire fraud, all actors in the financial sector owe transcendent duties to tell potential investors the complete truth with respect to all material facts. Once they speak to sell the investment product, they must offer the complete truth because half-truths will support a fraud finding. Furthermore, under federal law the sellers of securities must tell the whole truth about securities they peddle.

SEC Rule 10b-5, the core provision governing securities fraud, illustrates the point well. It prohibits false statements as well as half-truths: "It shall be unlawful for any person . . . to make any untrue statement of a material fact or to omit to state a material fact necessary in order to make the statements made, in the light of the circumstances under which they were made, not misleading" (17 CFR § 240.10b-5). Courts have similarly condemned half-truths under the mail and wire fraud statutes: "deceitful statements of half-truths or the concealment of material facts is actual fraud violative of the mail fraud statute" (*Lustiger v. United States*). Therefore, in the financial sector, sellers of securities hold an affirmative obligation to disclose all material facts completely and truthfully. Half-truths constitute fraud as much as affirmative lies.

Any firm that accesses public capital markets and trades on a securities exchange like the New York Stock Exchange or the NASDAQ marketplace must make certain truthful periodic disclosures to the investing public through disclosure filings with the SEC that the federal securities laws mandate. For example, Form 10-K requires an annual report that includes disclosure of all material facts and audited financial statements. Form 10-Q requires the quarterly disclosure of all material facts. If some major development—such as a change in auditors—occurs between the filing of these forms, then a publicly traded firm must file a Form 8-K. A firm also may decide to file a Form 8-K if it wishes to disclose important facts to the investing public (Choi & Pritchard 2008). All facts disclosed in these forms must be truthful. Frequently, firms will hold an investor conference call in connection with the release of these forms. All statements made in such conference calls also must be truthful.

The failure to make a truthful disclosure of material facts in connection with the purchase or sale of a security (such as stocks and bonds) can constitute securities fraud, and using the mail or wires (including the Internet) to further the fraud can also constitute mail or wire fraud. If a bank is the victim of the fraud, the crime amounts to bank fraud. The essential elements of all such criminal frauds are the following: a scheme or artifice to defraud or to obtain money or property by means of false or fraudulent material misrepresentations or promises. The criminal statutes punish the scheme, so that the prosecution need not prove (1) that the fraud was completed, (2) that the defendant gained any benefit from the fraud, or (3) adverse reliance by the victim or damages to the victim. The key and most difficult element to prove is the state of mind—intent to defraud, or "scienter." We address that element in the next section, in the particular context of criminal actions for various criminal frauds under federal law.

Scienter and Willfulness

The primary crimes we identify and discuss are various forms of fraud. Fraud simply means that one has schemed or used knowing misstatements or omissions of material facts to take money or property from another. Fraud in general requires proof of scienter—intent to defraud. Under civil law, courts may enter a finding of fraud and award recoveries to plaintiffs if the defendant recklessly proceeded without any care for defrauding a victim. Recklessness may suffice for scienter under civil law. Criminal convictions under federal law generally require a finding of willfulness or knowing misconduct. Legal scholars observe that courts take many different approaches to the proof required to secure a criminal conviction for federal fraud. Perhaps a relatively demanding level of proof for a criminal state of mind (or *mens rea* in legal jargon) makes the most sense for our project of assessing the government's response to manifest financial crimes.

As such, we use a standard identified by legal scholar Samuel W. Buell as on the more demanding side of the various formulations approved by courts. This standard requires proof that a defendant acted with a specific intent, including knowledge that the representation is false, willful blindness to its falsity, or deliberate disregard of the risk of falsity (Buell 2011). The courts define willful blindness to occur when a defendant "buries his head in the sand" and fails to investigate even when facts suggest wrongdoing. The evidence must support an inference of deliberate ignorance (*United States v. Gruenberg*). Recognizing its long-term application in federal criminal cases, the US Supreme Court identified two basic requirements to establish willful blindness articulated by federal appellate courts: "(1) the defendant must subjectively believe that there is a high probability that a fact exists and (2) the defendant must take deliberate actions to avoid learning of that fact" (*Global-Tech Appliances, Inc. v. SEB S.A.*). In sum, defendants will be found to have the required state of mind if they consciously avoided learning of their fraud.

While much of this analysis is rooted in criminal securities fraud, the need to prove intent also applies to prosecutions for federal mail, wire, and bank fraud. These federal statutory crimes all require very similar elements for a successful prosecution. Most importantly, all of these federal offenses require a showing of an intent to defraud, much like securities fraud. They also require knowing misconduct (Podgor et al. 2013). In particular, courts have approved willful blindness as an appropriate level of culpability for these federal offenses too (*United States v. Clay*).

This standard certainly creates a difficult evidentiary burden for any fraud-based federal conviction. Nevertheless, we will show that historically the government scored major successes against the most powerful financial titans notwithstanding this evidentiary burden. We will also show that much publicly available evidence of such an intent to defraud and willful blindness to the risk of defrauding investors already exists. We will see money changing hands based upon material lies in massive quantities, perhaps amounting to over $1 trillion. The key element of proof for purposes of criminal charges is identifying persons who made material misstatements with an intent to defraud.

The 10-Year Statute of Limitations for Crimes Affecting a Financial Institution

There is still time for the government to uphold the rule of law in the financial sector. In general, the federal government must pursue criminal charges within 5 years of a crime; however, the statute of limitations for crimes affecting a financial institution extends to 10 years.

Under 18 USC section 3293, the limitations period for criminal charges for bank fraud as well as wire fraud and mail fraud that "affects a financial institution" is 10 years (*United States v. Heinz*). This is twice as long as the 5-year statute that generally provides the limitations period for federal offenses and significantly longer than the limitations period applicable to securities violations and commodities fraud. The definition of a "financial institution" includes any insured depository institution and any holding company of any insured depository institution. Furthermore, federal frauds may involve schemes that continue beyond the fraudulent mailing or transmission that effectively will extend that period to 10 years after the scheme has ended.

Moreover, under relevant case law, frauds affecting a subsidiary of a financial institution "affect a financial institution." By the same logic, any loss to any subsidiary of a holding company also will affect a financial institution. Furthermore, any fraud committed within a financial institution clearly affects a financial institution and is subject to the 10-year statute of limitations because it exposes the financial institution to an increased risk of loss.

Interestingly, Congress added the term "mortgage lending business" to the definition of financial institution in the Fraud Enforcement Recovery Act of 2009. Courts have found that Congress may extend the period of limitations without running afoul of the Constitution's ex post facto clause, provided the original limitations period has not expired. In general, statutes of limitation are deemed procedural and are applicable to claims brought after the enactment of the statute. Thus, any criminal charges relating to a "mortgage lending business" brought after May 20, 2009, are subject to the new 10-year statute of limitations so long as they are not already time-barred as of that date (Ramirez 2013b).

This means that virtually all of the criminal conduct at the megabanks arising from the crisis of 2006 to 2009 is not time-barred until 10 years after the end of the fraudulent scheme—or 2016 at the earliest. Congress spoke comprehensively and with great clarity to the problem of fraud in the financial sector—financial frauds pose a great danger to the economy, and prosecutors can thus bring charges for such frauds far beyond the limitations period for other federal offenses. Therefore, with respect to the great weight of facts and misconduct detailed in forthcoming chapters, the statute of limitations will not bar the next administration from pursuing the Wall Street crimes that sank the economy.

Overview of Coming Chapters

In coming chapters we demonstrate that a historically unprecedented breakdown in the rule of law occurred in the years following the Great Financial Crisis. In chapter 1 we show that throughout the history of modern America (at least since World War II) white-collar criminals and their firms faced criminal sanctions under federal law regardless of their wealth and power. Prosecutorial discretion rested not on the power of the criminal but on transcendent policy considerations and the honest weighing of the evidence at the disposal of the government. Consequently, even the most powerful financial and corporate titans faced jail time in the years and decades prior to the Great Financial Crisis. Indeed, these criminals violated the very laws that we focus upon throughout this book, and therefore this chapter furnishes a short introduction to the development of white-collar crime.

Subsequent chapters will muster the most reliable sources possible in an effort to detail the most damaging misconduct at the firms that operated at the center of the crisis of 2008. We start at the beginning of the pipeline—the origination of subprime, even predatory, mortgages at the largest subprime lender in the United States, Countrywide Financial. Senior managers at Countrywide knew or should have known that the toxic mortgages they sold to public investors through pools of mortgage-backed securities posed a huge risk of default. Nevertheless, Countrywide's managers sold massive quantities of subprime mortgages into the financial system and rang up illusory profits. Ultimately, the firm crashed amid massive and predictable losses from defaulted mortgages. Management concealed these risks of default in order to attract capital to an otherwise deeply flawed business model.

The next stop in the pipeline of financial fraud takes us to the heart of Wall Street and the efforts of the largest Wall Street firms—the megabanks—to sell toxic mortgages in the form of mortgage-backed securities. Despite clear red flags, the megabanks sold hundreds of billions of dollars worth of toxic mortgages to investors worldwide without disclosing their true quality or the extraordinary risks of default these mortgages posed to investors. No megabanks, acting like lemmings following each other off a cliff, could resist selling toxic subprime mortgages as higher quality mortgages. Only recently has the scale of the fraud become clear as JPMorgan, Bank of America, Citigroup, and Morgan Stanley entered into settlements with the government for misrepresentations in connection with the sale of mortgage-backed securities. This massive fraud formed the foundation of the crisis of 2008 when the market realized that toxic mortgages infected the entire global financial system.

The failure of Lehman Brothers on September 15, 2008, marks the moment when the global financial system collapsed under the weight of the fraudulently originated and packaged mortgages. Lehman held huge amounts of debt on its balance sheet as it used massive leverage to invest in questionable real estate of all sorts. As the crisis progressed, the investing public became increasingly skeptical of firms with high levels of debt and leverage because they posed the highest risk of failure. In response, Lehman reassured its investors that all was well even while concealing huge amounts of debt on its balance sheet through dubious accounting machinations. Lehman's misrepresentations only postponed its day of reckoning, and its subsequent collapse sent the global economy into a historic tailspin.

Chapter 5 focuses on the collapse of the world's largest insurance company, AIG, right on the heels of the failure of Lehman. AIG facilitated the flow of subprime mortgages into the global financial system because of its willingness to enter into credit default swaps with subprime mortgage investors. The credit default transactions simply meant that AIG agreed to absorb the losses arising from subprime mortgage investments in exchange for fee income. Shortly before its collapse, AIG told its shareholders that the investments posed very low risk and senior managers could not conceive of scenarios where large losses would result. In 2008, when the subprime mortgage losses came home to roost, AIG lost over $60 billion, a record loss in US corporate history resulting from the credit default swaps. To save AIG (and the global financial system as a whole), the government expended hundreds of billions of dollars.

The frauds did not end there. Goldman Sachs settled a securities fraud lawsuit with the SEC for a record fine of $550 million. The scam at issue in that enforcement action involved a collateralized debt obligation fund that paid out proceeds to investors with different priorities based upon the tranche (a French word literally meaning a slice or part) held by a given investor. The riskiest tranche, called the equity tranche, is held by the sponsor of the investment fund. Goldman sold the investment without disclosing that the equity tranche investor assumed a short position in excess of its investment risk with respect to the senior tranches through credit default swaps, anticipating the collateralized debt obligation's failure and planning to profit from it. Goldman also failed to disclose the role that the equity tranche investor played in selecting the assets for the investment and thereby ensuring its failure. These nondisclosures meant that the senior tranche investors did not know that they invested in a vehicle that held assets selected by an investor who desired losses for the senior tranches. Unfortunately, this type of sabotaged investment became all too common on Wall Street, leading to a series of securities fraud settlements with the SEC by a parade of megabanks.

Since the end of the financial crisis, developments in the approach of the DOJ give greater meaning to its decisions not to prosecute the frauds of the financial crisis. Chapter 7 examines the HSBC and MF Global settlements with the DOJ in an effort to understand the recent devolution of the financial lawlessness plaguing the United States today. We posit that these instances of nonprosecution indicate that DOJ will not pursue powerful players in the financial sector regardless of crisis conditions and regardless of whether the failure of the financial institution where the criminality occurred is systemically important. Stated simply, some actors appear too powerful to prosecute even if there is no associated threat to the economy.

The conclusion proposes legal solutions for a more balanced and sound law enforcement approach to the megabanks and other ways to restore and secure lawful conduct in the financial sector. All of these would require political support for some degree of action on this front. In the end, if Americans demand a restoration of the rule of law in the financial sector they will get it; and these proposals appear to us as the most promising way to address and stem the new financial lawlessness. If Americans resign themselves to the idea that the most powerful financiers may commit financial frauds with impunity, then our financial sector will continue its corruption with all of its accompanying costs.

Obviously, it takes a criminal conviction in a court of law to determine if any particular individual committed a crime. This book cannot substitute for such criminal trials. Nevertheless, frauds and other crimes definitely occurred in the years preceding the Great Financial Crisis of 2008. This book shows that the evidence justified criminal charges against many Wall Street titans and firms. The evidence should have led to stringent grand jury investigations and jury trials. Juries could convict in such trials only based upon evidence proving the crimes beyond a reasonable doubt—including evidence of criminal intent. Only after such trials can citizens be satisfied whether any particular Wall Street leaders in fact broke the law or which banks committed crimes.

Lawlessness is always costly, and the American people have a right to understand precisely how their legal system functions, or whether the rule of law has broken down. The people can decide for themselves if our government has betrayed the rule of law and can choose to insist upon accountability through the power of the ballot.

1

A Short History of White-Collar Criminal Prosecutions

The savings and loan debacle was one-seventieth the size of
the current crisis, both in terms of losses and the amount
of fraud. In that crisis, the savings and loan regulators made
over 30,000 criminal referrals, and this produced over 1,000
felony convictions in cases designated as "major" by the Department of Justice. . . . [W]e, the regulators, worked very
closely with the FBI and the Justice Department. . . . We had
a 90 percent conviction rate, which is the greatest success
against elite white-collar crime (in terms of prosecution) in
history.
—Professor and former bank regulator William K. Black,
September 13, 2013

The recent legal indulgences granted to financial elites for financial
crimes stand without precedent in the modern American economy.
Between the end of World War II and the 2008 financial crisis, in the
United States even the most powerful business leaders faced criminal
accountability for significant financial crimes. A bipartisan consensus held that because white-collar crime could threaten the economy
and trigger financial instability that indulgences simply could not be
tolerated. This chapter first shows how this fact ensnared many high-
powered corporate executives and financiers as well as the firms they
led regardless of political connections prior to the Great Financial Crisis of 2008. Next the chapter provides an overview of how white-collar
crime in the United States evolved from the Great Depression onward
to impose more and more accountability upon business and financial
titans. Recent immunity for the most powerful financial elites is unprecedented and at odds with these historic realities.

Even as recently as 2001, in the wake of the Enron corporate scandals,
Congress acted to impose more accountability upon miscreant corporate

managers. For example, historically white-collar criminals have fared far better than street criminals during sentencing. At the point in time that the US sentencing guidelines went into effect, November 1, 1987, about half of all federal white-collar criminals (fraud, embezzlement, forgery/counterfeiting, bribery, tax offenses, and money laundering) received sentences of probation only. Congress responded to the perceived laxity in sentencing of white-collar criminals to stiffen the sentencing guidelines applicable to white-collar crime. Subsequent amendments to the sentencing guidelines placed additional weight on the economic loss to the victim or gain to the offender caused by financial crimes, and imprisonment became more likely and substantially more lengthy relative to prior to the amendments. The Sarbanes-Oxley Act of 2002 led to further sentencing enhancements for economic crimes. Changes to the federal sentencing guidelines substantially increased recommended terms of imprisonment by expanding the loss tables to reach high-dollar frauds exposed by accounting scandals, considering a greater number of victims and activity threatening the financial solvency of those victims, and adding an enhancement for jeopardizing the safety and soundness of a financial institution. Further enhancements were added for fraud committed by an officer or director of a publicly traded institution (M. Ramirez 2003). Once again a bipartisan consensus held that white-collar crime, particularly in the financial sector, posed unique economic dangers and required tough criminal accountability.

Statistics, to the extent available, also confirm this point. According to the *New York Times* the government indicted over 1,100 bankers in the wake of the savings and loan crisis of the 1980s and 1990s and achieved 839 convictions. White-collar crime prosecutions peaked in 1995 and declined thereafter, never returning to the 1995 peak. Financial crimes swelled throughout the 1990s, but the number of financial crime prosecutions since then has remained at a fraction of that elevated level. The financial crisis barely causes a blip on the *New York Times* graph. Financial regulators in general and the FDIC in particular contributed mightily to this problem due to their failure to make criminal referrals to DOJ; such referrals plunged as the megabanks grew in size and the banking sector became more consolidated (*New York Times* 2011).

Statistics and changes in law can explain only so much. We argue that the concentrated economic power of the megabanks provides the key to understanding the tepid response of the DOJ and the lack of criminal prosecutions at the federal level. Very high income inequality and concentration of wealth controlled by the largest banks combine to create a different outcome in criminal justice today compared to even the recent past. An unprecedented breakdown in the rule of law has emerged from the ability of those in control of this vast wealth to directly subvert law and regulation to avert criminal prosecutions. We show that such prosecutions occurred against similarly connected individuals and firms in the past. The history in support of this conclusion begins with the criminal prosecution of highly connected senior managers at Enron Corporation, right after the collapse of that firm in 2001.

Enron et al.

Few Americans have enjoyed the close personal and political relationships to presidents that Kenneth Lay, former chairman and CEO of Enron Corporation, enjoyed with three successive administrations. Lay first established a close relationship with President George H. W. Bush in 1990 when Bush called on Lay to help run the World Economic Summit in Houston. He then served as co-chairman of President Bush's 1992 reelection committee as well as the chairman of the Republican National Convention held in Houston that same year. Later, Lay enjoyed golfing with President Bill Clinton. He first forged close ties to future President George W. Bush when Bush served as governor of Texas. When the younger Bush began his quest to win the 2000 presidential election, Lay served as a major fund-raiser and contributed much of his own money to the campaign. After Bush won the presidency, Mr. Lay was considered for the job of Secretary of the Treasury. The first President Bush and his wife flew to their son's inauguration with Mr. Lay on an Enron jet (Bajaj & Eichenwald 2006).

Under Lay's leadership, Enron affiliates contributed more than $888,000 to the Republican National Committee in 2000 and another $1.3 million to the Republican Party. Enron's political contributions spiked in the 2000 election cycle just before the company's collapse in the wake of one of history's most infamous accounting frauds. Enron also gave huge sums to the Democratic Party, even though it clearly favored the GOP, by a factor of almost three to one (Center for Responsive Politics n.d.-a). According to the Center for Public Integrity, "Enron's employees and political action committee have given more than $600,000 to Bush over the course of his political career," more than any other George W. Bush supporter (Center for Public Integrity 2004). Lay and his wife Linda personally gave $238,000 to various George W. Bush campaign efforts and inauguration celebrations and raised another $100,000 from other supporters (Associated Press 2002). Bush even nicknamed Lay "Kenny boy" (*CNN* 2002b).

All of this support gave Lay and Enron very high access to the top of the George W. Bush administration. A House of Representatives inquiry reported on "Bush Administration Contacts with Enron." The report was prepared under the direction of Congressman Henry Waxman, by the minority staff of the Special Investigations Division of the House Committee on Government Reform. It found "at least 112 contacts between Enron and White House or other Administration officials during 2001. The largest number of known contacts—40 contacts in total—were between Enron and White House officials. The White House officials involved in these contacts included Vice President Cheney, presidential advisor Karl Rove, White House economic advisor Lawrence Lindsey, White House personnel director Clay Johnson, and White House energy task force director Andrew Lundquist" (House Minority Report 2002). Consequently, it is hard to imagine a business leader with greater White House access than Ken Lay.

Nevertheless, in July 2004, the DOJ indicted Lay and another former Enron CEO, Jeff Skilling, for securities fraud. In fact, as we will show, dozens of Enron executives faced criminal inquiries, and the company's auditor, storied accounting firm Arthur Andersen, effectively ceased operations as an auditor for public firms. Ultimately, a jury found both Lay and Skilling guilty. While Lay died of a heart attack prior to sentencing, after much legal wrangling Skilling was sentenced to 14 years in a federal penitentiary, where he remains today (Elkind 2013). The story of these prosecutions highlights that in the recent past not even the most economically and politically powerful could assume that they were above the law.

In 2001, Enron Corporation, ranked the seventh largest company by revenues in the United States, was a multinational corporation with operations on several continents. *Fortune* magazine named the firm the most innovative company in America from 1996 to 2001. Enron dominated energy markets, but had also expanded into to a wider array of businesses including fiber optics, natural gas, electricity, water, and derivatives trading. The success of the firm left Ken Lay an extremely wealthy man: in just one year he earned as much as $252 million (*BBC News* 2006).

Behind the broadly touted success of the corporation was a dense complex of interrelated companies supported by deceptive accounting practices. Simply stated, Enron lied about trading losses it hid in so-called special purpose investment entities. Stock prices for the corporation soared to an all-time high in August 2000, in response to earnings reports that turned out to be too good to be true. On December 12, 2001, the firm filed for bankruptcy.

The company began to unravel in August 2001, when Enron's CEO Jeff Skilling resigned a mere six months after taking the post, citing "personal reasons." In 1997, Skilling became president and chief operating officer of Enron, second only to then-CEO Kenneth Lay. Four years later, on February 12, 2001, Skilling ascended to CEO, while Lay remained as chairman of the board. The 48-year-old Skilling's abrupt resignation in August heralded the problems yet to come.

The resignation, along with plunging stock prices, aroused the interest of reporters and investors. Throughout the fall of 2001, news reports on Enron's questionable financial condition and accounting practices drove investors and creditors to seek assurances from Key Lay, who had returned as CEO. Lay repeatedly reassured investors (including Enron's own workers) that all was well. But by late fall, Enron's stock price swooned as it posted its first loss in years and restated its financial statements to reduce its previously reported profits (*CNN/Money* 2002).

The DOJ immediately began an aggressive series of criminal inquiries and prosecutions. Within six weeks of Enron's bankruptcy the DOJ's Criminal Division chief, Michael Chertoff, created the Enron Task Force, headed by Leslie Caldwell, then the chief of the Criminal Division for the San Francisco US Attorney's Office (Schoenberg & Farrell 2014). The Task Force drew on financial expertise from around the country, added experienced prosecutors from several offices, and worked closely with the FBI and the SEC, among others. After allegations of document shredding at Enron hit the news, the FBI began a nine-day search of the company's premises, seizing hundreds of boxes of documents and interviewing hundreds of witnesses. The Task Force's course was set as they diligently analyzed thousands of documents and pieced together complicated accounting schemes involving many participants through dozens of enterprises, some of which were created solely to disguise losses and create false appearances of a stable and financially successful corporation (FBI 2006).

In March 2002, just over three months after Enron declared bankruptcy, Arthur Andersen pleaded not guilty to charges of obstruction of justice for shredding documents related to its accounting services for Enron. That same week, Joseph Berardino, Arthur Andersen CEO, resigned in response to the Enron debacle. By early April 2002, David Duncan, the Arthur Andersen partner from its Houston office responsible for the Enron audit, pled guilty to ordering the document shredding and agreed to cooperate with investigators. Duncan admitted he ordered the shredding of documents to avoid criminal responsibility for his role in the scandal. He became the government's star witness in its Enron prosecutions (Raghaven 2002).

The criminal investigation next took full aim at Enron employees. In August 2002, a mere nine months after Enron's bankruptcy, Michael Kopper, the managing director of Enron Global Finance, pled guilty to charges of wire fraud and money laundering, becoming the first Enron executive to admit to criminal charges. Thereafter, the government obtained numerous guilty pleas (and agreements to cooperate) from senior executives from across Enron's business, ranging from energy trading (and manipulation of California's electricity market) to its broadband business (DOJ 2002b). Kopper's guilty plea and agreement to cooperate in the investigation proved the most helpful to the government's investigation. Kopper, who ultimately received a 37-month sentence, was a top assistant to CFO Andrew Fastow, and admitted providing assistance to Fastow in structuring special purpose investment vehicles that profited Fastow and hid losses from derivatives trading sustained by Enron (Hays 2006).

In October 2002, prosecutors charged Fastow with securities fraud, wire fraud, mail fraud, money laundering, and conspiring "fraudulently to both manipulate Enron's financial results and enrich [himself] at Enron's expense" (DOJ 2002a). Ultimately, the DOJ expanded these charges to 109 counts of federal crimes, including wire fraud, securities fraud, and money laundering. Fastow's indictment included charges against his spouse, another former Enron employee (DOJ 2003). This indictment of Fastow and numerous other Enron executives did not bode well for former chairman and CEO Ken Lay, nor for former CEO Jeff Skilling.

Two weeks after Fastow was charged, Timothy Belden pled guilty to conspiracy and agreed to cooperate with prosecutors. Belden was a top energy trader at Enron who is considered to be the "mastermind" of Enron's bid during 2000–2001 to drive up energy prices in the deregulated California energy market. Enron manipulated the California energy market over a nine-month period to create artificial energy shortages, leading to rolling blackouts in California, the bankruptcy of Pacific Gas and Electric Company, and federal investigations. Enron had manipulated the market by moving energy out of the state from California power sources to create the "shortage" and then returning the energy to the state at substantially inflated rates to "fix" the shortage.

Lawrence Lawyer, former Enron vice president of global markets, pled guilty in early December 2002 to failing to report income. In June 2003, two other former Enron energy traders, Jeffrey Richter and John M. Forney, were charged with criminal conspiracy and wire fraud. They pled guilty to manipulating California power markets and served two years on probation. Ben Glisan, a former Enron treasurer, pled guilty to conspiracy to commit fraud, and served two years of a five-year sentence. Glisan took copious notes of many key meetings among key Enron executives. David Delainey, former CEO of both the retail energy division and Enron's North American Trading Unit, pled guilty to insider trading and served a nine-month prison term. Timothy DeSpain, former assistant treasurer, pled guilty to conspiracy for lying to credit rating agencies about the financial health of Enron. In January 2004, Andrew Fastow, Enron's former chief financial officer, agreed to a 10-year prison sentence and cooperation with prosecution, in a joint deal that netted his wife, Lea Fastow, a former Enron assistant treasurer, with a five-month prison sentence for lying on a tax return.

At this point, prosecutors inspired sufficient cooperation that they could now strike at the top of the Enron hierarchy. Richard Causey, Enron's chief accounting officer, was charged with fraud, as was Skilling. In December 2005 Causey chose to plead guilty to securities fraud rather than face trial, in exchange for testimony against Lay and Skilling, and received a sentence of five and a half years. Skilling and Lay represented the most senior Enron managers. As such, at all times the two held decisive influence over Enron's prodigious political activities, in addition to the ability to direct their own significant wealth. Causey's defection to the government's prosecutorial efforts did not bode well for the former CEOs.

In July 2004, a federal grand jury indicted Ken Lay for lying to investors and shareholders about the company's finances throughout the fall of 2001. The pleas continued and supplied more evidence against Lay and Skilling. Ken Rice pleaded guilty to securities fraud in July 2004 and agreed to cooperate with the government. Rice was a co-CEO of Enron Broadband and a close friend of Skilling's. In all, seven employees from Enron Broadband were charged. Some were acquitted ultimately. But the noose was tightening around Lay and Skilling. Mark E. Koenig, head of investor relations, and Paula Rieker, managing director of investor relations, both pled guilty in August 2004 to securities fraud and insider trading, respectively. This methodical dissection of the crimes committed at Enron laid the ground work for the ultimate jury verdict against Lay and Skilling: guilty (*Houston Chronicle* 2011).

At trial, jurors were impressed by the parade of former Enron executives willing to plead guilty, face imprisonment, and testify against Lay and Skilling. The jurors also deemed the large profits earned by the executives during the fraud, particularly through sales of stock, to prove the requisite criminal intent. Jurors later stated that they relied heavily upon the detailed notes of former treasurer Glisan for evidentiary guidance. Although Lay and Skilling spent $60 million defending themselves against the government, the jury found Lay guilty on all counts and Skilling guilty on 19 of 28 counts of securities fraud and conspiracy. The verdicts against Lay and Skilling capped a government effort that had led to indictments of 33 Enron executives and 23 guilty pleas or convictions (Emshwiller et al. 2006). Essentially, the jurors looked through the complexity of the Enron frauds to see the simple lies told to raise capital and pump up the Enron stock price.

Both Skilling and Lay were convicted by a jury in May 2006, but Lay died of a heart attack and the conviction was vacated as a matter of law as a result of Lay's death. Facing more than 24 years of imprisonment,

Skilling appealed his conviction on several grounds, won a landmark Supreme Court case concerning the scope of so-called honest services fraud, and finally agreed to settle the case with no further appeals in 2013 for a reduction of 10 years off his sentence. He is expected to be released from prison in 2017 (Calkins 2013). The Enron story ends with two powerful business titans facing full criminal responsibility for their wrongdoing.

The investigation into the collapse of Enron occurred over five years, spawned criminal litigation over a dozen years, and resulted in criminal charges against 36 individuals, including 27 former Enron executives and two former chief executive officers. The government also charged accounting and banking personnel with crimes. The charges were primarily related to lying, cheating, and stealing. This is the simple essence of federal fraud-related charges such as securities fraud, mail fraud, wire fraud, insider trading, conspiracy, and obstruction. The tremendous investment of government resources paid off and were expended at the same time that the United States faced the challenge of investigating a significant physical threat to the security of the country after the 9/11 attacks. The collapse of Enron illustrates how the rule of law should address harmful financial frauds for even the most powerful.

Other large firms also became embroiled in accounting fraud investigations during 2001 and 2002, and their executives too faced a rational rule of law that meted out appropriate criminal accountability. For example, after merging with rival MCI, WorldCom had incurred a mammoth debt load and engaged in accounting fraud to cover up its weak position and maintain its stock price. WorldCom's fraud was stunningly simple: they booked expenses as assets, which effectively pumped up their profits. On June 25, 2002, WorldCom announced it had overstated its profits by over $3 billion over the past five quarters. WorldCom declared bankruptcy in July 2002, becoming the largest bankruptcy in history, exceeding Enron's bankruptcy less than a year earlier (Pulliam & Solomon 2002). The shareholders of the telecommunications giant lost their entire investment.

That fraud led to the convictions of several former WorldCom top executives, including controller David Myers, who admitted to his role in the fraud and was sentenced to a year and a day; Buford Yates, former director of general accounting, who was also sentenced to one year and a day; Betty Vinson, an accounting executive, who admitted to accounting fraud and was sentenced to five months in prison; and Troy Normand, another accounting officer, who was sentenced to three years of probation due to his lesser role in the fraud. CFO Scott Sullivan was sentenced to five years imprisonment having pled guilty to charges of securities fraud, conspiracy, and making false filings to the SEC. Sullivan testified against CEO Bernie Ebbers. Ebbers was convicted on all charges in 2005 and sentenced to 25 years imprisonment (Johnson 2005). Once again the government perfectly executed an investigation that involved prosecutions at progressively higher levels of corporate authority, culminating in the conviction of a CEO.

The Ebbers case led to an important precedent for the purposes of financial fraud. In *United States v. Ebbers*, the Second Circuit approved a conscious-avoidance jury instruction (or willful blindness instruction) against defendant Ebbers, charged with securities fraud. The court stated that "[a] conscious-avoidance charge is appropriate when (a) the element of knowledge is in dispute, and (b) the evidence would permit a rational juror to conclude beyond a reasonable doubt that the defendant was aware of a high probability of the fact in dispute and consciously avoided confirming that fact." The court concluded that the jury could find the defendant was consciously avoiding information that would reveal that the financial reports were inaccurate. CEO Ebbers signed "documents he didn't bother to read in full, including the 10-Ks [filed with the SEC], and tossing the management budget variance report in the trash without reading it." Thus, the mental element of knowledge may be proven by the conscious effort to avoid knowing and may be imputed to an individual or to a corporation (or both) depending upon the facts of the case. This is the equivalent of the willful blindness jury instruction approved by the Supreme Court, as discussed in the introduction.

While WorldCom was also politically active and was a larger company than Enron, it did not have direct connections to the White House that Ken Lay and Enron enjoyed. For example, it made $723,000 in so-called soft-money contributions to political parties rather than specific candidates. In addition, WorldCom affiliates funded both Democratic and GOP candidates about equally. Richard Gephardt, then House minority leader, stated, "No member will pull his or her punches. . . . I think the fact we have, not only not changed our rhetoric, we have not changed our actions on these issues are proof that the Democrats aren't affected by these money-raising activities" (Ambinder 2002). CEO Ebbers once made the *Forbes* 400 list of wealthiest Americans, with a net worth estimated at $1.4 billion, prior to the crash of WorldCom (Lewis 2002). The criminal convictions of the most senior officers of the bankrupt firm prove that as of 2002 the rule of law operated to hold even the most powerful corporate executives criminally accountable. Indeed, Bernie Ebbers remains in jail today (*Economic Times* 2015).

The Enron era of corporate scandals ended with many CEOs and other senior managers of major firms behind bars. Those highlighted above simply constitute the most economically and politically powerful to face criminal conviction. Some faced accountability under state law. The great majority faced accountability under federal law. One well-known commentator stated that these prosecutions proved that "the government has shown that juries are willing to hold the top officers of major corporations—executives who rarely are involved in the routine of daily operations—accountable for large-scale wrongdoing, even if the proof rests largely with the testimony of a single cooperating witness." These prosecutions inspired media reports that the CEO position had become a "hot seat" (Eichenwald 2005). The government did not win every case, and at least one high-profile trial resulted in acquittal. Some argued the government overstepped its bounds in some cases. Nevertheless, at the end of the Enron era commentators could confidently state, "When this era began, many people muttered that business leaders who committed fraud and other offenses would never be brought to justice. Investors would suffer losses because of their crimes, but the bosses would walk away because they were too big and too wealthy and had too many good lawyers. Nearly five years later, it's clear that that cynicism was unwarranted" (*Chicago Tribune* 2006).

In fact, with the changes to the sentencing guidelines for economic crimes discussed above, sentencing terms of imprisonment for financial crimes during the Bush administration far outpaced those in earlier administrations. Consider that in 1987 billionaire investor Ivan Boesky was convicted of insider trading (a variant of securities fraud) and was sentenced to only 3 years, serving only 22 months. Michael Milken, another billionaire and widely known as the junk bond king, was sentenced to 10 years and served only 22 months for securities fraud and regulatory violations. In comparison, the DOJ under George W. Bush obtained sentences of 25 years for Bernie Ebbers and 10 years for Andrew Fastow (Wong 2005).

Criminal Convictions of Powerful Bankers: The Savings and Loan Crisis

Among the best known prosecutions arising from the savings and loan crisis are the convictions of Charles H. Keating Jr., of Lincoln Savings and Loan in Arizona, and David Paul, of Centrust Bank in Florida. The US Department of Justice prosecuted Chairman and CEO Keating and his cohorts on 73 counts of racketeering and bank fraud in 1993, among other charges; Keating was convicted and served 4.5 years of a 12.5-year sentence in prison. The failure of Lincoln Savings was the costliest savings and loan failure in history (Black 2005).

Keating's case became well known in part because five US senators played a high-profile role in the ability of Keating and Lincoln Savings to deflect regulatory action. Each of the so-called Keating Five received substantial financial campaign support (totaling $1.4 million) from Keating and others affiliated with Lincoln. In one instance, the Keating Five approached the Federal Home Loan Bank Board (FHLBB), the agency responsible for overseeing savings and loan institutions, and asked the agency to forgo taking over Lincoln Federal. Although the FHLBB eventually took over Lincoln and prosecuted Keating, the delay in doing so led to a scandal concerning the senators and allegations they exercised inappropriate influence on behalf of Keating and Lincoln Savings.

After the deregulation of the savings and loan industry in the 1980s, savings and loans could take more risks with depositors' money, including making risky commercial real estate loans and even investing in junk bonds in an effort to maximize profits. The FHLBB instituted regulatory limits on these investments, found that Lincoln flagrantly exceeded theses limits, and began to press Lincoln to comply.

Before the FHLBB could use its enforcement arsenal, the Keating Five, John McCain, John Glenn, Alan Cranston, Donald Riegle, and Dennis DeConcini, intervened to delay the FHLBB. Keating and McCain were close friends and shared vacations and business investments. Ultimately the senators faced an ethics inquiry and one senator faced reprimand from the Senate. Senator McCain later termed the episode the worst mistake of his life.

Infamously, Keating, when asked if he thought his contributions gave him influence over the senators, stated, "I hope so" (Fetini 2008). Nevertheless, the Keating Five did not save Keating, as he faced both state and federal criminal jury trials and lost both. In the federal trial, the jury convicted him of 73 counts of fraud, for which he served over 4 years in federal prison. Although Keating prevailed on appeal, he pleaded guilty to bankruptcy fraud in 1999 and was sentenced to time served on the original conviction.

Another high-profile case from the savings and loan crisis that resulted in a powerful financier going to jail arose from the very costly failure of CenTrust Savings Bank. CenTrust failed in February 1990 at an ultimate cost to the taxpayer-backed FDIC deposit insurance fund of $1.7 billion, representing the fourth costliest savings and loan failure. CEO David Paul faced federal criminal charges for using bank funds to finance an extravagant lifestyle, complete with lavish treatment of a number of politicians. At the trial, witnesses testified that Paul used CenTrust funds to improve a $9 million waterfront estate and make his $7 million yacht more luxurious. The mayor of Miami testified that Paul paid him a bribe of $35,000 in CenTrust funds to get an exemption for his residential boat dock. Prosecutors also charged that Paul defrayed $3.2 million in personal expenses in the construction of a $140 million tower for the bank in downtown Miami.

At trial, the jury convicted Paul of virtually all counts. This included 47 counts of bank fraud, nine counts of misapplication of bank funds, five counts of tax violations, four counts of mail fraud, two counts of obstruction of regulators, and one count each of conspiracy and making false entries in the bank's books. The jury acquitted Paul of only a single mail fraud count (*New York Times* 1993). In another criminal action Paul was convicted of a wide array of racketeering and fraud charges, 97 crimes in all. A federal judge ultimately sentenced him to 11 years in prison, along with $65 million in fines and restitution orders (*New York Times* 1994).

The staff of Senator Orrin Hatch led a Senate inquiry into the failure of CenTrust. They found that Paul helped raise funds for the Democratic Senatorial Campaign Committee. He steered over $300,000 into the effort to get more Democrats into the Senate. He also entertained a US senator at one of his lavish parties that included chefs flown in from France, and several senators used his private airplane and sailboat for fund-raising and recreation (Hatch 2002). Needless to say, none of these connections saved Paul from criminal accountability.

While it is true that banks in the 1980s were smaller than today's megabanks, and therefore posed little threat to financial stability, that cannot explain individual criminal immunity. Recently, the DOJ indicted and convicted a member of the Goldman Sachs board of directors for insider trading, a form of securities fraud. His incarceration in 2014 did not lead to any financial instability (Hurtado 2016). Individual criminal accountability promotes financial stability by providing investors the confidence of the rule of law. On the other hand, insider trading typically does not threaten entire political networks, as the wide-ranging frauds we detail herein would. Hence, we posit that the real barrier to the prosecution of criminality at the megabanks is the preservation of various forms of political advantage. The next section expands on this by focusing on the missed opportunity to cut the megabanks down to size despite serious criminal misconduct.

DOJ and the Corporate Death Penalty: They Did It Before

On at least two occasions in recent decades the DOJ pursued criminal actions with little regard for the collateral consequences on a corporate defendant—including the essential demise of the corporation's business viability. Effectively, the DOJ criminal prosecutions have yielded the corporate death penalty in the past without calamitous disruption to the industry.

The global accounting firm of Arthur Andersen provides the most recent example. Arthur Andersen rolled the dice and lost, as a jury found in June 2002 that it obstructed justice by destroying documents in connection with its audit of Enron. While the conviction was ultimately reversed by the Supreme Court (for flawed jury instructions), the damage was done because a convicted felon cannot act as an auditor. Arthur Andersen surrendered its auditing license and thus its right to practice before the SEC on August 31, 2002. This put the firm out of the accounting and auditing business. Many of its accountants joined other firms, and parts of its operations were sold to other auditing firms.

DOJ specifically argued at trial that the motive for obstructing the government's investigation and shredding documents arose from prior bad acts that Arthur Andersen had committed that would operate to disqualify it from auditing practice before the SEC if one more bad act was found. In June 2001, Arthur Andersen had settled an SEC complaint based upon its audit work with Waste Management and was enjoined from committing any further violations. In July 2001, the company faced another SEC complaint related to its audit work for Sunbeam Corporation (*Arthur Andersen LLP v. United States* 2005). Within six months, Arthur Andersen faced a third case, this one for shredding Enron documents. The DOJ proceeded to prosecute the company on obstruction for the Enron shredding knowing that a conviction would put the firm out of business (Weil & Barrionuevo 2002). In essence, DOJ sought the corporate death penalty against the world's largest accounting firm, denying the corporation a third dodging of criminal liability.

Another case where a DOJ criminal prosecution led to a firm's demise involved the long-standing investment bank Drexel Burnham Lambert. Drexel became highly dependent upon Michael Milken's success as junk bond king and ultimately became fully embroiled in his frauds. Drexel agreed to pay Milken's legal costs when he was criminally charged. With the case against Milken proving quite strong and with the emergence of the cooperation of a number of Drexel employees, the criminal investigation easily led to Drexel as corporate defendant. In December 1988, the firm pleaded guilty to six felonies and settled SEC claims in a consent decree. The firm agreed to pay $650 million in fines and to install retired SEC Chairman John Shad as chairman of Drexel. The consent decree further required the firm to buy out the Milken brothers' equity and break off contact with them. On February 13, 1990, Drexel filed for bankruptcy, unable to recover from the loss of its reputation, the Milken ouster, and the large fine. Once again, the DOJ did not stand down simply because of the likelihood of demise of a large and storied financial firm (Eichenwald 1990).

In fact, quite to the contrary, the DOJ obtained its guilty plea from Drexel in part because it threatened to pursue a criminal case that would include racketeering charges under the Racketeer Influenced and Corrupt Organizations Act (RICO). RICO charges would empower the DOJ to seize assets before trial, and almost certainly end Drexel's ability to do business. This proved too much for Drexel to bear, and immediately before being indicted under the racketeering laws Drexel agreed to plead guilty. Even without the racketeering counts, the prosecution materially ended Drexel, as a felony conviction dooms firms in a business requiring trust and confidence such as investment banking (Paltrow 1988).

Today, as we will show, the government affirmatively acts to negate this type of corporate death penalty. As the *Economist* observes, "Admitting to criminal behaviour in America was once a guarantee of bankruptcy. That, at any rate, was the fate of big names such as Drexel Burnham Lambert, an investment bank, and Arthur Andersen, an accountancy firm, which had to shut up shop after losing both operating licences and clients that were restricted from doing business with felons. Yet the Department of Justice and other regulators seem to have magicked this consequence away" (*Economist* 2015).

Large financial firms also suffered legal fragmentation in the past, albeit not expressly for criminal behavior. In the aftermath of the Great Depression, Congress passed the Glass-Steagall Act, which mandated the separation of commercial and investment banking. As a direct result, J.P. Morgan & Company spun off Morgan Stanley, an investment bank, to its shareholders in order to preserve its ability to pursue its commercial banking business. The slow erosion and ultimate repeal of Glass-Steagall allows today's megabanks to continue to exist in their current form (Carpenter et al. 2016). Yet, this history of legally mandated divestment in the financial sector directly supports the notion that megabanks can suffer fragmentation with little or no economic harm.

History provides other examples of legally mandated spin-offs to shareholders, to the benefit of a firm's shareholders. Both AT&T and Standard Oil faced federally mandated breakups under US antitrust laws. Stockholders receiving shares in the firms these behemoths spun off under the breakup saw their total investment double. The financial services industry could see similar benefits for current shareholders of the megabanks. The megabanks trade at a discount compared to the price of shares of large regional banks relative to the book value (a measure of underlying assets) (Bair 2012). This dovetails with evidence from the introduction suggesting that megabanks underperform due to their complexity and inclination toward criminality. Much shareholder value could actually be unlocked if criminal megabanks faced compelled breakups. In fact, recently General Electric reduced the size of its financial services affiliate by selling hundreds of billions in assets, which allowed it to shed its Too-Big-to-Fail status—and its shares soared relative to the market and peer firms (Cox 2016).

White-Collar Criminal Liability and the Financial Crisis

The financial crimes that figure largely in the financial crisis of 2008 and beyond are straightforward in their roots: lying, stealing, and fraud. As the US economy became more advanced and interstate transactions became a more pronounced reality, Congress responded to the threat that financial scams could cause financial instability and recessions or depressions with a more expansive federal arsenal to combat financial frauds and scams. The new indulgences for financial crimes committed by financial elites are directly at odds with this legal reality.

Stealing money through financial frauds (or through dishonesty about material facts) has been criminalized under federal law since at least the Great Depression. The Securities Act of 1933 and the Securities Exchange Act of 1934 both outlaw fraud in connection with securities transactions. The Exchange Act also created the SEC, which Congress empowered to investigate and prosecute violations of securities laws in general and securities fraud in particular. After the enactment of these landmark laws, the federal government mandated truthful disclosure of material facts in a broad array of financial and investment transactions.

The breadth of this federal criminal authority extends to all transactions in securities. In general, a securities transaction occurs any time a promoter seeks to pool money from passive investors with the promise of profits. Thus, transactions involving shares of corporate stock, investments in corporate bond transactions, and investments in pools of mortgages all fall within the scope of securities transactions. Any such transaction triggers an obligation for issuers of securities to tell the truth, the whole truth, and nothing but the truth to potential investors, for which there is no exemption under federal law. This broad affirmative disclosure obligation supplemented state laws because Congress found that securities fraud threatened the entire national economy.

In tandem with this expansion in disclosure obligations, and as briefly discussed in the introduction, Congress further required all publicly traded firms to periodically and truthfully disclose all material facts to the investing public. Once a stock is publicly traded on a stock exchange, the firm must provide all material facts about its business in periodic reports. The annual report is called Form 10-K and must include audited financial statements. Quarterly reports, Form 10-Q, also must disclose all material facts. Firms also file a Form 8-K when important events occur that require disclosure. Under these federal laws, therefore, affirmative disclosure obligations are imposed on issuers and public firms. This disclosure regime also addressed state law failures to require such disclosures.

Congress took this action to secure truthfulness in investment transactions in the wake of the Great Depression and the manifest frauds that drove all facets of that economic catastrophe. State law proved inadequate to prevent such massive frauds in the nationwide business of securities transactions. The Great Depression convinced Congress to act to criminalize securities fraud, and this determination that federal interests in financial markets justified a federal solution has never been reversed over the 80 years since the passage of these landmark laws (Ramirez 2014). Prior to imposing this federal disclosure regime, securities markets and exchanges operated like giant betting parlors where the house always won because investors rarely had access to the truth about the firms and securities they invested in.

Aside from securities laws, financial scams that use the mail or wires also constitute federal offenses. Mail fraud under 18 USC section 1341 applies to all frauds that utilize the mail in furtherance of the fraudulent scheme and has been a federal crime since 1872. Later, Congress outlawed fraudulent schemes that utilized the wires, including telephone lines or the Internet. Since the Great Depression Congress has broadened the scope of criminal financial frauds in response to manifest needs that appeared in the wake of some new financial crisis. For example, Congress criminalized bank fraud when it enacted 18 USC section 1344 in 1982 at the beginning of the savings and loan crisis.

The Enron frauds discussed above similarly demanded a congressional response. In an effort to hold key managers accountable for the honesty of corporate financial reports, Congress included a new statute in the Sarbanes-Oxley Act of 2002, requiring corporate officers to certify financial reports, thereby placing responsibility for the underlying assertions of such documents on the corporate leaders and conveying the obligation to verify and inform themselves of the financial stability of the corporation. After the Sarbanes-Oxley Act, senior corporate managers could no longer colorably claim that they did not know about frauds at their firm because this law requires them to certify the accuracy of their disclosure statements. The upshot of these legal developments is a constant effort at the federal level to rid the financial sector of fraud through a broad array of antifraud statutory provisions.

Other elements of modern federal criminal law impose even greater accountability. Even before the Great Depression, federal law had already outlawed conspiracies to violate laws. In fact, criminal law had proscribed conspiracies as early as the 1600s in England. Historically, a conspiracy is simply an agreement between persons to violate a law or engage in criminal misconduct together. The conspiracy need not succeed, but under the federal general conspiracy statute, 18 USC section 371, some affirmative action by any member of the conspiracy must be taken in furtherance of such a conspiracy. Therefore, any person participating in a scheme to defraud commits a federal crime at an early stage in the scheme, simply by agreeing to the scheme and by the overt act of any conspirator in furtherance of the scheme, whether or not the scheme succeeds or results in some defrauded victim.

The federal antifraud statutes also prohibit schemes to defraud as well as actual frauds. Fraudulent statements made in furtherance of a scheme to defraud may include false assertions of past, present, or future acts and are criminalized even if the scheme fails. This means that the government need not prove reliance by the victim on any false claim of a past, present, or future fact. The federal statutes punish the scheme to defraud, whether or not the scheme is actually completed or successful, and do not require proof of reliance upon the false statement by the victim (*Neder v. United States*). Thus, the scope of the above statutes has been effectively broadened beyond general criminal law concepts. Similar legal developments hold corporations and their senior managers to heightened accountability.

Early writers on common law posited that a corporation could not commit a crime, although its agents could be held criminally responsible. Yet, over 100 years have passed since the Supreme Court first recognized that "modern authority, universally, as far as we know, is the other way," and rejected a challenge to holding a corporation criminally responsible for the acts of its agents in *New York Central & Hudson River Railroad Company v. United States.*

In that case, the Court addressed due process arguments of the corporate defendant that criminal punishment of the corporation "in reality punishes the innocent stockholders" and "deprive[s] them of their property without opportunity to be heard." In holding the corporation criminally responsible for acts of its agents done for its benefit, the Court affirmed policy interests in protecting the public by refusing to "shut its eyes to the fact that the great majority of business transactions in modern times are conducted through these bodies, and particularly that interstate commerce is almost entirely in their hands, and to give them immunity from all punishment . . . would virtually take away the only means of effectually controlling the subject-matter and correcting the abuses" at which the criminal law is aimed.

While it is easy to understand how a person can form the criminal intent that satisfies the requisite elements of the federal antifraud crimes, corporations or other organizations are nonhuman legal entities and thus have no mind with which to form intent. Instead, corporations act through their agents and employees. Thus, the law has imputed to corporations the acts and intentions of agents acting within the scope of their employment. The federal courts have explained that under the doctrine of *respondeat superior* corporations can be held criminally responsible for the acts of their agents, acting within the scope of their authority and with the intent, at least in part, of benefitting the corporation. This means that if any employee of a corporation harbors the intent to defraud, the corporation can be found criminally liable.

Corporations may also be held criminally liable for the collective knowledge of their employees. Thus, in *United States v. Bank of New England*, the First Circuit found that the bank "willfully" failed to file credit transactions reports "as part of a pattern of illegal activity involving transactions of more than $100,000 in a twelve-month period" in violation of federal law. The court observed that the collective knowledge jury instruction was especially pertinent to the case because "[c]orporations compartmentalize knowledge, subdividing the elements of specific duties and operations into smaller components. The aggregate of those components constitutes the corporation's knowledge of a particular operation."

The bank had compartmentalized its departments, but proof of knowledge was supported by the collective evidence of willfulness, including knowledge by a head teller, an internal memorandum on the bank's reporting obligations under law, instructions on government-authored currency transaction report forms, a bank auditor's instructions to the head tellers, and bank employees' awareness of the numerous unreported transactions. Thus, in proving the mental element of knowledge, the courts have held a corporation criminally liable for its agents' acts by considering the collective knowledge of its employees.

Not only can the corporation be held liable for the acts of its agents, but criminal law may also hold corporate officers responsible for omissions of oversight in some circumstances through the "responsible corporate officer" doctrine. In *United States v. Park*, the Supreme Court concluded that Park, then president and chief executive officer of Acme Markets, Inc., a national retail food chain with headquarters in Philadelphia, could be held criminally responsible for violations of the Federal Food, Drug, and Cosmetic Act, when food held for sale in a warehouse in Baltimore was found to be adulterated within the meaning of the statute because it was exposed to contamination by rodents.

Although Acme pleaded guilty, Park did not, asserting that he had delegated responsibility for overseeing the warehouses to Acme's Baltimore division vice president, who had taken steps to remedy the unsanitary conditions at Baltimore and earlier at a second warehouse in Philadelphia. The Court held that Park could be held liable for the contamination even if he did not personally participate and found the jury was fairly advised that "to find guilt it must find respondent 'had a responsible relation to the situation,' and 'by virtue of his position . . . had . . . authority and responsibility' to deal with the situation." Given that the statute involved was intended to protect the public food supply from contamination, the Court adopted the reasoning articulated in *United States v. Dotterweich* that "the interest of the larger good . . . puts the burden of acting at hazard upon a person otherwise innocent by standing in responsible relation to a public danger." The responsible corporate officer doctrine also may apply to corporate managers in those cases where *mens rea* is required; however, the prosecution must prove that the officer had supervisory responsibilities for the matter in question and acted with the requisite level of *mens rea* required by the applicable statute.

In recent history, other federal criminal statutes have assumed a high profile and bear upon the key issues addressed in this book. For example, perjury, obstruction of justice, lying to a federal agent, and lying to Congress also constitute federal offenses. Statutes related to these offenses address efforts to obstruct investigations into unlawful conduct, so that in some instances the cover up becomes a prosecutable crime. Powerful individuals with wealth and/or political connections have faced criminal prosecution for these crimes, including Scooter Libby (former chief of staff to Vice President Dick Cheney), billionaire entrepreneur Martha Stewart, and Colonel Oliver North (a White House aide in the Reagan administration) (Green 2007).

Finally, federal money laundering statutes along with transaction reporting requirements and the Bank Secrecy Act are purely statutory creations of relatively new origin intended to impede the use or movement of funds obtained through illegal misconduct. Large sums of money are unwieldy to transport in cash, so criminal organizations seek the services of financial institutions to move it seamlessly and invisibly across borders and even continents as desired. Financial institutions, therefore, have been tasked through criminal statutory requirements with monitoring large incoming sums of money and reporting them to the government. Notification can provide leads to discovering and seizing the proceeds of illegal gains from dangerous criminal organizations such as violent international drug cartels and terrorist organization fronts.

Prosecutorial Discretion and Its Abuse

Of course, the government holds discretion to decline criminal prosecutions. That discretion, however, cannot be applied for improper ends, such as political advancement or monetary rewards. The Department of

Justice provides guidelines to its prosecutors to aid in making the discretionary decision of whether and whom to prosecute. The US Attorneys' Manual (USAM), though it does not afford defendants any additional rights, is available online. Consequently, potential defendants can review it and often structure their arguments against prosecution with an eye toward its considerations. White-collar criminals often have ready access to legal defenses long before ordinary street criminals. Thus, a key task for white-collar defense attorneys is to work to prevent a case from reaching the point where the prosecution seeks indictment from a grand jury. Knowing the factors that prosecutors consider before seeking indictment allows the defense counsel to shape arguments against indictment accordingly.

All prosecutors consider the legal sufficiency of a case as a starting point. The nature of the case, the gravity of the harm, and the strength and admissibility of the evidence, including the credibility of the likely witnesses, are key considerations because unless the defendant pleads guilty, the prosecutor must prove every element of the crime beyond a reasonable doubt. Absent legal sufficiency, or probable cause, a prosecutor should not move forward with a criminal prosecution both for practical reasons and ethical reasons.

USAM 9–28.000, revised in 2008, sets forth the Principles of Federal Prosecution of Business Organizations, and 9–28.300 sets forth the factors to be considered by prosecutors in determining whether to charge a corporation (DOJ 1997, 2008). While many of the considerations are the same as those for an individual, the section identifies factors unique to business entities as well. Prosecutors are advised to consider "the pervasiveness of wrongdoing within the corporation, including the complicity in, or the condoning of, the wrongdoing by corporate management." Other factors include considering whether the corporation has engaged in similar misconduct addressed through criminal, civil, or regulatory enforcement actions, whether the corporation voluntarily disclosed its wrongdoing, and the efforts it has taken to cooperate and remediate. In particular, "efforts to implement an effective corporate compliance program . . . , to replace responsible management, to discipline or terminate wrongdoers, to pay restitution, and to cooperate" with the government should be considered. Especially unique to corporate entities are factors considering "collateral consequences, including whether there is disproportionate harm to shareholders, pension holders, employees, and others not proven personally culpable, as well as impact on the public arising from the prosecution."

Certainly to the extent that the corporation benefitted, at least initially, from the criminal misconduct, so have the shareholders, pension holders, and employees. However, due to the potential for a criminal prosecution to devastate the value of the company's shares, a prosecutor is directed to consider whether any consequential loss disproportionately harms such stakeholders. Should a corporation be convicted of a crime, depending upon the charges, it could face an effective death penalty. A bank convicted of money laundering, for example, could lose clients such as pension funds that would be prohibited by law from investing in it, and the bank would potentially lose its charter to operate.

Federal prosecutors are further instructed to also consider whether there are adequate alternatives to indicting a corporation, such as prosecuting individuals responsible for the corporate malfeasance or seeking civil or regulatory remedies. The prosecutor should weigh the factors as relevant to the case and with a view toward ensuring the general purposes of criminal law warrant the anticipated punishment.

Addressing the criminality incurred by large, publicly traded companies has contributed to a rise in the use of deferred prosecution agreements (DPAs) and nonprosecution agreements (NPAs) that had originated as a form of diversion for individual offenders. A DPA allows a prosecutor to obtain criminal charges against a corporation; the charges are then filed with the court. The prosecution agrees to withhold pressing forward on litigation in exchange for promises on the part of the defendant. Ordinarily, such promises would include avoiding further criminal conduct, reforming current business and ethical practices, firing managers and other employees responsible for the criminal conduct, hiring a monitor to implement or oversee such changes, and possibly agreeing to pay restitution or comply with other civil or regulatory agreements. The agreements may also include admissions of wrongdoing on the part of the defendant and promises not to contradict those admissions or undermine the cooperative nature of the agreement. The cooperative development of such agreements allows the parties to shape the agreement to fit the nature of the offense, the situation of the offender, and the needs of the victims. The parties agree that the deferral will extend for a defined period (typically one to five years), with the possibility to extend the period should a question regarding compliance be raised during the agreed upon period. The DPA effectively stays the timing on the criminal proceedings. Once the deadline expires, the prosecution moves to dismiss the case from court if the defendant has complied. An NPA is similar in effect, except that no charges are filed, so the agreement occurs outside the judicial process and no agreement is filed with the court. Once the deadline expires, the agreement has been fulfilled and no criminal case is filed.

The past 15 years have witnessed a dramatic upturn in the use of DPAs and NPAs by the Department of Justice that have substantially usurped the dichotomous choice of pursing a civil or criminal case against a major corporation. Although data on such prosecution alternatives are not tracked by the DOJ, Brandon Garrett reported in his book, *Too Big to Jail*, that he was able to locate only 14 DPA and NPA cases prior to 2001; however, from 2001 through 2012, 255 companies received DPA or NPA agreements. During that same period, 2,000 corporations were convicted of federal crimes, but "large and public corporations increasingly received agreements allowing them to avoid a conviction . . . and generally, banks and other financial institutions received deferred prosecution or non-prosecution agreements, not convictions" (Garrett 2014, 65). The use of these agreements has continued to swell, with fewer than a third of 434 agreements currently identified in Brandon Garrett and Jon Ashley's database occurring before 2009. Moreover, close to one-third of the post-2008 recent agreements involved financial institutions (Garrett & Ashley 2016).

Central to the concept of avoiding collateral consequences by declining prosecution of the corporation is the expectation that those corporate agents most directly involved and those managers most responsible for oversight would be held individually liable for their personal conduct and the harm it caused. Since corporations can act only through their agents, it stands to reason that agents engage in criminal conduct when a DPA or NPA is reached. Even if one accepts that a corporation may be too big to fail or to jail, there is no single person who is essential to the success of a major publicly held corporate entity. Furthermore, permitting such individuals to avoid accountability for criminal activity creates the moral hazard that encourages further risk taking and law breaking by those individual corporate managers and others who might take their place. Garrett's study revealed that where the corporation avoided criminal prosecution by entering into a DPA or NPA from 2001 to 2012, "[i]n about two-thirds of the cases no individual officers or employees were prosecuted for related crime," whereas in about one-third of such cases individuals were prosecuted (Garrett 2014, 83). The type of offense mattered, however, so that "in antitrust cases, individuals were prosecuted in three of four antitrust cases. In contrast, no individual officers or employees were prosecuted in cases involving banks violating laws related to money laundering." By comparison, 25 percent of the convicted publicly traded companies during this period also saw officers or employees face prosecution (Garrett 2014, 84).

The striking fact is that no criminal cases have been brought against managing executives of the top banking firms following the financial crisis of 2008. A justification for some, such as Lehman Brothers, is that the firm is defunct, rendering criminal charges useless; other participants in the crisis, such as Countrywide, have been acquired by another company, so it is unfair to impose criminal liability on the successor corporation. A more prominent assertion is that civil recovery through settlement is more expedient in that it is less costly and provides certainty of recovery, even if incomplete. Combined with the recent upswing in DPAs, the result of this is vanishing accountability for the most powerful financial elites.

Early reaction to the evolving mortgage crisis suggested DOJ was taking an aggressive stance on prosecutions. From March 1 to June 18, 2008, the DOJ charged more than 400 defendants for their roles in mortgage fraud schemes as part of a multiagency collaborative nationwide investigation called Operation Malicious Mortgage. Moreover, in conjunction with the announcement in 2008 that two senior managers of failed Bear Stearns hedge funds had been charged with conspiracy, securities fraud, and wire fraud, the DOJ declared it was "committed to investigating and prosecuting cases of mortgage-related securities fraud," highlighting that "[m]ortgage fraud and related securities fraud pose a significant threat to our economy" and that by holding perpetrators accountable the government would "help restore stability and confidence in our housing and credit markets" (DOJ 2008). As we will abundantly demonstrate in coming chapters, after 2008 the DOJ failed to pursue criminal accountability for the real misconduct at the center of the financial crisis and opted to leave the megabanks undisturbed rather than restructured.

That Was Then, This Is Now

The historic reality emerging from the above facts consists of an increasing criminal accountability of corporate executives for serious wrongdoing from the Great Depression forward, over a period of eight decades—regardless of the personal wealth and political influence of a given CEO or senior manager. Indeed, on the cusp of the Great Financial Crisis of 2008, the Corporate Fraud Task Force, created by President George W. Bush in the immediate aftermath of the Enron-era scandals, reported that between its formation in July 2002 and 2008, more than 200 chief executive officers and corporate presidents, more than 120 corporate vice presidents, and more than 50 chief financial officers had been convicted for financial frauds. The multiagency unit successfully oversaw a six-year effort to crack down on white-collar crime with a specific focus on corporate crime committed by top executives (Corporate Fraud Task Force 2008).

The Bush administration did in fact seek to distance itself from important corporate sponsors. Only one month after Enron declared bankruptcy, Attorney General John Ashcroft recused himself from the Enron investigation because it and CEO Ken Lay had been significant financial supporters in his tight Missouri Senate campaign, and Ashcroft's chief of staff, David Ayers, bowed out as well. The Bush Justice Department thereby avoided the appearance of impropriety (*CNN* 2002a).

In contrast, Attorney General Holder and the chief of the DOJ Criminal Division, Lanny Breuer, failed to avoid the appearance of impropriety. Specifically, Reuters reported in 2012 that both officials hailed from the same major law firm, Covington & Burling, which included among its clients some of the major financial institutions at the center of the financial crisis, including Bank of America, Citigroup, and JPMorgan Chase (Paltrow 2012). Subsequently, a major international newspaper out of London published a story that raised questions regarding these links to the megabanks and the lack of criminal prosecutions of megabanks or their senior managers (Dayen 2014a). Thereafter, the *Columbia Journalism Review* chided mainstream news outlets for failing to report the links between Holder, Breuer, and the banks and the lack of criminal prosecutions (Chittum 2014).

One outlet, *Newsweek*, did report on the revolving door problems plaguing the DOJ and the political power of the megabanks. It documented that when Eric Holder became US attorney general in 2009, he had been co-chairing the white-collar defense unit at Covington & Burling. Holder had already enjoyed prior stints at DOJ and lucrative compensation at Covington for helping clients navigate DOJ-related matters. Holder tapped Lanny Breuer, another white-collar defense attorney from Covington & Burling, as the assistant attorney general of the DOJ Criminal Division in April 2009, along with others from Covington for other senior positions (Boyer 2012).

There are other distinctions between the Obama administration and the Bush administration on this issue. Under the new DOJ leadership of Holder and Breuer, the two former Bear Stearns traders were acquitted by a jury after a three-week trial in a case initiated under the Bush administration. Both traders later settled a related civil suit brought by the SEC, collectively agreeing to pay $1.05 million and accepting limited bans from the securities industry for misleading investors. With the jury acquittal in the criminal case, the DOJ seemingly abandoned efforts to hold major banks or investment firms or their employees criminally accountable for securities fraud. Instead the government entered into dozens of civil settlements involving each of the major institutions engaged in the trading activities that led to the near collapse of global financial markets. Only in rare instances were individuals held even civilly accountable by the government (Cassidy 2014). Despite occasional losses in the prosecutions during the accounting fraud crisis, the DOJ under the Bush administration did not allow such setbacks to intimidate it from enforcing the law.

To believe that one acquittal explains the weak-kneed response of DOJ to the massive frauds we detail herein begs credulity, in light of a staff of experienced DOJ financial crime prosecutors who had racked up convictions earlier that same decade. As Bill Black has noted, the government achieved high conviction rates against even elite white-collar criminals in the aftermath of the savings and loan crisis (Black 2013a).

Instead, the history of white-collar crime prosecutions suggests that a historic break in the accountability of financial elites has occurred.

No prior administration would allow the lawlessness underlying the financial crisis to untrack such an important enforcement mechanism as criminal accountability under law to impose appropriate incentives and disincentives in the financial sector. History shows that the stakes loom too large to permit such lawlessness in finance. That is why Congress equipped DOJ with such broad antifraud statutes and other tools to combat corruption in finance. In the past, DOJ used these tools aggressively even against the richest corporate and financial titans. The only thing that has changed is the soaring inequality in the United States and the massive resources controlled by financial elites at the megabanks. We will return to this point in later chapters. However, in the next few chapters we will present the best evidence available to show the utter criminality that pervaded the financial sector beginning in the years prior to the 2008 financial crisis. It is not a pretty picture and demands a response from the DOJ in the form of criminal prosecutions.

Following Attorney General Holder's April 2015 departure from the DOJ, returning to Covington & Burling in July 2015, as Lanny Breur had in 2013, Holder's replacement, Loretta Lynch, announced a shift in policy at the DOJ to address individual accountability for corporate wrongdoing, at least prospectively "to all future investigations" (Yates 2015). Indeed, shortly after Holder's departure, the parent companies of five major banks pled guilty to financial market manipulation. Deputy Attorney General Sally Quillian Yates issued a DOJ memorandum dated September 9, 2015, that summarizes changes to its policy toward pursuing individual accountability, both criminally and civilly, for corporate wrongdoing. The memo explains the policy change as maximizing the DOJ's "ability to deter misconduct and to hold those who engage in it accountable" (Yates 2015). The memo provides explicit guidance regarding these "policy shifts," setting forth six "key steps" to pursuing individual accountability. Among other policy changes, the memorandum identifies hinging credit for corporate cooperation upon full provision of relevant facts of individual wrongdoing and memorializing declinations as to individuals only with approval by the US attorney or assistant attorney general for the relevant DOJ division.

A true shift in policy would be a welcome relief. The memorandum, however, while not expressly dismissing the possibility of prosecutions arising from the subprime crisis, appears to operate prospectively, meaning that it may implicitly dismiss the option to revisit substantial corporate misconduct that led to the financial crisis.

In November 2015, the Principles of Federal Prosecution of Business Organizations of the USAM were revised and new sections were added to reflect the new guidance expressed in the memo (DOJ 1997, 2015). The question remains whether these principles will be applied faithfully when moneyed interests are investigated and civil remedies are expedient. After all, Lynch was the US attorney in Brooklyn at the time the HSBC deferred prosecution was negotiated in 2012. Just as the DOJ assured the American public for six years following the financial crisis that appropriate action would occur, the rule of law hangs on the promise of the latest US attorney general and the broad discretionary power she wields. No effort is even suggested to redress the extraordinary hubris of an attorney general who appears to have discarded 80 years of congressional statutory authority to deter and punish criminal wrongdoing while hiding behind prosecutorial discretion. At least one commentator suggests that this preserved his lucrative private practice position (Taibbi 2015b).

Lest history repeat itself, it is worth reviewing the bold misconduct that led to the financial crisis and the disregard for imposing the rule of law by the agency tasked with enforcing it. The more aggressive DOJ tone is encouraging, but the underlying forces that may explain the disinclination to enforce the laws remain in place.

2

Angelo Mozilo and Countrywide's "Toxic" Subprime Mortgages

This settlement resolves the fourth enforcement action I have brought against Bank of America to fight the widespread fraud that was at the root cause of the economic crisis. Bank of America, and in particular Countrywide, were major players in virtually every aspect of the market that caused the crisis, from shoddy loan originations and discriminatory lending to African Americans and Latinos to fraudulent marketing of mortgage-backed securities.
—Illinois Attorney General Lisa Madigan, August 21, 2014

Countrywide Financial originated more subprime loans than any other firm, $97 billion between 2005 and 2007, ultimately generating billions and billions in losses. Unfortunately, Countrywide failed to disclose to borrowers, purchasers of the loans, or its own investors the true nature of the loans even though officers at the corporation knew the loans were "toxic." As the leading subprime lender in the United States during the height of the subprime bubble, Countrywide pushed more poisonous mortgages into the global financial system than any other firm (Center for Public Integrity 2014). Nevertheless, in early 2011 the Department of Justice reportedly dropped its criminal inquiry against former Countrywide chairman of the board and CEO Angelo Mozilo, who personally profited from the demise of Countrywide to the tune of $521.5 million in compensation payments from 2000 to 2008 (Morgenson 2011). The government has pursued no criminal charges against any senior officer at Countrywide.

If Countrywide had truthfully disclosed the risks of its subprime loans, shareholders, investors, borrowers, and loan purchasers would have fled. By logic, fewer subprime originations would have followed as both demand and supply would have declined. Countrywide's publicly traded securities would have plunged in value. Countrywide would have faced real challenges peddling its subprime mortgages to investors looking to purchase prime mortgage-backed securities. In short, Countrywide's lies regarding the true risks of its subprime lending drew much more capital into its business for a much longer time than would have been the case had it told the truth. As the truth of its subprime loans became known, the inevitable crash inflicted more pain than otherwise because the bubble grew under the influence of Countrywide's fraud.

A jury found Countrywide civilly liable for a massive fraud totaling over $1.2 billion through a scheme to sell mortgages to the government-sponsored enterprises (GSEs)—Fannie Mae and Freddie Mac—in the final stages of the subprime debacle. In addition, former Countrywide CEO Mozilo settled civil securities fraud claims brought by the SEC for $77 million. Countrywide also engaged in serious misconduct against borrowers. Countrywide settled the largest predatory lending lawsuit in history and the largest race-based lending lawsuit in history. Furthermore, Congress found that Countrywide ran a massive influence peddling scheme known as Friends of Angelo, whereby influential individuals obtained VIP benefits from Countrywide in the form of sweetheart mortgages not otherwise available to the public. This chapter reviews the current facts known regarding the pattern of potential crimes committed by Countrywide.

All of these unlawful acts arose from one fundamental goal: maximizing the ability of senior management to soak investors for as much cash as possible for as long as possible. Frequently in white-collar crime cases defendants do not limit their dishonest behavior to a single crime. As we demonstrate in this chapter, Countrywide engaged in a variety of unlawful acts, arguably operating as a classic racketeering enterprise. Evidence now known from civil cases and government investigations reveals that Countrywide's senior officers were well aware of much of the conduct. Even without RICO charges, Countrywide's senior managers could face criminal charges for frauds affecting a financial institution. The statute of limitations for such crimes will not expire until 2018, as we outline.

Countrywide's Operation Hustle

The strongest evidence of criminality at Countrywide arises from its misrepresentations to Fannie Mae and Freddie Mac in connection with the sales of mortgages to these GSEs as mounting mortgage defaults suddenly shut down the subprime mortgage market in 2007. The GSEs enjoyed US government backing and could continue to purchase prime loans even as the market collapsed. Since the mortgage market was approaching a total collapse, Countrywide wanted to generate as many mortgages for sale as quickly as possible. That meant underwriting shortcuts regardless of the risks. The GSEs, however, purchased only prime mortgages, so Countrywide needed to portray its risky mortgage products as prime mortgages.

Inside Countrywide this program was called the High Speed Swim Lane (HSSL), or the Hustle. A jury found Countrywide guilty of civil fraud against the GSEs arising from the Hustle. The federal district judge called the fraud "brazen" when assessing civil fines against Countrywide. The fraud essentially centered on the testimony of a former Countrywide senior executive who blew the whistle on the practice. More specifically, according to former Countrywide senior vice president and executive vice president Edward O'Donnell, Countrywide shifted to defrauding the GSEs after the market for subprime mortgages collapsed in mid-2007 by misrepresenting the quality and riskiness of the mortgages.

The GSEs bought mortgages originated under the Hustle program and packaged them into mortgage-backed securities (MBSs), which the GSEs guaranteed. The GSEs impose certain clear guidelines on loans eligible for purchase and packaging into MBSs, requiring that all loans sold to them include detailed representations and warranties as to loan quality. These requirements essentially mandate that only prime loans qualify for sale to the GSEs and that the loans meet these investment quality standards. Furthermore, the GSEs require that all sellers of mortgages impose quality control mechanisms including postclosing review and reporting of any underwriting defects. If any loans default, the GSEs undertake their own quality review and in appropriate circumstances, if a defect is found, demand repurchase of the loan. Countrywide knowingly circumvented all of these requirements (*United States ex rel. O'Donnell v. Countrywide Home Loans, Inc.* 2012).

Operation Hustle started with a pilot program in 2006 and extended until 2008. It involved a deliberate plan to defraud the GSEs by selling subprime mortgages with very minimal underwriting (or assessment) for risk of default, contrary to their express misrepresentations to the GSEs. Ultimately, the US government lost more than $1 billion through its guarantee of the GSEs' mortgage loans. More losses cascaded through the financial system due to the failure of the GSEs and Countrywide's subprime loans, thereby directly contributing to the failure of the GSEs as well as the failure of banks invested in the securities of the GSEs.

The Hustle program sought to accelerate loan production through the elimination of "toll gates," including qualified underwriter review for certain high-risk loans, underwriting checklists, and compliance specialist audit prior to loan funding. The program also shifted compensation incentives to bonus payments based solely upon loan volume. In short, Countrywide eliminated nearly all quality control mechanisms and focused simply on originating as many loans as quickly as possible. Instead of disclosing the underwriting and audit lapses, Countrywide reassured the GSEs that it was tightening—not loosening—loan underwriting.

Countrywide pursued the Hustle loan program despite clear warnings it would lead to obvious and severe loan quality control problems. A number of senior managers at Countrywide told the senior officers running the Hustle program (the president of Countrywide Home Loans as well as its chief operating officer) that it risked higher fraud and lower mortgage quality. An internal quality control review early on confirmed that the loans generated under the Hustle program had exceptionally low quality. In particular, an internal review of Hustle in 2006 found that stated income loans (loans where the borrower's income is not documented or verified) were too risky for inclusion in the underwriter-free Hustle process. Still, Countrywide continued the program and included the dreaded stated income loans in the program.

Operation Hustle began in earnest on August 13, 2007, with the collapse of the subprime mortgage market that month (*United States ex rel. O'Donnell v. Countrywide Home Loans, Inc.* 2012). Countrywide realized that summer that only Fannie Mae and Freddie Mac survived as purchasers of mortgages. CEO Mozilo testified that August 2, 2007, constituted Countrywide's 9/11 because the credit markets suddenly shunned subprime mortgage exposure. Mozilo emailed Federal Reserve governor and former Countrywide board member Lyle Gramley: "Fear in the credit markets is now tending towards panic. There is little to no liquidity in the mortgage market with the exception of Fannie and Freddie. . . . Any mortgage product that is not deemed to be conforming either cannot be sold into the secondary markets or are subject to egregious discounts." Thus Countrywide desperately needed to sell loan products that conformed to the GSE loan guidelines (FCIC 2011).

Whistleblower Edward O'Donnell himself directed that underwriters conduct quality reviews on Hustle loans prefunding, and initially this was approved by senior officers so long as it did not slow down loan production. This quality review would ensure that the loans sold to the GSEs conformed to the prime quality standards imposed by the GSEs. They found a staggering defect rate of 57 percent and an even higher defect rate of nearly 70 percent for stated income loans. Rather than alter or end the Hustle program, senior management told O'Donnell to keep the findings of his audit within the Countrywide division running Hustle. Predictably, this quickly proved catastrophic. The US government lost over a billion dollars from Operation Hustle.

The loans from the Hustle program often featured grossly overstated borrower income. Appraisals used to value homes as collateral for mortgage loans were based on substandard practices contrary to GSE guidelines. This, in turn, meant unacceptably high loan-to-value ratios. Some borrowers listed employment with nonexistent businesses or misrepresented their employment. The GSE loan standards that Countrywide short-circuited were specifically intended to uncover such loan defects and misrepresentations. Not surprisingly many of the borrowers of these loans defaulted in the course of just a few months.

Compounding its fraudulent sales of low-quality subprime loans to the GSEs, Countrywide (as well as its successor in interest, Bank of America) refused to repurchase defaulted loans as agreed in the face of manifest defects in loan quality and other misrepresentations, even though Countrywide had known of the loan defects that triggered its legal repurchase obligation. One postfunding audit found defects in up to 40 percent of Countrywide's loans. Ultimately, the GSEs proved too undercapitalized to withstand mortgage losses, and the government placed them into conservatorship. By 2011, the government had spent $183 billion to bail out Fannie and Freddie (*United States ex rel. O'Donnell v. Countrywide Home Loans, Inc.* 2012).

Unlike much of the evidence discussed in this book, this case was decided by a jury. Reporters interviewed jurors from the civil case after the verdict finding the Hustle program constituted fraud under civil law. One juror cited as persuasive the testimony of John Boland, a former Countrywide supervisor, who testified that some Countrywide loan officers were not allowed to go home for the night unless they approved a loan. Jurors asked for Boland's videotape deposition just minutes before announcing their verdict. The juror told *Bloomberg* that "Boland's testimony was shocking. . . . Those employees were told to do '30 in 30,' or 30 loans in 30 days. I will say in my opinion the bank and these employees were just passing off unsatisfactory loans as prime loans and Fannie and Freddie got stuck." The jury readily comprehended the essence of the fraud (Hurtado 2013).

The US district judge in that same case stated during the damages part of the case that "[w]hile the [Hustle] process lasted only nine months, it was from start to finish the vehicle for a brazen fraud by the defendants, driven by a hunger for profits and oblivious to the harms thereby visited, not just on the immediate victims but also on the financial system as a whole." Judge Jed S. Rakoff also found that "[t]he HSSL fraud, simply by itself, more than warrants a penalty of $1,267,491,770." While it is impossible to predict if a jury would find that the Hustle program amounted to criminal fraud, surely the jury finding of civil fraud and the statement that the program amounted to "brazen" fraud are sufficient basis for convening a grand jury investigation to find probable cause for a criminal indictment (*United States ex rel. O'Donnell v. Countrywide Home Loans, Inc.* 2014). Yet, we have not found any public indication of a grand jury inquiry, and no criminal charges or pleas have been filed.

The US Court of Appeals for the Second Circuit reversed the judgment of the lower court for civil federal mail and wire fraud, based upon a narrow and unprecedented legal interpretation of federal statutory law. Specifically, although not required by the mail and wire fraud statutes, the court held that the DOJ's theory of liability required proof of fraudulent intent not just as of the date of the transfer of the Hustle loans to the GSEs, but also at the time of the formation of the contract. The appellate court found the jury was asked to find the required fraudulent intent only as of the date of transfer. While acknowledging that the evidence showed defendants knew the loans did not meet the representations required under the contract as of the time the loans were transferred to the GSEs, and that Countrywide held an intent to defraud as of the time of transfer, the appellate court required more. "The Government adduced no evidence and made no claim that Countrywide had fraudulent intent" while negotiating or signing the contracts (*United States ex rel. O'Donnell v. Countrywide Home Loans, Inc.* 2016). Consequently, the Second Circuit reversed the judgment of fraud. Even the courts themselves exercise seemingly extreme caution in holding bankers to account. The Second Circuit's reversal is novel.

Some observers argue that the failure of the GSEs caused the financial crash (Kaletsky 2010). Certainly, once the GSEs failed the financial system cratered thereafter. We now know Operation Hustle contributed to the insolvency of the GSEs. While we cannot know that Countrywide inflicted sufficient losses on the GSEs to cause their insolvency, at the very least Operation Hustle depleted the capital of the already thinly capitalized GSEs. Indeed, because Countrywide produced more subprime loans than any other firm, it stands to reason that it contributed the most to the real estate bubble and crash that destroyed the GSEs' economic viability.

The DOJ's civil case addresses only the GSEs' losses due to Operation Hustle. But they were not the only victims, and HSSL was not the only Countrywide scheme, as we discuss below. Countrywide also originated other toxic loans outside of the Hustle loans that no doubt inflicted additional losses on the GSEs, directly or indirectly, through the investment of the GSEs in nonprime loans. Ultimately, Countrywide's toxic loans led to $33 billion in losses to its acquirer, Bank of America. Shareholders of Countrywide also suffered substantial losses resulting from the reckless lending. Shareholders lost 80 percent of their value compared to share prices prior to the credit crisis (Ramirez 2009). As described in the next section, these other "toxic" mortgage loans also rested on fraud at Countrywide and further destabilized the financial system.

Angelo Mozilo's Fraud Settlement

On October 15, 2010, on the verge of a scheduled trial in Los Angeles, the Securities and Exchange Commission announced that former Countrywide Financial CEO Angelo Mozilo would pay a record $22.5 million civil penalty to settle SEC charges that he and other former Countrywide executives misled investors as the subprime mortgage crisis first emerged. Mozilo further paid $45 million in disgorgement of ill-gotten gains to settle the SEC's claims of securities fraud. Terms of the settlement stipulated that Mozilo be permanently barred from serving as an officer or director of a publicly traded company.

Former Countrywide chief operating officer David Sambol, a co-defendant, paid $5 million in disgorgement and a $520,000 penalty and agreed to a three-year bar from serving as a director or officer of a public firm. Former chief financial officer Eric Sieracki settled for a $130,000 penalty and a one-year bar from practicing before the commission. The SEC therefore investigated securities fraud at Countrywide and alleged that the company's senior management team engaged in securities fraud. The SEC also obtained significant monetary recoveries from its enforcement action.

According to the SEC's director of enforcement, "Mozilo's record penalty is the fitting outcome for a corporate executive who deliberately disregarded his duties to investors by concealing what he saw from inside the executive suite—a looming disaster in which Countrywide was buckling under the weight of increasing risky mortgage underwriting, mounting defaults and delinquencies, and a deteriorating business model." The associate regional director of the SEC's Division of Enforcement added, "This settlement will provide affected shareholders significant financial relief, and reinforces the message that corporate officers have a personal responsibility to provide investors with an accurate and complete picture of known risks and uncertainties facing a company" (SEC 2010a).

Despite the SEC's self-congratulatory press release, the message to corporate officers likely missed its mark. The commission failed to mention that Mozilo actually paid only a fraction of the total financial sanction and that Bank of America's totally innocent shareholders covered the rest. The *Los Angeles Times* reported that Bank of America and insurance proceeds (of policies paid for by the shareholders) covered all but $22 million. Furthermore, the SEC allowed the Countrywide officers to settle without admitting or denying guilt—which means the SEC settlement would provide no help to private shareholder claimants in any civil lawsuit for damages against these senior officers (Hamilton and Reckard 2010). We will see this pattern repeatedly with respect to government settlements and levied fines—almost always wrongdoers pay at most a token amount of their gain while innocent shareholders cover the rest. For example, the SEC was seeking to recover profits from sales of shares totaling $141.7 million from Mozilo (and $18.3 million from Sambol). A $22 million fine for $141.7 million in proceeds for stock sales does not qualify as even a slap on the wrist. Instead, it simply allowed Mozilo to reap great profits from his alleged fraud and sent the message to other financial elites that crime does in fact pay.

Congress empowered the SEC, unlike ordinary parties to litigation, to issue subpoenas and take sworn testimony before litigation. Thus, even before it files a complaint it already knows much more than an ordinary party to litigation because of these investigative powers. An SEC complaint therefore represents a report of a quasi–grand jury investigation. Consequently, the SEC's allegations enjoy the support of the findings of the SEC pursuant to its investigative powers.

The SEC's complaint filed against the Countrywide officers was well supported, referencing emails, internal documents, and other records that the SEC obtained during its investigation. The complaint details the representations that Countrywide made in its Form 10-K with respect to its loan underwriting standards. For the 2005, 2006, and 2007 annual reports Countrywide told the investing public that it managed its "credit risk through credit policy underwriting, quality control and surveillance activities." Countrywide generally disclosed its level of subprime loans and showed that its exposure to subprime loans increased from 2001 to 2006. Yet, Countrywide did not disclose that it had relaxed its guidelines for what it considered to be "prime" loans.

The SEC complaint stated that from 2005 to 2007, Mozilo, Sambol, and Sieracki "held Countrywide out as primarily a maker of prime quality mortgage loans, qualitatively different from competitors engaged in riskier lending." In fact, Countrywide specifically decided to expand its underwriting guidelines to include virtually all borrowers who would qualify for loans at other firms. "Countrywide engaged in an unprecedented expansion of its underwriting guidelines from 2005 and into 2007." Internal documents and emails show that even as early as June 2005, senior officers warned that this strategy put Countrywide at the "frontier" of risky lending. Basically, Countrywide decided it would match the underwriting standards of any competitor so as not to lose any potential borrower to another firm. The chief risk officer, John McMurray, predicted that this would result in "high expected default rates and losses." He further stated that the matching strategy would put Countrywide "among the most aggressive" lenders in the marketplace. This proved prescient, and the "matching strategy" of Countrywide ultimately proved unsustainable.

The SEC found similar emails to the entire Countrywide senior management team, including Mozilo, Sambol, and Sieracki, throughout 2006 and 2007. For example, on June 2, 2006, Sambol received a message that summarized the findings of Countrywide's quality control audit, which showed that 50 percent of stated income loans audited by the bank showed a significant variance in actual borrower income per IRS records. Of those, 69 percent overstated their income by more than 50 percent. Sambol also received an email from McMurray in late 2006 that argued that the matching strategy led to Countrywide ceding its risk policies to its competitors. In early 2007 McMurray told Sambol "[w]e've simply ceded our risk standards and balance sheet to whoever has the most liberal guidelines." He also warned that this would not likely "play well with investors, credit rating agencies, etc."

In early 2006, another bank insisted that Countrywide buy back certain defective loans that essentially allowed borrowers to buy homes with no down payment. In March 2006, CEO Mozilo sent an email to Countrywide's senior managers that demanded corrective action. He stated that the no-down-payment loans were "the most dangerous product in existence and there can be nothing more toxic." Later Mozilo called the loans "poison." On April 17, 2006, Mozilo called this type of home mortgage the most "toxic" home mortgage he had ever seen. Thus by mid-2006, CEO Mozilo and senior management at Countrywide knew that the company had exposed itself to inordinate risks of loan defaults.

On December 6, 2006, Mozilo circulated a memo drafted by Chief Risk Officer McMurray to the entire board and all senior managers, including Chief Operating Officer Sambol and Chief Financial Officer Sieracki. In the memo, Mozilo highlighted the fact that vintage 2006 mortgages had already defaulted at rates higher than in years past and the trend would continue. This arose from Countrywide's aggressive expansion of underwriting standards, which lowered required FICO scores, raised maximum loan amounts, raised loan-to-value ratios, and expanded stated income loans. In fact, Mozilo noted that 62 percent of Countrywide's 2006 loans had a loan-to-value ratio of 100 percent. Countrywide never disclosed these facts to its shareholders or other investors.

Another product that Mozilo found highly problematic actually allowed the borrower to determine the amount to be paid within certain limits and allowed negative amortization so that borrowers could owe significantly more than the value of their homes. These so-called pay-option ARM loans also featured adjustable rates with low initial teaser rates that would increase over time, making repayment increasingly more difficult for borrowers. Mozilo found the pay-option ARM loans so risky that he advocated that Countrywide sell the entire portfolio of those loans. Countrywide's originations of pay-option ARMs constituted between 17 and 21 percent of its total originations. It retained the majority of these loans in its own portfolio. Nevertheless, in its disclosures to investors it classified these loans as prime loans, making it impossible for investors to determine the risks posed by such loans.

In fact, the definition for prime loans for purposes of its SEC filings was astonishingly broad. Countrywide's "prime nonconforming" category included loan products with very low FICO scores. Banking regulators considered loans whose borrowers had a credit score of 660 or lower to be subprime. Others drew the line at 620. Unbeknownst to investors, Countrywide did not consider any FICO score to be too low for "prime." It also did not include stated income loans or low documentation loans—where much borrower financial information is not verified—to be subprime. Even loans to borrowers with recent bankruptcy or borrowers with late mortgage payments could be "prime."

With respect to its admittedly nonprime loans, Countrywide reached for the highest levels of credit risk. As Mozilo himself stated, on April 17, 2006, with respect to one such product that piggybacked a 20 percent second mortgage on top of a subprime first mortgage, "In all my years in the business I have never seen a more toxic prduct [*sic*]. It's not only subordinated to the first, but the first is subprime. In addition, the FICOs are below 600, below 500 and some below 400[.] With real estate values coming down . . . the product will become increasingly worse." Mozilo also called these loans "poison." Unfortunately, no investor could find such deep levels of credit risk referenced in any of Countrywide's disclosures. Sambol, Mozilo, and Sieracki did not take steps to disclose the material facts that they knew were buried in their "prime" loan portfolio, even though one senior officer urged more thorough disclosures.

The SEC specifically alleges that McMurray lobbied consistently throughout 2006 and 2007 for more disclosures regarding Countrywide's increasingly risky loan underwriting standards in its periodic disclosure statements to investors. For example, in January 2007, McMurray urged the inclusion in Countrywide's annual report (Form 10-K) of an outline he prepared of where precisely the enhanced credit risk would affect Countrywide's balance sheet and sent it to CFO Sieracki and the financial reporting staff. He again urged more expanded disclosures of the lowered underwriting standards in August 2007 in Countrywide's quarterly report to shareholders (Form 10-Q) via an email to the Sieracki's deputy. Ultimately, Sambol and Sieracki decided not to include the expanded disclosures of Countrywide's risky lending. Indeed, at no time did Countrywide's Form 10-K annual reports or the Form 10-Q quarterly reports ever include any such disclosures from 2005 to 2008.

Not only was the record replete with evidence demonstrating the executives' knowledge of the risk and affirmative refusal to inform investors as legally obligated, but Mozilo, Sambol, and Sieracki each had a powerful motive to pursue high subprime lending profits regardless of ultimate losses to Countrywide shareholders and to conceal this fact as long as possible from the investing public. According to the SEC, Mozilo sold $139 million worth of Countrywide shares from November 2006 to October 2007, as the subprime market started to swoon. From May 2005 to the end of 2007 Sambol sold $40 million of Countrywide stock.

In the end, the SEC complaint shows that the SEC's investigation uncovered document after document that demonstrates that senior management knew that it had dramatically lowered its loan underwriting standards. By 2006 and 2007, Countrywide's increasingly subprime lending led to mounting losses, as predicted in many of the internal memos and emails discussed above. Unfortunately, while the Countrywide insiders cashed out to the tune of hundreds of millions of dollars in stock sales, they never affirmatively disclosed crucial information to shareholders, including the fact that the company's basic business plan of expanding the permissiveness of its loan underwriting led to greatly enhanced risk of losses (SEC 2009). The SEC's investigation, in short, provided sufficient evidence of probable cause to seek indictment of CEO Mozilo, COO Sambol, and CFO Sieracki.

Notably, the SEC did not pursue claims based upon Operation Hustle, as discussed above. The DOJ could still pick up the SEC's investigation and add the jury's fraud findings to a more expansive criminal case. That case would allow the government to put senior managers on the stand to convince a jury that Countrywide engaged in securities fraud. Two of these senior managers—Chief Risk Officer McMurray and Executive Vice President O'Donnell—blew the whistle on Countrywide's reckless lending and fraudulent practices. Indeed, whistleblowers have been instrumental in other lawsuits against Bank of America, Countrywide's successor, for the unlawful activities at Countrywide. Their testimony, along with evidence from those cases, could be used to prove a pattern of conduct to support RICO claims against Countrywide and its leaders.

Whistleblower Kyle Lagow brought a *qui tam* lawsuit on behalf of the government under the False Claims Act alleging that the company systematically undermined the appraisal process for mortgages in order to close as many loans as possible. Lagow claimed that Countrywide blacklisted appraisers who did not conform to Countrywide's demands to maximize loan closings. He also claimed he was fired for reporting appraisal deficiencies to Countrywide's senior management. When the Federal Housing Authority settled with Bank of America over Federal Housing Administration insurance payments, the $1 billion settlement included a $75 million settlement to Lagow (Currier 2012).

Lagow's allegations about appraisal manipulation comport with another whistleblower. Robert Madsen, a former employee at Countrywide's appraisal affiliate, sued the firm in 2011 claiming that the bank deliberately used "improper appraisal practices" that overstated the value of the homes backing Countrywide's portfolio of nonperforming loans by $6.6 billion for an extended period of time until 2011. According to news reports, Madsen ultimately collected roughly $56 million for blowing the whistle on Countrywide's appraisal practices. He had filed a confidential complaint against Countrywide's successor, Bank of America, in 2011, alleging that improper appraisals at the bank's LandSafe appraisal subsidiary systematically overstated property appraisals to make the bank "appear to be more profitable and financially stable" than it actually was (Goldstein 2014b). Madsen contended that his bosses started cutting his hours after he raised concerns about properties potentially being overvalued at the expense of borrowers and investors.

Another Countrywide whistleblower, Michael Winston, won a lawsuit against Bank of America for retaliatory discharge, although an appellate court later reversed the jury's decision. Winston worked as chief leadership officer at Countrywide and earned two promotions in 14 months while building and supervising a team of 200 corporate strategists. He has summarized Countrywide's lending standards in a variety of media outlets: "If they can fog a mirror, we'll give 'em a loan." Winston complained to senior managers to no avail. He also complained about toxic working conditions and filed a complaint with a state agency. He claims that COO Sambol asked him to meet with Moody's to misrepresent corporate governance standards at Countrywide. He refused. CEO Mozilo terminated Winston three weeks thereafter (Dayen 2013b). Retaliation against whistleblowers at Countrywide would support a finding that the Countrywide executives attempted to "consciously avoid" facts that would reveal knowledge of potential schemes to defraud at Countrywide. Eliminating the messengers, who were warning managers about excessive risks and were rebuffing fraudulent conduct, is a deliberate act that may suggest actual knowledge even more than willful blindness to intentionally defraud for purposes of securities, bank, wire, and mail frauds, as discussed in the introduction and chapter 1.

In all, the *Wall Street Journal* reported that Countrywide whistleblowers collected $170 million from Countrywide or its successor Bank of America. The whistleblowers accuse Countrywide of misdeeds ranging from inflating the value of mortgage properties to misrepresenting defective loans to investors (Rexrode & Martin 2014). These whistleblowers have made allegations broadly consistent with the key point this chapter emphasizes: Countrywide committed pervasive fraud in an effort to maximize profits and to keep its fraudulent business going for as long as possible with the full knowledge of its most senior managers.

The SEC also settled its securities fraud claims prior to the publication of the FCIC report. The FCIC uncovered more facts that support the claim that Countrywide's disclosure statements to its shareholders failed to disclose material facts about the riskiness of its mortgage lending. Most particularly, the FCIC highlighted internal Countrywide discussions regarding the pay-option ARM loans that were the focus of the SEC lawsuit. The FCIC found that, contrary to its public disclosures, Countrywide switched its charter to the Office of Thrift Supervision (OTS) specifically because the Federal Reserve (its previous regulator) found the pay-option ARM mortgages too risky.

The FCIC report references more emails that support the SEC's case (and by extension criminal charges) that Countrywide did not disclose material risks to its shareholders and that its senior officers knowingly allowed this. For example, as early as August 1, 2005, Angelo Mozilo sent an email to the former chief operating officer of Countrywide and its chief of banking operations warning that Countrywide's riskiest subprime loans would lead to a "financial and reputational catastrophe." On April 16, 2006, Mozilo warned the entire senior management team that "there was a time when [s]avings and [l]oans [w]ere doing things because their competitors were doing it. They all went broke." On August 12, 2006, Mozilo argued in favor of moving more quickly to an OTS charter to escape regulation by the Fed, which would have imperiled the huge profits and volume attributable to the pay-option loans. These email threads went out to all Countrywide senior managers, including COO Sambol and CFO Sieracki (FCIC 2011). It could not be clearer from these emails that Mozilo and other senior managers knew that Countrywide's strategy of matching its subprime competitors would lead to precisely the disaster that befell the company. Countrywide never disclosed such risks to its investors.

The SEC's action against Countrywide's senior managers led to settlement payments that pale in comparison to private plaintiff recoveries for essentially the same misconduct. Shareholders recovered $624 million against Countrywide and its auditor for claims similar to those pressed and settled by the SEC (Stemple 2010). Notably, the SEC is not subject to a draconian law passed in 1995 called the Private Securities Litigation Reform Act, which creates heavy burdens on private litigants but not the SEC. In particular, private litigants must allege facts giving rise to a strong inference of scienter (intent to defraud) without the benefit of any pretrial discovery. The SEC, on the other hand, can subpoena witnesses prior to filing claims. The SEC may also seek disgorgement of ill-gotten gains rather than be limited by provable damages. The huge recovery in the private litigation suggests that the SEC did not vigorously press its claims against Mozilo and the other Countrywide senior managers.

We will see further securities fraud settlements with respect to Countrywide's sale of MBSs to investors worldwide in chapter 3. Further allegations and claims also can be added from the manifest and undisclosed predatory lending that occurred at Countrywide, particularly targeting African American and Latino borrowers, as discussed next.

Countrywide's Predatory and Race-Based Lending

Countrywide faced multiple legal and regulatory inquiries regarding its lending practices from even before the financial collapse. Multiple claimants alleged it had engaged in predatory and race-based lending. Predatory lending results from loan originations that seek to profit from loan defaults through high fees and seizure of collateral, or loans made without regard to repayment ability because the originator knows it can sell the loan at a profit regardless of repayment prospects through, for example, fraud. While there is no generally accepted definition of predatory lending, it invariably involves fraud because few victims would borrow if they knew the lender intended to profit from the borrower's default and the foreclosure of the borrower's home. These inquiries led to multibillion-dollar settlements. Countrywide never disclosed any of these practices to its investors, to the purchasers of its loans, or to borrowers themselves.

Countrywide ultimately settled allegations of predatory lending asserted by 11 states for over $8 billion—the largest such settlement in history. The states alleged that Countrywide lied about its "no closing cost loans," misled consumers with respect to hidden fees, structured loans with risky features, paid brokers more to sell more risky loans, and frequently lent based upon inflated borrower income (without borrower involvement) (Morgenson 2008). As stated by Illinois Attorney General Lisa Madigan, "This settlement holds the number-one mortgage lender in the country accountable for deceptively putting borrowers into loans they didn't understand, couldn't afford and couldn't get out of. These are the very practices that have created the economic crisis we're currently experiencing" (Illinois Attorney General 2008).

The *New York Times* interviewed former employees who corroborated (and documented) many of these allegations. The interviews revealed disturbing facts even as of late summer 2007. The profits generated through lax lending standards and high fees were so substantial that Countrywide continued its reckless lending even after delinquency rates soared. Countrywide routinely lent to people with low credit scores, personal bankruptcies, missed mortgage payments, and even home foreclosures. Because Countrywide sold the loans into the secondary market it focused on generating fees, not repayment ability.

Former employees and sales representatives also told the *Times* that Countrywide's compensation system incentivized risky, high-cost loans. Brokers that put people into subprime loans could double their commission relative to prime quality mortgages. Adding a three-year prepayment penalty to a loan resulted in an extra 1 percent in commission payments, even while making it difficult for borrowers to refinance the loan. Loans with a low teaser rate at the beginning of repayment and a higher rate at reset also led to greater commission payments. The commission structure at Countrywide rewarded salespeople for pushing whatever loans made the most money for Countrywide without regard to loan default risk. Accordingly, as the *Times* noted, "the company is Exhibit A for the lax and, until recently, highly lucrative lending that has turned a once-hot business ice-cold and has touched off a housing crisis of historic proportions" (Morgenson 2007).

Yet another Countrywide whistleblower emerged who further corroborated Countrywide's brazen predatory lending. In 2007, the executive vice president of fraud risk management, Eileen Foster, investigated Countrywide's subprime lending branches in greater Boston. Her inquiry found that Countrywide loan officers forged signatures of borrowers, falsified documentation of borrower income and assets, and circumvented Countrywide's automated underwriting systems in order to get loans approved regardless of risk of default. Foster investigated after receiving a tip from a former employee who was fired after objecting to these fraudulent practices. After Foster's investigation, Countrywide terminated dozens of employees and closed six of its eight Boston branches.

In 2008, Foster found similar frauds in Chicago, Cincinnati, San Diego, Las Vegas, Los Angeles, Miami, and San Diego, among other metropolitan areas. Foster ultimately concluded that this fraud was systemic in Countrywide, abetted by management. Production trumped fraud prevention. Countrywide personnel garnered payments for production not loan quality. Countrywide thereby saddled huge numbers of borrowers with loans they could not qualify for or afford. According to Foster fraud was a way of business at Countrywide. Management did not want to know about the wrongdoing its compensation system spawned.

In fact, according to Foster in a *60 Minutes* interview, Countrywide managers told representatives to report fraud not to Foster but to the Employee Relations department. Such reports routinely led to transfer, demotion, or discharge. Foster asked Countrywide's Internal Audit department to investigate Employee Relations. The company instead asked Employee Relations to investigate Foster. Countrywide terminated Foster in the fall of 2008. Ultimately, she recovered nearly $1 million in a whistleblower lawsuit against Countrywide (*60 Minutes* 2011).

Foster concludes that the government's response to her testimony regarding clear criminal misconduct at Countrywide was stilted to say the least. As she wrote in *Rolling Stone,* "The Department of Justice has failed, inexplicably, to tap into the intelligence that financial whistleblowers like myself have tried to offer them." More disturbingly, "I've found there were scores of whistleblowers inside Countrywide and then B of A. Trumped-up investigations were widely used to discredit us. The inner circle at both corporations operated like the mob: company staff, including attorneys, often worked to silence employees, using weapons like blacklisting, hush money and confidentiality agreements." Amazingly the DOJ never bothered to contact Foster, at least through the late summer of 2012. She states, "The DOJ needs to investigate our allegations, and prosecutors could start by contacting whistleblowers like me" (Foster 2012). It appears that DOJ failed to contact even obvious witnesses to frauds against mortgage borrowers.

Countrywide also settled allegations of race-based predatory lending with the US Department of Justice. DOJ's complaint alleged that Countrywide discriminated by charging more than 200,000 African American and Hispanic borrowers higher fees and interest rates than white borrowers. The complaint also alleges that these borrowers were charged more because of their race or national origin, not because of their creditworthiness or other factors related to default risk. Furthermore, Countrywide discriminated by steering thousands of African American and Hispanic borrowers into subprime mortgages while white borrowers with similar credit profiles received prime loans. This undisclosed discrimination occurred coast to coast in over 180 markets and 41 states. Countrywide paid $335 million to settle claims regarding this mortgage discrimination, which started in 2004 and ended only in late 2008, when Countrywide ceased to exist as an independent entity.

The government's complaint highlights the damage caused to American families as a result of these predatory loans. The government reviewed 2.5 million loan files and, with access to nonpublic information, conducted a rigorous regression analysis accounting for credit scores, income, loan-to-value ratio, and other credit risk factors and still found large race-based differences in Countrywide's lending. As a result of Countrywide's discrimination, minority borrowers faced twice the likelihood of getting saddled with subprime mortgages relative to similarly situated white borrowers. A borrower of a subprime mortgage, according to the Office of Comptroller of the Currency, is over five times more likely to default (DOJ 2011a).

Countrywide agents made these predatory loans based upon raw greed rather than racial hostility. The incentive-based compensation system in place at Countrywide encouraged loan officers to put borrowers generally in more costly, high-risk loans. Minority borrowers suffered traditionally from credit starvation due to discrimination and redlining by lenders for decades prior to the subprime bubble. Thus, minority communities and families did not have the same level of sophistication and experience regarding mortgage transactions, all else being equal. After being denied credit for generations, minorities proved too eager to take on too much debt and too trusting that legal protections would operate to save them from lender abuses.

Countrywide particularly abused Latino borrowers, who constituted two-thirds of their victims. If English was not a borrower's primary language, Countrywide could pounce (Weissmann 2011). Essentially Countrywide preyed upon the most vulnerable citizens in order to make predatory loans to maximize profitability.

Countrywide's senior managers knew about the discrimination and predatory lending but did nothing to stop or to disclose the practice. Countrywide owed an obligation under law to record and disclose its lending practices regarding race to the government under the Home Mortgage Discrimination Act (HMDA). The HMDA data would have alerted senior management to the problems that ultimately were uncovered by the government. Yet Countrywide's internal monitoring resulted in no change in policy and no reimbursement of victims, even after finding discrimination, until forced by the government to make restitution.

Indeed, Countrywide could profit from these loans so long as they could be pawned off to investors in the MBS market. Countrywide encouraged its employees to raise rates on mortgage loans pursuant to "risk-based adjustments." At no time did Countrywide provide any "written guidance in . . . risk-based adjustments" to mortgage prices. Instead, it simply incentivized loan volume and high-cost loans. This left loan officers with abilities and incentives to loan to those who could be most easily exploited, whether based on income, education, or familial experience with home mortgages.

Importantly, from January to November 2008, Countrywide funded substantially all of its home loans through Countrywide Bank—a federally chartered thrift under the supervision of the Office of Thrift Supervision. Prior to that Countrywide Bank was a national bank regulated by the Office of the Comptroller of the Currency. Furthermore, Countrywide Financial Corporation was a bank holding company regulated by the Federal Reserve. According to the DOJ, however, throughout the entire time of its discriminatory misconduct Countrywide made loans with essentially the same policies, procedures, and personnel. In fact, regulators found the predatory lending and alerted senior management.

In 2006, the Fed initiated a review of Countrywide's home lending practices and found "reason to believe that Countrywide . . . engaged in a pattern or practice of discrimination based on race and ethnicity" in violation of law. In 2008, the OTS made essentially the same finding. Thereafter the DOJ entered into tolling agreements with Countrywide under which the company waived the running of the statute of limitations regarding potential legal violations until December 2011, when DOJ filed its complaint.

The discriminatory lending occurred on a systemic basis throughout the nation in Countrywide's most high-volume markets: Los Angeles, Chicago, New York, Miami, Atlanta, Houston, and Phoenix. Such systemic discrimination on a nationwide basis in the face of manifest warnings of illegal behavior could only be the result of a determination by Countrywide's senior managers that the short-term profitability of such odious lending policies justified the lawlessness rather than any innocent explanation. The government's allegations state this point well: (1) Countrywide's senior management promulgated and ratified lending policies that gave wide discretion to its loan officers; (2) it incentivized high-volume, high-cost loans; and (3) it knew or had reason to know these policies were leading to mortgage discrimination based upon race and ethnicity (DOJ 2011a). Yet the company did nothing to stop these illegal violations.

For purposes of securities, bank, mail, and wire frauds, this predatory and race-based lending simply spawned even more nondisclosures of material facts and more fraud victims. Countrywide did not disclose (1) the risks of these predatory loans to its shareholders and other investors, (2) the risks of these predatory loans to investors in MBSs, or (3) the risks of the high-cost loans to borrowers too numerous to quantify. As Eileen Foster stated, at Countrywide fraud was a core business. Indeed, as the next section details Countrywide worked hard to keep its core business of fraud going as long as possible.

Friends of Angelo?

Perhaps the most intriguing loans that Countrywide made, at least in terms of investigating and explaining the lack of criminal investigative response of the DOJ to the manifest illegal activity underlying the financial crisis, are those pursuant to a program called Friends of Angelo. These loans consist of special mortgage loans with very favorable terms that Countrywide routinely disbursed to power politicians and to managers at the GSEs.

According to the *Wall Street Journal*, Senate Banking Committee Chairman Chris Dodd and Senate Budget Committee Chairman Kent Conrad were among the politicians who received favorable mortgages under the Friends of Angelo program (*Wall Street Journal* 2009). The

New York Times reported that four members of the House of Representatives were referred to the House Ethics Committee for potential violations of House ethics rules, which require members take out only loans on terms generally available to the public. The lawmakers referred to the House Ethics Committee included Republicans Howard McKeon and Elton Gallegly; GOP congressional campaign chair Pete Sessions; and Edolphus Towns, Democrat from New York. All denied participating in or even knowing about Countrywide's Friends of Angelo program (*New York Times* 2012a).

According to an in-depth investigation by the House Committee on Oversight and Government Reform, the program consisted of a 12-year effort to target and influence powerful Washington policy makers through favorable loans. More specifically, "Between January 1996 and June 2008, Countrywide's VIP loan unit made hundreds of loans to current and former Members of Congress, congressional staff, high ranking government officials, and executives and employees of Fannie Mae." VIPs enjoyed more lax underwriting standards and paid lower fees. The standard discount was 0.5 percent of the loan amount. Countrywide also typically waived junk fees that saved these VIP borrowers hundreds more. Finally, Mozilo or other senior Countrywide officers guaranteed loan approval for most policy makers in the program.

The House committee found internal Countrywide emails in which senior Countrywide officers expressly weighed a given politician's political influence against the cost of the loan discount. In another email, with respect to a prominent senator, Mozilo personally directed the VIP Unit at Countrywide to "take off 1 point, [charge] no extra fees and approve the loan." The House investigation specifically found that "Countrywide used the VIP loan program to cast a wide net of influence." Thus, there is little question that the entire Friends of Angelo program constituted influence peddling at its worst.

Nevertheless it probably did not constitute illegal bribery. Under 18 USC section 201(b), "whoever directly or indirectly, corruptly gives, offers or promises anything of value to any public official . . . with intent to influence an official act" commits a federal felony. Courts generally require an express or understood quid pro quo to violate this provision. Countrywide never expressly requested that participants give Countrywide anything in exchange for its favorable loans. As the House Committee found, "Angelo Mozilo and Countrywide's lobbyists may have skirted the federal bribery statute by keeping conversations about discounts and other forms of preferential treatment internal" (Staff Report, US House of Representatives 2012). In other words, Countrywide did not insist upon an express commitment of favorable action.

Under section 201(c) of the same statute, however, the discounts and promises of favorable treatment to Friends of Angelo with a specific goal of obtaining additional influence and goodwill to sway future official action on a particular issue may well qualify as unlawful gratuities so long as they can be linked to some official act (*McDonnell v. United States* 2016). And there are internal emails suggesting such a link, specifically to possible predatory lending and GSE reform legislation. Proof of unlawful gratuities does not require a showing of a deal, or a quid pro quo. The practice constitutes a federal felony but carries a much lighter prison term than bribery (Podgor et al. 2013).

These potential felonies may be time-barred, however, since the government failed to act on this clear effort to corrupt government lawmakers. On one hand, if these crimes are subject to the general federal statute of limitations (rather than a crime affecting a financial institution), it is possible any criminal charge arising from the Friends of Angelo program lapsed under the governing federal statute of limitations. On the other hand, this kind of systematic corruption certainly could have adversely affected the bank and bank holding company subsidiaries of Countrywide that were central to all of Countrywide's operations. The corrupt loans could have exposed the bank and bank holding company to losses and reputational losses. Certainly, there was no disclosure of this program to Countrywide shareholders. Consequently, it is arguable whether the statute of limitations has expired on these unlawful gratuities.

The government may still pursue criminal charges against Countrywide or its agents because under 18 USC section 1961 any violation of the bank, mail, and wire fraud statutes may operate as a predicate act under the RICO Act. The RICO Act provides for a 10-year statute of limitations. Given that the pattern of Countrywide frauds discussed above (Operation Hustle, predatory lending, Friends of Angelo) no doubt affected financial institutions that may have ultimately taken losses on Countrywide-originated loans, and its invariable use of the mail and wires, a clear pattern of violations of predicate acts occurred within Countrywide and its various divisions.

RICO charges are difficult to prove. But essentially a pattern of predicate acts—violations of certain laws including bank, wire, and mail fraud—within a given enterprise constitutes a violation (Podgor et al. 2013; 18 USC § 1962). The US Supreme Court interprets the RICO Act to also require a relationship that gives a common purpose to the criminal conduct. The Court described this required relationship as "continuity plus relationship," explaining that the predicate criminal acts "have the same or similar purposes . . . or otherwise are interrelated by distinguishing characteristics and are not isolated events" (*H.J. Inc. v. Northwestern Bell Telephone Co.* 1989).

Here, there is little doubt that Countrywide's wide-ranging illegality focused on a singular purpose: keeping the compensation gravy train rolling by maximizing the ability of senior managers to earn money and cash out stock for as long as possible and for the highest possible price. As such, the violations of law discussed above occurred over several years and fulfill all of the essential elements of the RICO law, including common purpose and a related pattern of criminality. The gratuities paid to federal officials to fend off federal predatory lending legislation and GSE reform allowed the enterprise to continue its predatory lending and fraud on the GSEs unfettered by federal legislation. Similarly, the sweetheart loans to Fannie Mae officials helped ensure Countrywide a channel to sell their admittedly toxic loans to investors. And the lies to Countrywide's shareholders were necessary to keep the market for Countrywide's shares as high as possible so that the senior managers could cash out their shares. If the DOJ were to criminally charge Countrywide, a jury could well conclude that the company engaged in a pattern of criminality in order to maximize the compensation paid to senior managers regardless of losses to shareholders, harm to borrowers, losses to MBS investors, or damage to the global economy.

As a potential criminal enterprise, Countrywide inflicted massive losses on the global economy. As the largest mortgage lender in the United States, Countrywide exerted a profound influence on the entire US mortgage market. The more aggressive they "expanded" their underwriting standards to permit, ultimately, every borrower to qualify for a loan, the more Countrywide's competitors needed to respond by lowering their credit standards. Countrywide led a veritable arms race to subprime oblivion—and expressly intended to do so. That was the whole point of the matching strategy—to always be at the most aggressive lending frontier. The individual acts of the Countrywide enterprise may not have been as violent and heinous as those of the Corleone family, but the global damage far eclipsed any potential harm done by a Mafia family or organized crime syndicate.

The RICO Act includes strong criminal and civil legal sanctions including treble damages for aggrieved civil litigants (18 USC §§ 1963, 1964). Such suits would unquestionably follow a criminal conviction, potentially bankrupting all defendants. Furthermore, all of those participating or conspiring in the conduct of racketeering enterprises are subject to criminal conviction under RICO. The act also provides for criminal and civil forfeiture of assets, so prosecutors could use it to cast a broad net and indict a wide array of Countrywide's senior managers and seize their assets through criminal forfeiture (Podgor et al. 2013).

Despite the pervasive frauds that Countrywide perpetrated, RICO charges may strike some as too aggressive. The mere threat of RICO charges against Drexel Burnham Lambert essentially forced the firm to capitulate to the government, eventually closing the firm, as discussed in chapter 1. Nevertheless, the Countrywide frauds proved quite aggressive, and the associated damage counsels in favor of a vigorous rather than conservative government response. Uncountable families suffered the economic devastation of predatory subprime lending and shareholders lost fortunes. The entire financial system essentially bought Countrywide's mortgages and buckled under the weight of the toxic loans.

Furthermore, the downside risk to such a prosecution is minimal. Operation Hustle operated as a "brazen fraud" according to a federal judge, and it certainly involved a financial institution, which would trigger the 10-year statute of limitations. Countrywide's corporate structure included a federal thrift and a bank holding company. The Friends of Angelo program specifically intended to influence policy makers with sweetheart loans and specifically sought to influence specific legislation according to Countrywide's own internal emails. The victims of the firm's predatory loans literally cannot be counted, but the lives devastated by its racially targeted predatory loans must be huge based on the settlements it paid to resolve such charges. These facts would no doubt influence any jury, and even if the government lost its RICO criminal charges against Countrywide and its senior officers, it could still prevail on lesser counts of mail, wire, and bank fraud.

Based upon the facts we know today and the applicable law, the government's decision not to pursue criminal charges against any Countrywide managers makes no sense. Certainly, the explanation offered by President Obama that reprehensible but not illegal misconduct drove the crisis is simply wrong. Furthermore, the attorney general need not fear that pursuing the individuals at the center of Countrywide's misconduct would somehow destabilize the economy. Angelo Mozilo and the other senior managers at Countrywide simply cannot be considered too big to jail from a global economic point of view. After all, Countrywide no longer exists as an independent financial institution. There is zero chance that any prosecution of Countrywide's senior executives would spawn financial instability.

One lurking explanation for the government's indulgence of such severe criminality here involves Countrywide's political influence. The congressional inquiry into the Friends of Angelo program concluded that Countrywide made favorable loans to many hundreds of borrowers in influential positions. There is no complete list, and so there is no way to know the identity of all of Angelo's friends. However, the program does not represent the totality of Countrywide's influence peddling activities. According to the Center for Public Integrity, Countrywide spent nearly $10 million lobbying the government for indulgences and influence. Countrywide and individuals affiliated with the company spent another $1.2 million on campaign contributions (Center for Public Integrity 2014). Thus, while we may never know the true dimensions of Countrywide's political clout, we do know that it is formidable. Mozilo no doubt learned from the mistakes of Charles Keating and his Keating Five senators, discussed in chapter 1. Rather than a small cadre of attentive senators whom Keating hoped would give him influence, one appears better served by spreading the wealth around to a broader array of potential influence. Investments in the Friends of Angelo program, substantial lobbying, and campaign contribution largesse produced a surprising amount of security from criminal charges for pennies on the dollars earned by Countrywide's top executives.

Given that Countrywide no longer exists as an independent entity, the corporate death penalty is not justified against Countrywide in any form. Nevertheless, the individuals responsible for the misconduct discussed above should face criminal accountability, and if some still work in the financial services industry, the government should exercise its power to impose the career death penalty of barring them from the financial services sector, as discussed in the introduction. Along these lines, it is noteworthy that the jury in the Hustle case specifically asked the court why no senior managers (particularly two credit managers) other than Rebecca Mairone had been sued. The court noted that issue was simply not before the jury. Naturally, this book similarly cannot assess who within Countrywide should be found responsible (criminally or otherwise) for the frauds in that case. Our position is simply that the government should investigate this very point.

3

Wall Street's Fraudulent Sales of Toxic Mortgages

The recent financial crisis was caused by a number of factors,
including, among others . . . at the heart of it all, the worst
mortgage underwriting in our nation's history.
—John C. Dugan, former comptroller of the currency, July
21, 2010

John Dugan knows mortgage underwriting. As the former comptroller
of the currency he supervised the activities of every national bank in
the United States. Loan underwriting is a core function of every bank
that attempts to control the risk of nonpayment (or default) through the
assessment of borrower creditworthiness and the analysis of collateral.
Mortgage underwriting constitutes the primary way bankers control the
risk of nonpayment when they make mortgage loans. During the years
before the financial crisis Wall Street bankers increasingly threw caution
to the wind and made more risky loans than ever before, ultimately toppling the global financial system. The megabanks then packaged these
mortgages into mortgage-backed securities and sold them to investors
around the world.

The worst mortgage underwriting in history, however, did not occur
accidently or inadvertently. It occurred through fraud, as demonstrated
in the last chapter and highlighted again in this chapter through the huge
settlements the megabanks agreed to, and the stories of the whistleblowers behind those settlements. No investor willingly invests in loans that
offer little chance of repayment. Instead, Wall Street sold hundreds of
billions of dollars of toxic loans to unsuspecting investors through deception. These toxic loans posed much greater risks of default than the
banks disclosed to the investing public. In the run-up to the financial
crisis, the megabanks systematically sold high-risk loans through misrepresentations that they were lower risk loans. Without these material
misrepresentations, the crisis would have been far less serious, if not

completely averted. The Great Financial Crisis of 2008 arose primarily from the most massive securities fraud in history. The government's own actions now confirm this, as we detail below.

Countrywide led the pack of subprime lenders and set the pace for peddling subprime mortgages as less risky than they actually were, as demonstrated in chapter 2. We now know that virtually all Wall Street firms participated in pawning off high-risk mortgages as lower risk mortgages to investors around the world, especially to Fannie Mae, Freddie Mac, and other government-sponsored agencies. From major banks to the credit rating agencies, securities fraud became a core part of Wall Street's business. These firms knowingly bundled mass quantities of mortgages into mortgage-backed securities without full disclosure of material facts for great profit. As such, Wall Street became the center of a giant securities fraud, sucking in investment capital from the four corners of the world. Ultimately, these toxic loans poisoned the entire global economy through the distribution of the loans into mortgage-backed securities to investors around the world.

Mortgage-backed securities simply consist of pools of mortgages that are sold to investors interested in interest income and the relative safety of real estate mortgages. As the name itself suggests, they still operate as securities in that investors passively receive interest and debt repayment while some other entity administers the pool of mortgages. Each specific mortgage-backed security offering is backed by a specific pool of mortgages. As such, federal securities laws apply to the sale of mortgage-backed securities. This means that sellers must tell the truth, the whole truth, and nothing but the truth when selling this investment in mortgages. Failure to do so constitutes at least federal securities fraud, as discussed in greater detail in the introduction.

Furthermore, banks typically invest in mortgage-backed securities, and when sellers misrepresent material facts and expose banks to enhanced risk of loss, they commit bank fraud. That enhanced risk translated into billions in actual losses suffered by banks across the nation due to fraudulently sold mortgage-backed securities. Similarly, when fraudfeasors use wires and the mail to further fraudulent schemes, they commit wire and mail fraud. Thus, as discussed in more detail in the introduction and chapter 1, the frauds we discuss in this chapter violated long-standing federal antifraud statutes and regulations.

The Department of Justice investigated just enough that today there can be no dispute that Wall Street sold hundreds of billions in fraudulent mortgage-backed securities. This jumbo-sized fraud occurred most markedly in 2006 and 2007. Remarkably, the identity of the securities fraudfeasors remains concealed from the public, resulting from DOJ's decision not to pursue criminal charges against the megabanks and their influential senior managers. The anonymity also stems from the failure of financial regulators (the FDIC, the Fed, and the SEC, most notably) to pursue the individuals responsible (including senior managers who participated in the misconduct or approved it) for these crimes and expel them from the financial services industry. The only remaining issue is which individuals at which megabanks acted with scienter—or intent to defraud.

The public is left to speculate why DOJ declined to enforce the criminal laws despite overwhelming proof that securities fraud occurred and involved the sale of hundreds of billions in toxic mortgages. Instead, DOJ contented itself with billions in civil and regulatory fines paid by innocent shareholders. The financial regulators contented themselves with taking no action. Citizens must now accept that the government allowed the persons behind the most costly fraud in our history to shirk all criminal and regulatory responsibility. While DOJ and the regulators certainly hold discretion over prosecuting crimes, they do not maintain discretion to do so for political reasons or to exempt an entire class of individuals from law enforcement based upon wealth and power.

In the course of its civil recoveries, the DOJ enjoyed much help from willing whistleblowers who risked career advancement and even termination yet fought to bring recklessness and criminal misconduct to light. Nevertheless, many of these whistleblowers maintain that the government did not want the information they offered, at least insofar as criminal actions are concerned. Indeed, we spoke to several whistleblowers (or their representatives) identified in this book and could not find any who would confirm that they were even called to testify before a grand jury. Generally, the whistleblowers we contacted maintained instead that they never heard from government prosecutors or testified before any criminal inquiry or grand jury. One attorney for a whistleblower declined to speak to the issue based upon attorney-client privilege.

The upshot of this is that while Countrywide originated and sold more subprime loans than any other firm through misrepresentations, the Wall Street megabanks packaged these and other toxic loans into mortgage-backed securities and sold them to investors across the financial sector and global economy through yet more misrepresentations. These toxic mortgages ultimately crashed the entire global economy. While we do not know the identity of the bankers who acted with the requisite scienter, it is exceedingly unlikely that the misrepresentations occurred by happenstance and that the happenstance coincided with billions in revenue for the megabanks. This chapter demonstrates that the megabanks have all but admitted to this fraud and that consequently the DOJ and financial regulators would have less difficulty pursuing criminal indictments and disqualifications from the financial services industry.

Citigroup

Citigroup's CEO Chuck Prince infamously remarked in 2007 that if liquidity dried up in financial markets "things will be complicated" but that "as long as the music is playing you've got to get up and dance" (Ramirez 2014). Today we know from publically available settlements that Citigroup kept the music playing through apparent securities and bank fraud. A full-blown criminal trial would certainly enhance our knowledge of wrongdoing at Citigroup. Facts known today strongly suggest such a trial should occur. Indeed, the FCIC made two criminal referrals to the DOJ against Citigroup's most senior officers related to the facts discussed below (Black 2016).

For example, on July 14, 2014, the DOJ (and other law enforcement partners including the FDIC) announced a $7 billion settlement with Citigroup to resolve civil claims related to the company's mortgage business. The settlement covered misconduct extending through January 1, 2009. Citigroup essentially admitted it made serious misrepresentations to the investing public about the mortgage loans it securitized and sold during the subprime bubble and bust. The settlement included a record $4 billion civil penalty (under the Financial Institutions Reform, Recovery, and Enforcement Act) and certain relief to homeowners. Although the settlement did not absolve Citigroup or its employees of criminal misconduct, DOJ has failed to pursue any such charges. Nor has the FDIC, Fed, or SEC taken any regulatory action to disqualify any individual or the firm from the financial sector.

As part of the settlement, Citigroup acknowledged it made serious misrepresentations to investors. An agreed-to statement of facts describes its misrepresentations to investors in mortgage-backed securities that it sold. Citigroup represented lower risks to investors than the actual high-risk mortgages they sold. The company did not follow its own underwriting criteria as disclosed to investors, and the "due diligence" teams uncovered these underwriting deficiencies. Contrary to its representations regarding the quality of the loans it securitized, Citigroup knew the mortgage loans it sold had "material defects." According to the statement of facts, one Citigroup trader stated in an email that he "went through the Diligence Reports and think[s] [they] should start praying." He estimated that as many as half of the loans would default. He concluded, "It's amazing that some of these loans were closed at all." Citigroup nevertheless securitized such loans and sold the resulting mortgage-backed securities to investors for billions of dollars without disclosing the true risks (DOJ 2014d). Given these admissions, one wonders why the government has refused to pursue any criminal charges, disqualifications, or spin-offs.

Another civil settlement establishes further fraud in Citigroup's mortgage operations. Specifically, on February 15, 2012, Citigroup, Citibank, NA, and CitiMortgage, Inc. entered into a $158 million settlement with DOJ and a whistleblower named Sherry Hunt, who worked as a vice president and chief underwriter at CitiMortgage. As part of that settlement Citigroup stipulated to the following facts: (1) it falsely certified loans for Federal Housing Administration (FHA) insurance; (2) it failed to properly conduct postdefault reviews on loans that defaulted rapidly as it represented it would and to buy back defective loans; and (3) FHA suffered losses as a result of these misrepresentations. Disturbingly, this misconduct did not end with the financial crisis of 2008. Rather, it began in 2004 and *continued* through to the date of the settlement in 2012 (DOJ 2012d).

According to whistleblower Sherry Hunt, CitiMortgage routinely misrepresented the quality of its mortgages to investors. Citi did not adhere to the underwriting standards and controls that were disclosed to investors. "The quality control and risk management function there had been compromised, coerced and manipulated." CitiMortgage covered up and failed to investigate indications of possible fraud that its quality control underwriters had found. Hunt alerted the ethics and human resources departments at Citigroup of her concerns and followed Citi's Code of Conduct by alerting her supervisor of the same concerns. The only response was that she was "demoted and relegated to a corner with barely any responsibilities and then to a back room position in [quality control]."

In May 2011, she blew the whistle on Citigroup's misconduct to the SEC. In August 2011, she filed a whistleblower lawsuit against Citigroup, Citibank, NA, and CitiMortgage (*United States ex rel. Hunt v. Citi-Mortgage* 2012). Ultimately the government took over the lawsuit and Hunt collected $31 million under a Civil War–era whistleblower statute known as the False Claims Act (Ivry 2012). This lawsuit culminated in the above-referenced $158 million settlement payment by Citigroup and its affiliates.

One of the people whom Hunt blew the whistle to was her supervisor, Richard Bowen, who served as a senior vice president at Citigroup. Bowen was the chief underwriter of the Consumer Lending Group. Bowen testified to the Financial Crisis Inquiry Commission (FCIC) that he supervised loan quality for over $90 billion per year of mortgages underwritten and purchased by CitiFinancial. Citi in turn sold these mortgages to Fannie Mae, Freddie Mac, and other investors. Bowen therefore had a front-row seat on Citi's entire mortgage operation.

In June 2006, Bowen learned that as many as 60 percent of the mortgages that Citi was buying included defects in that the loans did not comply with Citigroup's loan guidelines. By 2007 that number had climbed to 80 percent. Citi represented to loan investors that the loans did, in fact, comply with Citi's underwriting requirements when it knew the loans were defective. The large number of defective loans presented a risk that Citi could be legally obligated to repurchase the loans. Bowen told top managers at the firm of this large financial risk, but got no meaningful response. He testified that instead "there was a considerable push to build volumes, to increase market share" (Bowen 2010).

He ultimately took his warnings to the highest level of Citigroup's management including Robert Rubin, the chairman of the Executive

Committee of the Board of Directors and former Treasury Secretary during the Clinton administration. He sent Rubin and three other senior managers a memo with the words "URGENT — READ IMMEDIATELY" in the subject line. Sharing his concerns, he stressed to top managers that Citi faced billions of dollars in losses if investors were to demand that Citi repurchase the defective loans. Rubin told the FCIC that "I do know factually that that was acted on promptly and actions were taken in response to it." Bowen testified to the FCIC that after he alerted management by sending emails, he faced effective demotion, his bonus was reduced, and his performance review was downgraded (FCIC 2011). Consequently, the very top level of senior management at Citigroup seemingly acted to silence the whistleblowers — a telltale sign of willful blindness.

The music that kept playing for Citigroup's mortgage business thus included a drumbeat of deceptive sales of securities, at a minimum. Citi lied to investors (or in DOJ's words made "serious misrepresentations") about the quality of its mortgage-backed securities in order to dupe investors into purchasing mortgages that were not otherwise sellable. That is the point of securities fraud — to attract capital through lies. These "serious misrepresentations" go to the heart of the subprime debacle. They explain the "worst mortgage underwriting in our nation's history." But Citi's apparent fraud did not stop with its sales of mortgage-backed securities.

According to the allegations of a class action complaint, Citigroup also worked to keep the music playing by including "liquidity puts" in its securitized pools of subprime mortgages it sold to investors. The liquidity puts required Citigroup to repurchase interests in subprime mortgages in the event of turbulence in the subprime market. In the fall of 2007, Citigroup learned that its subprime exposure amounted to about half of its total capital, but concealed these facts from the investing public. Thus, investors in Citigroup shares and bonds did not know of the associated risks.

Only in November 2007 did Citigroup publicly disclose for the first time that it had $55 billion in subprime mortgage exposure and anticipated losses of about $8 billion to $11 billion. CEO Prince resigned shortly thereafter. In December 2007, Citigroup announced it would assume $58 billion of debts that had been carried by structured investment vehicles (SIVs) it had sponsored; the SIVs had been invested in long-term assets (including mortgage-related assets) with short-term funding. The liquidity puts required Citi to make good on the SIV assets if market disruptions occurred. The risks of these losses went undisclosed to shareholders until no earlier than November 2007.

In the class action litigation revolving around these undisclosed risks, a federal judge found that the plaintiffs successfully alleged a "strong inference" of scienter in connection with Citigroup collateralized debt obligations against an array of senior managers at Citigroup, including CEO Prince, CFO Gary Crittenden, and vice chair of the board, Robert Rubin (*In re Citigroup Securities Fraud Litigation* 2010). By failing to truthfully disclose its subprime exposure, Citigroup, like many other Wall Street firms, was able to draw more capital into its mortgage-related activities than would otherwise have been the case. It fooled its shareholders and bondholders into capitalizing subprime mortgage activities they otherwise would not have invested in. Given the scale of a megabank like Citigroup, this materially contributed to the Great Financial Crisis of 2008.

The losses proved so staggering that the US government was forced to bail out Citigroup, injecting $45 billion in capital and guaranteeing $306 billion in asset values. During 2007, Citigroup's shareholders lost more than 95 percent of their value. Its stock traded at $55 per share in 2006, before crashing to less than $4 per share in early 2009, later falling below $1. CEO Chuck Prince fared much better: his compensation amounted to $66.8 million over his last three years, and he was paid a bonus of $10.4 million for his last 10 months of work, which were marked by huge losses. He exited Citigroup with $40 million in severance pay. The outcome at Citigroup follows a familiar pattern that animates this book: massive compensation payments to senior executives while shareholders and investors suffer much greater losses. Based upon such facts, juries could well conclude that the financial crisis was no accident and that instead senior managers should be held personally responsible for intentionally lining their own pockets at the expense of all others, including investors.

The securities class action based upon a failure to disclose exposure to subprime mortgages settled for $590 million. The SEC settled a similar securities fraud claim for $75 million (SEC 2010c). Counsel for Citigroup could not recommend such large settlements without serious evidence of wrongdoing. The SEC's investigatory powers supported its civil enforcement action and the settlement of that action. The massive class action settlement resulted only after a federal judge found "a strong inference of scienter." Despite Citigroup's acknowledgment of wrongdoing in connection with its massive settlement payment for selling dodgy mortgage-backed securities, the testimony of whistleblowers like Sherry Hunt and Richard Bowen, and the settlements paid in connection with the undisclosed liquidity puts, the government has not sought grand jury indictments against Citigroup or its senior managers.

It is not too late for DOJ to pursue criminal charges. Many financial institutions certainly lost millions from Citigroup's frauds. For example, the FDIC settled securities fraud claims on behalf of failed banks for $208.25 million. No fewer than three banks invested in Citi's fraudulent mortgage-backed securities and ended up in FDIC receivership (FDIC 2014a). Many other banks that did not end up in FDIC receivership doubtlessly invested in the mortgage-backed securities that even Citigroup itself admits were sold through misrepresentations. The fact that banks lost money as a result of Citigroup's admitted misrepresentations triggers the 10-year statute of limitations for frauds affecting a financial institution.

All of Citigroup's misconduct ultimately involved financial institutions. The settlement payments that Citigroup and its various affiliates made directly involved Citibank, NA, a national bank, and Citigroup Inc., a bank holding company. These institutions and their affiliates paid out billions in settlements arising from the misconduct in mortgage operations. As a result there can be no question that the bank and bank holding company faced an enhanced risk of loss arising from the skullduggery in Citigroup's mortgage operations. That fact also triggers the 10-year statute of limitations under 18 USC section 3293, discussed in more detail in the introduction.

Therefore the statute of limitations for any crimes the government may prove in connection with the above facts will not expire any earlier than 2018. That is 10 years after the last of its fraudulent mortgage-backed securities offerings underlying the massive DOJ settlement discussed above. Similarly, the class action period for purposes of the settlement relating to the undisclosed liquidity puts extended until April 18, 2008. If the government pursued criminal claims based upon Sherry

Hunt's allegations of senior managers at Citigroup ignoring red flags of severe underwriting deficiencies, that settlement encompassed conduct extending into 2012. Such a criminal prosecution would not be time-barred under the statute of limitations until 2022.

Of course, as discussed in the introduction, the government could allege that all of the above misconduct shared a common purpose and pattern of selling very high-risk mortgages as lower risk mortgages, as alleged by Citigroup's own employees. Citigroup seemed intent upon generating short-term profits to boost incentive compensation through mortgage misrepresentations, regardless of long-term costs. The settlement of the claims arising from Citi's misrepresentations in connection with government-insured mortgages continued until 2012. If this is viewed as a part of a common scheme, that would extend the statute of limitations to 2022 for all of Citi's misconduct.

There can no longer be any question that this misconduct continued to draw capital into the subprime bubble for much longer than would have occurred had Citigroup told the truth. This made the crisis much worse. As Attorney General Eric Holder stated with respect to Citigroup's mortgage fraud, "This historic penalty is appropriate given the strength of the evidence of the wrongdoing committed by Citi. The bank's activities contributed mightily to the financial crisis that devastated our economy in 2008. Taken together, we believe the size and scope of this resolution goes beyond what could be considered the mere cost of doing business" (DOJ 2014d). Holder offered no specific explanation at any time during his tenure as attorney general why no single individual at Citi faced any criminal indictment. Nor has DOJ offered any explanation for why the far-flung misconduct of Citigroup did not involve a multiagency effort to break up the megabank under current law, as discussed in the introduction. The silence of bank regulators with respect to all of this misconduct has been deafening—no expulsions or disqualifications from the banking industry against any Citigroup banker.

One can certainly imagine that a jury could conclude that Citi's senior managers acted with an intent to defraud investors in the mortgage-back securities that Citi peddled across the world. Once Citi's senior executives learned from whistleblowers such as Sherry Hunt and Richard Bowen that serious misrepresentations were being made in connection with the sale of mortgage-backed securities, they did nothing to halt the practice. Instead Bowen and Hunt effectively faced demotion and retaliation. This type of willful blindness or conscious avoidance could support a jury finding of criminal intent.

Importantly, Citigroup holds tremendous economic and political power. According to the *Wall Street Journal*, Citigroup paid the sitting Secretary of the Treasury, Jack Lew, a bonus to leave the company for a "high level position with the United States government or regulatory body." Similarly, Peter Orszag left the Obama administration as budget director to become the current vice chairman of Citigroup. Treasury Secretary Robert Rubin left the Clinton administration to become vice chairman of Citigroup and ended up earning $115 million at that post (*Wall Street Journal* 2013). More recently, the *Journal* reported that five senior economic policy makers in the Obama administration hail from Citigroup (Armour & Raice 2014). Of the 61 Citigroup lobbyists in 2014, 53 previously held government jobs. Citigroup exemplifies the revolving door between regulators and high-paying jobs with the regulated.

Of course, real political influence requires bipartisan influence peddling. In 2008, while Citi-affiliated persons contributed $755,000 to future President Obama, Citigroup contributed over $330,000 to Senator John McCain. In that same election year, persons affiliated with Citigroup contributed about $1.5 million to GOP candidates for office. Citigroup-affiliated persons contributed more than twice as much (over $491,000) to the Romney presidential bid in 2012 than to the Obama campaign (around $200,000). In the 2014 election cycle, Citigroup officials made $2.5 million in political campaign contributions, split about evenly between the GOP and the Democratic Party, and spent over $5 million on lobbying. Simply stated, Citigroup epitomizes a political heavy hitter (Center for Responsive Politics 2015a).

JPMorgan Chase

Citi's toxic mortgages mirrored the activity of many other Wall Street firms including JPMorgan Chase (Chase). On November 19, 2013, the DOJ, along with other law enforcement partners, announced a $13 billion settlement with Chase to resolve federal and state civil claims arising from the packaging, marketing, sale, and issuance of toxic mortgage-backed securities. The settlement also involved misconduct at Bear Stearns and Washington Mutual, both of which Chase acquired in the course of the financial collapse in 2008. The settlement covered every Chase, Bear Stearns, or Washington Mutual offering of mortgage-backed securities in which any one of the firms participated as an issuer, sponsor, depositor, or underwriter from 2003 to 2007. Therefore, this settlement demonstrates the degree to which fraud pervaded the Wall Street toxic mortgage machine and how systemic the misconduct was within these firms (DOJ 2013a).

JPMorgan Chase acknowledged that it made "serious misrepresentations" to the investing public in connection with its sales of many pools of mortgage-backed securities. Terms of the settlement required that Chase acknowledge an agreed statement of facts, including "that it regularly represented to [mortgage] investors that the mortgage loans in various securities complied with underwriting guidelines. Contrary to those representations, JPMorgan employees knew that the loans in question did not comply with those guidelines and were not otherwise appropriate for securitization, but they allowed the loans to be securitized—and those securities to be sold—without disclosing this information to investors." Again, Chase did not admit that it committed fraud, or that any particular employee committed fraud. Nevertheless, Chase effectively admitted that fraud occurred in the sale of these mortgage-backed securities because, as seller of such securities, it had an affirmative obligation to make true and complete disclosures of material facts, as discussed in the introduction. Once Chase admitted that it made "serious misrepresentations," that disclosure obligation had been breached.

In one sampled mortgage-backed securities offering, 27 percent of the loans did not meet underwriting representations regarding loan quality and risk. More specifically, JPMorgan Chase acknowledged, "According to a [report] prepared . . . by one . . . due diligence vendor . . . of the 23,668 loans the vendor reviewed for JPMorgan, 6,238 of them, or 27 percent, were initially graded Event 3 loans," those not meeting underwriting standards, having no compensating factors for any deficiencies, or missing critical documentation. Such loans directly violate the representations Chase made to mortgage investors. Chase nevertheless included more than half the loans in mortgage-backed securities pools. The admitted statement of facts makes plain that Chase systematically lied about important loan risk factors, that its own staff and third-party vendors flagged the misrepresentations, and that Chase senior executives allowed the bank to sell the securities to unsuspecting buyers anyway.

There is similarly no question that investors and banks incurred massive damages from these misrepresentations. Of the $13 billion that Chase paid under its settlement agreement, $1.4 billion went to settle securities claims with the National Credit Union Administration and $515.4 million was paid to settle such claims by the Federal Deposit Insurance Corporation (FDIC). This necessarily means that insured depository institutions including banks and credit unions took large losses. According to the FDIC, for example, no fewer than six banks (all of which failed and wound up in FDIC receiverships) invested in Chase mortgage-backed securities and sustained losses (FDIC 2014b).

The US attorney for the Eastern District of California echoes this point: "Abuses in the mortgage-backed securities industry helped turn a crisis in the housing market into an international financial crisis. The impacts were staggering. JPMorgan sold securities knowing that many of the loans backing those certificates were toxic. Credit unions, banks and other investor victims across the country, including many in the Eastern District of California, continue to struggle with losses they suffered as a result." As with the Citigroup settlement, Chase promised to provide mortgage relief to underwater homeowners and distressed communities. The essential point is that Chase caused massive damages in many different ways to investors, borrowers, banks, and entire communities.

Moreover, according to the negotiated statement of facts, Chase acknowledged that "[p]rior to JPMorgan purchasing the loans, a JPMorgan employee who was involved in this particular loan pool acquisition told an Executive Director in charge of due diligence and a Managing Director in trading that due to their poor quality, the loans should not be purchased and should not be securitized. After the purchase of the loan pools, she submitted a letter memorializing her concerns to another Managing Director, which was distributed to other Managing Directors. JPMorgan nonetheless securitized many of the loans. None of this was disclosed to investors." This admission implicates senior management in the decision to knowingly market interests in mortgage-backed securities without full disclosure of all material facts (DOJ 2014c).

The evidence of wrongdoing gets even stronger. A former Chase employee, Alayne Fleischmann, witnessed "massive criminal securities fraud" while working as a due diligence manager on mortgage-backed securities. Fleischmann warned that the bank was peddling very risky mortgage loans as safe mortgage-backed securities to investors. Her superiors responded by "yelling until they [got] the answer they want[ed]" because "they just wanted these [loans] pushed through." Fleischmann also maintains that there is clear and substantial documentary evidence of wrongdoing: "There are emails. There are reports that were ignored. There are vendor reports that were ignored. There are emails from diligence managers, from myself. There's a letter that sets out exactly who did what and what's wrong in our diligence process and how that's going to cause problems in the security" (Hayes 2014). A few short months after reporting the wrongdoing, in February 2008, Alayne Fleischmann lost her job at Chase (Cohan 2015).

The SEC also alleged fraud in one of its investigations into mortgage-backed securities fraud. The SEC alleged that in December 2006, in a prospectus supplement for an offering of $1.8 billion worth of mortgage-backed securities, JPMorgan Chase represented that only 4 loans (or 0.04 percent of the total loans offered to investors) were delinquent by 30 to 59 days. In fact, the firm actually had information showing that more than 620 loans (more than 7 percent of the total loans) had already suffered delinquencies. Moreover, the 4 loans represented as being 30 to 59 days delinquent were in fact 60 to 89 days delinquent. Chase settled these securities fraud claims for $296 million (SEC 2012).

Like Citigroup, Chase also abused the government mortgage guarantee programs. Chase paid $614 million to settle claims that the government brought through information provided by a whistleblower. The period covered by the settlement runs from 2002 to January 31, 2014. As part of the settlement, JPMorgan Chase admitted that it approved thousands of loans that were not eligible for FHA or Veterans Affairs (VA) insurance because they did not meet applicable agency underwriting guidelines. Chase further admitted that it failed to inform the FHA and the VA when its own internal reviews discovered more than 500 defective loans that did not qualify for insurance. In order to participate in these programs, Chase assumed the obligation to notify the government agencies of loan defects (DOJ 2014c).

The whistleblower turned out to be Keith Edwards. He recovered over $63 million for alerting the government to Chase's misrepresentations in connection with FHA and VA loans. Edwards worked for JPMorgan from 2003 to 2008, as a supervisor in JPMorgan Chase's government-insured residential lending department. He alleged that when he informed his supervisors of problems with loans in his unit they reacted with anger and threats that slowing down the volume of insured loans could result in termination (*United States ex rel. Edwards v. JP Morgan Chase Bank, N.A.* 2013). Yet he refused to silently acquiesce to Chase's false certifications. Clearly, he would be able to attest that the bank sold defective loans to the two agencies in contravention of Chase's representations and warranties (Chaudheri 2014a).

JPMorgan Chase and Chase Bank, NA both qualify as financial institutions for purposes of 18 USC section 3293, meaning the statute of limitations for any criminal charges of bank, wire, or mail fraud would not lapse for 10 years following criminal wrongdoing. Certainly, the frauds discussed above exposed both entities to an increased risk of loss, as proven by the massive fines paid. Thus, as discussed in the introduction, the ongoing effort to sell toxic subprime loans as higher quality loans, which continued through at least 2007, would not expire until 2017 at the earliest. Furthermore, the bank continued its fraudulent sales of mortgages to the government through 2014. Any crimes involving that aspect of Chase's mortgage fraud would not expire until at least 2024.

It also appears that senior management either acquiesced to the fraud or at least acted with willful blindness. Chase ignored the two whistleblowers, and both ultimately faced demotion and termination. The senior executives who ignored this information acted with willful blindness sufficient to support an allegation that they acted with an intent to defraud (or scienter)—that is, the state of mind necessary to show criminal fraud.

Bank of America

Bank of America (BOA) entered into the largest settlement in history to resolve claims of securities fraud in connection with the sale of mortgage-backed securities—agreeing to pay over $16 billion to the government in the summer of 2014. The settlement included mortgages originated and packaged into mortgage-backed securities by firms BOA acquired, specifically including Countrywide and Merrill Lynch. While this settlement resembles the massive fraud settlements related to the Citibank and Chase cases, it also includes many new insights into the depths and pervasiveness of wrongdoing in the mortgage business of the megabanks prior to and throughout the financial crisis.

DOJ required that BOA agree to a statement of facts declaring that it sold billions in mortgage-backed securities through material misrepresentations regarding loan quality and risk of default. When the deals collapsed, investors suffered billions in losses. Federally insured banks were among the victims. BOA also conceded that it originated risky mortgage loans and sold many to Fannie Mae, Freddie Mac, and the FHA without accurate disclosure of loan riskiness. Thus BOA's massive settlement establishes once again that Wall Street duped investors into purchasing mortgage-backed securities without the full disclosure of risks mandated under law.

In one $850 million securitization, BOA represented the investment as being backed by "prime" mortgages originated by BOA and underwritten in accordance with its underwriting guidelines. In fact, BOA knew that up to 70 percent of the loans consisted of "wholesale" mortgages originated through mortgage brokers and not through BOA's underwriting process. BOA knew that these wholesale loans suffered from underwriting defects and poor performance. The loans were supported by problematic appraisals, inadequately documented income, and indicia of potential mortgage fraud. In fact, BOA's own CEO termed these loans "toxic waste." Internal documents showed that BOA sought to "shift the risk" of these loans to outside investors. BOA sold these mortgage-backed securities to investors (including federally backed financial institutions) without sufficient due diligence on the securitized loans and without disclosing in the offering documents all material facts (SEC 2013b and 2014).

BOA also paid to settle claims against firms it acquired such as Merrill Lynch. According to the agreed statement of facts, Merrill Lynch made material misrepresentations to investors in 72 mortgage-backed securities offerings during 2006 and 2007. Specifically, the company represented to investors that the loans it was securitizing benefitted from borrowers who were willing and able to pay back the loans. Merrill Lynch knew, however, based on its own due diligence on samples of the loans, that as many as 55 percent of the loans had material underwriting defects. The firm failed to conduct due diligence on many other loans and simply ignored its own due diligence and securitized loans identified as defective. This practice led one Merrill Lynch consultant to "wonder why we have due diligence performed" if the company was going to securitize the loans "regardless of issues" (DOJ 2014b).

The SEC settled administrative proceedings against BOA on the same day as the record settlement with DOJ. As part of that settlement, BOA admitted that it failed to disclose known risks arising from potential obligations to repurchase mortgage loans arising from more than $2 trillion in residential mortgage sales from 2004 to 2008. BOA made contractual representations and warranties about the quality of the mortgage loans, and if a loan buyer claimed a breach of a representation or warranty, the bank could be obligated to repurchase the mortgage loan. BOA failed to properly disclose the repurchase obligation risks in its financial reports for the second and third quarters of 2009 (SEC 2014).

According to Attorney General Holder, "This historic resolution—the largest such settlement on record—goes far beyond 'the cost of doing business.' Under the terms of this settlement, the bank has agreed to pay $7 billion in relief to struggling homeowners, borrowers and communities affected by the bank's conduct. This is appropriate given the size and scope of the wrongdoing at issue." Yet, the failure of Holder's DOJ to bring any criminal cases from these massive multibillion-dollar settlements stands in stark contrast to that statement (DOJ 2014b).

Certainly, Holder did not face any challenges in terms of the statute of limitations for pursuing criminal claims. As the DOJ press release announcing the massive settlement stated, $1.03 billion of the total settlement amount was paid to settle federal and state securities claims by the FDIC. Consequently, numerous banks suffered losses as a result of BOA's misconduct. Furthermore, the settlement directly impacted Bank of America Corporation and Bank of America, NA, both of which are financial institutions and signatories to the settlement agreement with the government (DOJ 2014b). The statute of limitations would be 10 years from the completion of any fraud.

The statute of limitations for a criminal case based upon BOA misrepresentations made to sell its mortgage-backed securities would not expire until 2018, as many of its offerings occurred as late as 2008. The claim against BOA for failing to disclose repurchase obligations would expire in 2019. The statute of limitations for crimes at Merrill Lynch would expire in 2017.

The Rating Agencies

The credit rating agencies were essential to the massive frauds of the Wall Street banks in peddling higher risk loans than represented by giving the mortgage-backed securities an artificially high rating. If the rating agencies had acted in accordance with the representations they made to public investors that they exercised independent professional judgment, lenders would not have made many of the worst mortgages underlying the financial crisis because they would not have been able to sell them as easily on the mortgage-backed securities market. In fact, some investors are restricted by law from investing in securities unless they receive high credit ratings from nationally recognized statistical ratings organizations (FCIC 2011). Without the high ratings the mortgage pools would not have been as marketable or desirable.

In February 2015, the Department of Justice announced a $1.37 billion settlement with S&P over claims that the rating agency engaged in a scheme to defraud investors in various mortgage-backed securities. The settlement included an agreed statement of facts, according to which

> S&P admits that its decisions on its rating models were affected by business concerns, and that, with an eye to business concerns, S&P maintained and continued to issue positive ratings on securities despite a growing awareness of quality problems with those securities. . . . S&P promised investors at all relevant times that its ratings must be independent and objective and must not be affected by any existing or potential business relationship; S&P executives have admitted, despite its representations, that decisions about the testing and rollout of updates to S&P's model for rating [mortgage-backed securities] were made, at least in part, based on the effect that any update would have on S&P's business relationship with issuers; Relevant people within S&P knew in 2007 many loans in [mortgage-backed securities] transactions S&P were rating were delinquent and that losses were probable; S&P representatives continued

to issue and confirm positive ratings without adjustments to reflect the negative rating actions that it expected would come. (DOJ 2015c)

Clearly, S&P further duped unsuspecting investors.

The rating agencies played a key role in the toxic mortgage machine. Essentially they license investment products for certain institutional investors and therefore act as gatekeeper for billions and billions in investment capital. As Acting US Attorney Stephanie Yonekura stated,

> S&P played a central role in the crisis that devastated our economy by giving AAA ratings to mortgage-backed securities that turned out to be little better than junk. Driven by a desire to increase profits and market share, S&P blessed innumerable securitizations that were used by aggressive lenders to offload the risks of billions of dollars in mortgage loans given to homeowners who had no ability to pay them off. This conduct fueled the meltdown that ultimately led to tens of thousands of foreclosures in my district alone. This historic settlement makes clear the consequences of putting corporate profits over honesty in the financial markets. (DOJ 2015c)

S&P and Moody's also settled private claims asserted under New York State law for fraud. In the spring of 2013, the two largest rating agencies entered into a confidential settlement with 14 plaintiffs led by Abu Dhabi Commercial Bank and King County in Washington State. The plaintiffs sought to recover about $700 million in losses that the plaintiffs claimed resulted from misrepresentations in connection with the sale of mortgage-backed securities. The case settled only days before the trial was scheduled to begin (Raymond & Stempel 2013). The *Wall Street Journal* later reported that the case settled for $225 million, to be split among three defendants including the two rating agencies and Morgan Stanley, a bank holding company (Neumann 2013).

Prior to the settlement, a federal judge found that the plaintiffs produced sufficient evidence of fraud and scienter to proceed to trial. This evidence included emails and text messages that demonstrated that the rating agencies recklessly rated the securities at issue without an adequate basis. The judge cited one email from a Moody's analyst that stated that there were "no actual data backing the current model assumptions" for the purpose of the Moody's rating. As for S&P, an analyst declared that the methodology for rating the investments was "totally inappropriate." S&P representatives also engaged in a text message exchange with respect to the investment, in which one stated that "the deal is ridiculous" and that the model used by S&P did not capture "half the risk." He concluded that S&P should not rate the deal. The other analyst responded, "we rate every deal. . . . It could be structured by cows and we would rate it." Consequently, the judge found sufficient evidence of fraud to proceed to trial (*Abu Dhabi Commercial Bank v. Morgan Stanley & Co. Inc.* 2012). Once again the US government failed to act in light of these facts.

"The Magnitude of Falsity, Conservatively Measured, Is Enormous"

The settlement payments outlined in this chapter, amounting to tens of billions of dollars, belie any argument that while some conduct in the run-up to the Great Financial Crisis of 2008 was reprehensible, no laws were broken. Laws were certainly broken even if DOJ declines to criminally prosecute and the financial regulators refuse to use their power to expel criminals from the financial sector. Given the scale of the apparent frauds, it is hard to overstate the degree of corruption that pervaded the mortgage business in the United States from 2006 to 2008. Yet there is still further powerful evidence of this pervasive fraud in connection with the packaging and sales of mortgage-backed securities.

For example, US District Judge Denise L. Cote ruled that two large international megabanks, Nomura and Royal Bank of Scotland, sold mortgage-backed securities through massive material misrepresentations to Fannie Mae and Freddie Mac. Judge Cote decided the case instead of a jury because of the nature of the claims pursued by the government. The bench trial (in which the judge makes both legal and factual findings) lasted from March 16 to April 9, 2015, and involved dozens of witnesses. In the end, Judge Cote concluded, "This case is complex from almost any angle, but at its core there is a single, simple question. Did defendants accurately describe the home mortgages in the Offering Documents for the securities they sold that were backed by those mortgages? Following trial, the answer to that question is clear.

The Offering Documents did not correctly describe the mortgage loans. The magnitude of falsity, conservatively measured, is enormous." The judge therefore once again found that the megabanks used the "big lie" to peddle their subprime mortgages to unsuspecting investors.

While the precise claims pursued by the government in that case did not require a finding of scienter, and therefore Judge Cote did not find that the defendants committed securities fraud, the judge did make findings of importance to any fraud claims. She found for example that one element of fraud—material misrepresentations—was factually and legally supported. She also rejected the defendants' effort to blame the government's losses on the real estate bust and the recession of 2007 to 2008. Instead, she recognized that the material misrepresentations the defendants made contributed to those very events. Thus, the judge did find some important elements of a criminal fraud claim, while not making a finding on the issue of fraud itself (*Federal Housing Finance Authority v. Nomura Holding America, Inc.* 2015).

The SEC alleged even more fraud in the mortgage-backed securities market as it sued mortgage securitizers in connection with the sale of mortgage-backed securities and collected very large fines, even if lesser than the settlements discussed above. These SEC settlements further highlight both the pervasiveness and the depth of the fraud driving the subprime mortgage market. Some of these settlements seem to allege borderline theft in the subprime market.

For example, the SEC charged Bear Stearns with the "failure to disclose its practice of obtaining and keeping cash settlements from mortgage loan originators on problem loans that Bear Stearns had sold into [residential-mortgage-backed securities, RMBSs] trusts. The proceeds from this bulk settlement practice were at least $137.8 million." Essentially Bear Stearns collected money from loan originators for the bum loans that the company had packaged into RMBSs and sold to investors; Bear then pocketed the cash, with no disclosure of this practice to investors. The SEC made similar allegations with respect to Credit Suisse. These "bulk settlements practices" by Wall Street no doubt fed the demand for very low-quality mortgages that could be sold to investors who would suffer massive losses while the Wall Street bank pocketed money from the loan originator for the failed loans (SEC 2012 and 2013a). Not only did Credit Suisse reap additional profit by misrepresenting the quality of the RMBSs it sold, it also recovered through settlements for losses on loans it had already sold. This sordid scheme further highlights the fraudulent practices pervading the mortgage-backed securities market in the years prior to the financial crisis.

The FCIC found that the mortgage market in the United States was pervaded by fraud in connection with the purchase and sale of mortgage-backed securities immediately prior to the meltdown of 2008. Indeed, the FCIC reported that up to $1 trillion of mortgage loans were tainted by fraud, leading to losses of $112 billion. By any measure, the Great Financial Crisis of 2008 originated in massive securities fraud involving mortgage-backed securities (FCIC 2011).

The government's nonprosecution of the banks and senior managers involved in the serious misconduct that occurred in the subprime mortgage crisis is inexplicable. The civil and regulatory settlements discussed above provide substantial evidence of knowing misrepresentations. Given the scale of the transactions tainted by strong indicia of fraud, criminal accountability or at least investigations and trials should follow. Broad promises from the attorney general to hold accountable those responsible have morphed into broad criminal immunity for financial crimes involving the megabanks and their senior executives. It appears that the government deliberately set out to stifle criminal accountability.

The RMBS Working Group, part of the Financial Fraud Enforcement Task Force that President Obama established in November 2009, supervised many of the civil cases discussed in this chapter and featured an array of senior law enforcement agencies at both the federal and state levels. The Obama administration created the Task Force to hold accountable those whose misconduct contributed to the financial crisis. Yet as late as 2016, the Task Force's website lists only a single annual report on the Task Force, from 2010 (DOJ 2016).

One member of that Task Force reportedly complained, however, that it did not focus enough effort on building criminal cases. New York Attorney General Eric Schneiderman told the *Washington Post*, "I've seen evidence that indicates that criminal cases might have been brought if some investigations had begun earlier than they did. There has been no release of any criminal liability. None of the civil settlements negotiated by the working group I co-chaired have released any individual or institution from criminal liability" (vanden Heuvel 2014). Earlier reports suggested Schneiderman thought the Task Force allowed politics to get in the way of bringing criminal charges. Senator Carl Levin said that Schneiderman argued to him that the DOJ lacks the "political will" to forge ahead with prosecutions of high-ranking financial executives and large financial groups (Grim & Nasiripour 2013).

The sad reality in the United States today is that it does take "political will" to aggressively enforce the law against megabanks like Citigroup, JPMorgan Chase, and Bank of America. These banks simply control such huge aggregations of wealth that pursuing criminal indictments quickly becomes unthinkable. According to *CNBC*, "five institutions—JPMorgan Chase, Bank of America, Wells Fargo, Citigroup and U.S. Bancorp—had just under $7 trillion in total assets as of the end of 2014. That's good for 44.61 percent of the industry total" (Cox 2015a). The CEOs of the megabanks sit atop the largest capital aggregations in our society, if not the world.

Such huge firms provide government officials with lucrative job opportunities, large campaign contributions, and other lobbying largesse. Combined with the personal wealth of the senior managers at such huge firms, the degree of political power concentrated in just one firm becomes a threat to the enforcement of criminal law and to the rule of law generally. Indeed, this concentrated power explains the systemic nature of the problem. DOJ does not stand alone in apparent capitulation before financial elites. The FDIC, the Fed, and the SEC are all complicit to say the least. The subprime crisis stands as testament, and the lack of law enforcement will in the aftermath of the crisis bears further witness, to the breakdown in the rule of law.

4

Lehman's Phantom Cash

Lehman Brothers [engaged] in a massive accounting fraud, involving the surreptitious removal of tens of billions of dollars of securities from Lehman's balance sheet in order to create a false impression of Lehman's liquidity, thereby defrauding the investing public. Called "Repo 105," these transactions, hatched in 2001, allowed Lehman to park tens of billions of dollars of highly liquid fixed income securities . . . for the sole purpose of reducing Lehman's balance sheet leverage, and painting a false picture of an important financial metric for investors, stock analysts, [and] lenders.
—*People v. Ernst & Young, LLP*, December 21, 2010

Lehman Brothers' fraud occupies ground zero for the Great Financial Crisis of 2008. Its bankruptcy on September 15, 2008, the largest bankruptcy in history, sparked the meltdown of global capitalism. Indeed, the collapse of Lehman Brothers, the fourth largest investment bank in the world, led to the largest financial crisis our nation has ever seen. It initiated a chain reaction of fear in financial markets requiring massive government assistance for the entire global economy and world of finance, as well as a global economic downturn that continues today.

Securities fraud lies at the root of Lehman's downfall. The firm made leveraged bets on real estate at the wrong time, immediately before the investing public's skepticism of such a business plan peaked. Lehman assured its investors throughout its downward spiral in 2008 that it held sufficient cash and equity to withstand any financial turbulence. In fact, through a program of dubious accounting-driven transactions Lehman masked the degree of its debt and artificially reduced its leverage ratio—the ratio of debt to equity on the balance sheet.

These accounting transactions, known inside Lehman as Repo 105, climaxed during the bank's struggle to stay afloat after the initial shock waves of the 2008 crisis hit the financial sector. The bank engaged in a "shell game" using these transactions to conceal its true debt levels and mislead its investors. It accepted cash to pay down debt and never disclosed its obligation to repurchase the assets for a higher price. Lehman was highly leveraged, holding 44 dollars of debt for every dollar of equity, meaning losses of just under 2.5 percent of its assets would sink the firm. For a firm heavily invested in real estate in 2008, this degree of leverage translated into a high risk of failure, and a very dangerous investment for creditors and stockholders.

The government bailout of Bear Stearns in March 2008 set the stage for Lehman's troubles. Financial markets in early 2008 became uneasy with the basic investment bank model of using high levels of debt to make leveraged investments in real estate. Creditors no longer wanted to finance the operations of highly leveraged investment banks and withdrew short-term funding, resulting in an electronic bank run on the most leveraged investment banks. The most leveraged banks with the most illiquid assets—such as real estate investments—suffered the most from this capital flight. Bear Stearns merely served as the initial victim of capital starvation. By the spring of 2008, Lehman's use of high levels of debt to fund investment bank activities—especially real estate investments—created a death spiral toward failure. Lehman Brothers sought bankruptcy protection on September 15, 2008 (Gasparino 2009).

After the firm filed for bankruptcy, the federal bankruptcy court appointed the former US Attorney for the Northern District of Illinois, Anton Valukas, as bankruptcy examiner to investigate what went wrong and potential claims for recovery of losses. Valukas investigated Lehman's demise for 18 months, interviewing hundreds of employees and reviewing tens of millions of documents. Ultimately Valukas produced a 2,200-page, nine-volume report. Valukas explicitly concluded that "colorable claims of fraud" existed against both Lehman's top officials and its accountant, Ernst & Young. These potential fraud claims could support enforcement action by the SEC or DOJ for securities fraud. The government failed to follow up on Valukas's investigation and bring any fraud claims (Valukas 2012). As a consequence, the statute of limitations bars some claims, but not the key fraud claims, as we will explain.

We argue below that the publicly available evidence would support a grand jury finding of probable cause to indict senior managers, including CEO Richard Fuld, at the very least. Beyond that, certain senior officers should be barred from the securities industry, but only a full investigation would reveal the most culpable senior managers. The story of Lehman's apparent fraud begins in late 2007 with the growing instability in the financial sector, which arose from megabanks' reckless investment in subprime real estate assets based upon a foundation of debt, and ends on September 15, 2008, with Lehman's bankruptcy.

Lehman Brothers' Repo 105

Throughout 2008, the global economy fell further into recession as subprime mortgage losses mounted in the financial sector. Lehman Brothers worked to reassure its investors—creditors and stockholders—that it held enough liquidity and capital to weather the storm. As the crisis deepened throughout 2008, investors became increasingly concerned about capital levels and leverage at the largest banks. The entire financial sector found its very survival at risk by the fall. Firms with high leverage faced the prospect of electronic bank runs like that which essentially shuttered Bear Stearns.

Investors rationally feared that leverage and high-risk assets weakened the balance sheets of many Wall Street banks. Lehman responded by structuring accounting transactions to improve the appearance of its financial stability to regulators and investors, among others. These transactions lacked economic substance, however, and even within Lehman senior officers recognized they constituted "window dressing." Such transactions thereby misled investors and violated the law.

A standard repurchase agreement involves a transfer of assets in exchange for cash, with a future obligation on the part of the cash recipient to repurchase the assets in the future. As such, repurchase agreements resemble loans, with the interest rate for the cash determined by the difference in the price of the asset transfers at the beginning and end of the repurchase agreement. Firms must disclose the repurchase obligation to investors, and basic accounting requires that disclosure in a firm's financial statements.

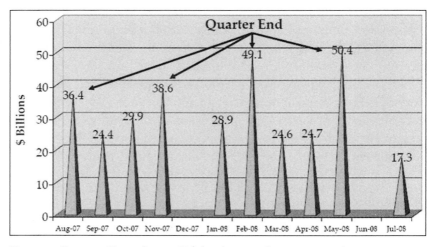

Figure 4.1. Repo 105 Usage. Source: Valukas (2010, 875).

Lehman treated the Repo 105 transactions not as loans but as sales of assets without disclosure of the obligation to repurchase the assets. Such treatment of the Repo 105 transactions gave Lehman accounting benefits. Lehman treated the cash received in these transactions as if it carried no repurchase obligation. That cash was then used to reduce debt. This effectively reduced the size of Lehman's balance sheet, making it look like it held more capital and liquidity relative to the size of its debt. This, in turn, made Lehman's leverage ratio look far less dangerous. In fact, other than their accounting impact, the Repo 105 transactions had no economic purpose.

Demonstrating the true nature of the Repo 105 transactions, the transactions spiked at the end of each quarter when Lehman disclosed its quarterly financial statements to its investors. Thus, in the final quarter of 2007, Lehman listed $38.6 billion in Repo 105 transactions; by the second quarter of 2008, the figure stood at $50.38 billion. As shown in Figure 4.1, at each and every quarter end Lehman engaged in tens of billions of dollars of transactions for the purpose of distorting its debt levels, the strength of its capital base, and its liquidity levels. As shown in Table 4.1, these transactions materially influenced Lehman's key metric of survival—its net leverage ratio (Valukas 2010).

Table 4.1 Impact of Repo 105 on Net Leverage Ratios

Date	Q4 2007	Q1 2008	Q2 2008
Repo 105 usage	$38.6 billion	$49.1 billion	$50.38 billion
Reported net leverage	16.1	15.4	12.1
Leverage without Repo 105	17.8	17.3	13.9
Difference in net leverage ratios	1.7	1.9	1.8

Source: Valukas (2010, 748).

Lehman never disclosed that it undertook these transactions primarily right before the end of each quarter and for the specific purpose of manipulating its leverage ratio to lower, less dangerous levels. Nor did the company disclose that it owed a legal obligation to repurchase the assets soon after the quarter closed for a higher price than it received on the assets. In other words, the transactions had no economic substance other than to fool the investing public (and to pay counterparties money in the process). As one internal email stated, "The recent increase in 105 business was urgently transacted to improve the [f]irm's balance sheet profile over . . . quarter end." Another candidly admitted, "We only focus on meeting our quarter end balance sheet targets. The intra month targets haven't historically been actively managed" (Valukas 2010).

In the United States, firms with publicly traded securities, like Lehman Brothers, must adhere to generally accepted accounting principles, or GAAP. In addition, the financial statements of every publicly held firm must be audited by an accounting firm that certifies they follow GAAP rules. The federal securities laws mandate that public firms file these audited financial statements in an annual report called a Form 10-K. In addition, firms must file quarterly financial statements in a report called a Form 10-Q. There is no required monthly reporting obligation.

The state of New York sued Lehman's accounting firm, Ernst & Young, for securities fraud and alleged that the Repo 105 transactions were not properly accounted for under GAAP. The state sought disgorgement of the $150 million in fees Lehman paid Ernst between 2001 and 2008. Essentially the state claimed that Lehman stretched GAAP beyond its breaking point by accounting for the Repo 105 transactions as if they were true sales of the underlying assets without any obligation to repurchase the assets in the near future (*People v. Ernst & Young, LLP*

2010). As discussed below, this case ultimately settled, as did a private plaintiff lawsuit, with significant payments from Ernst & Young.

GAAP rules were promulgated under the authority of the SEC by the Financial Accounting Standards Board. Under Financial Accounting Statement 140, Lehman's treatment of the Repo 105 transactions could comply with GAAP only under certain circumstances. One condition is that the transaction must amount to a "true sale." Unable to find a US law firm willing to attest that such transactions were "true sales," Lehman obtained an opinion letter from a London law firm opining that specified Repo 105 transactions by Lehman's London affiliate would be "true sales" under English law. Lehman then used this narrow opinion letter directed to the London affiliate to treat all of its Repo 105 transactions as "true sales" and applied it to all such transactions whether or not they involved the London affiliate (*People v. Ernst & Young, LLP* 2010).

Furthermore, a bedrock principle of GAAP is that "the presentation of financial statements in conformity with generally accepted accounting principles includes adequate disclosure of material matters" (AU § 431). Auditors have further obligations beyond just GAAP compliance (AU § 411.04). Mere adherence to GAAP accounting creates only a presumption that financial statements are not misleading (17 CFR § 210.4–01). Lehman entered into these Repo 105 transactions with the intent to mislead investors regarding leverage. According to Lehman's global financial controller, Martin Kelley, the only purpose or motive for the Repo 105 transactions "was reduction in the balance sheet" and that otherwise there was "no substance to the transactions." Another Lehman senior officer stated that the Repo 105 transactions were "basically window dressing" and could be termed "true sales" only due to "legal technicalities." Yet another officer called the transactions an "accounting gimmick" (Valukas 2010). As such, the Lehman financial statements were materially misleading.

Whether the transactions technically complied with certain provisions of GAAP is thus irrelevant. GAAP requires complex judgments, and even the chair of the Financial Accounting Standards Board declined to opine to a congressional inquiry whether Lehman's Repo 105 transactions "complied with the particular standards relating to accounting for repurchase agreements" due to insufficient information (Herz 2010). Violation of GAAP accounting principles, however, creates only a presumption of materially misleading financial statements. The key legal standard goes beyond GAAP to focus on whether financial statements materially misled investors. At the very least, regardless of the formal accounting treatment, Lehman should have fully disclosed the transactions elsewhere in its public filings so that investors would have been completely informed.

As courts consistently recognize, because GAAP has an overall goal of fair disclosure to investors, GAAP tolerates no loopholes. In the final analysis, the question always remains whether the financial statements accurately depict the financial condition of the firm. "Fair presentation is the touchstone for determining the adequacy of disclosure in financial statements. While adherence to generally accepted accounting principles is a tool to help achieve that end, it is not necessarily a guarantee of fairness" (*In re Global Crossing Ltd. Securities Litigation* 2004). Or, as stated by the SEC's chief accountant, "even if there are colorable arguments that GAAP has technically been complied with, if the financial statements taken as a whole are misleading and are not fairly presented, [the SEC Division of] Enforcement will be investigating and you can expect us to recommend charges to the Commission if the evidence suggests that investors were materially misled and the persons acted with the requisite intent" (Scheck 2010).

Aside from the lack of economic substance, the Lehman financial statements made it impossible for any investor to understand the impact of the Repo 105 transactions. For example, Valukas interviewed Lehman's outside disclosure counsel, Andrew Keller, the partner at Simpson, Thacher & Bartlett who worked on Lehman's SEC disclosure documents, including its financial statements. Keller was aware of neither the Repo 105 transactions nor their effect on the financial statements. His assumption was that repos in general are disclosed as secured financings, which would mean they are disclosed as the debts they in fact represent. Lehman's own global controller, Martin Kelly, also told the bankruptcy examiner that he could not find any trace of the Repo 105 repayment obligation in the Lehman financial statements. If these experts, with intimate knowledge of the Lehman financial statements, could not find any hint of disclosure of the Repo 105 transactions, and most particularly the undisclosed obligation to repay, no ordinary investor could possibly have uncovered the truth. Lehman's global head of accounting policy also stated that Lehman made no disclosures regarding the Repo 105 program. The lead partner for Ernst & Young, Lehman's auditor also agreed that Lehman's financial statements made no disclosure of the Repo 105 transactions, although there was general discussion in the financial statements of GAAP compliance (Valukas 2010).

Lehman Brothers Reassures Investors

Lehman sought to calm investor concerns about its leverage through assurances within the course of its quarterly earnings conference calls with securities analysts who would ultimately inform the investing public about Lehman's financial stability. Statements from these calls are central to any potential fraud claim. Unfortunately, at no point in these investor conference calls did any Lehman representative ever mention the effect of Repo 105 transactions on the leverage, capital, or liquidity level of the firm.

At year-end 2007, Lehman's global head of risk management, Chris O'Meara, told the investment community that the leverage ratio at Lehman held steady, but the firm's liquidity position was "very strong." Lehman's chief financial officer, Erin Callan, told investors that although market conditions posed challenges, the firm held ample liquidity and capital to meet the challenges. She also stated, "We ended the quarter with a net leverage ratio of approximately 16.1 times, in line with last quarter" (Lehman Brothers 2007b).

These themes continued into early 2008. In the first quarter conference call with investors, Callan stated that the firm "very deliberately" took leverage down, strived to enhance balance sheet transparency, and benefitted from a robust liquidity position. Net leverage reportedly declined from 16.1 to 15.4. She also emphasized that Moody's reaffirmed Lehman's credit rating due to the strength of its capital base and its liquidity. She concluded by noting that Lehman had no expectation that the "extremely challenging period" gripping financial markets would end soon but that the firm's capital strengths and liquidity would permit it to "ride out the cycle" (Lehman Brothers 2008a).

At the end of the second quarter of 2008 Lehman announced a $2.8 billion loss. This unpleasant announcement caused CEO Richard Fuld to participate in the earnings conference call. Fuld told investors that the firm reduced its balance sheet by $147 billion in assets and raised additional capital of $10 billion. Fuld also assured investors that the firm decided to "aggressively delever" during the quarter. He stated, "Our capital and liquidity position have never been stronger." Ian Lowitt, the CFO who had succeeded Callan, echoed this, stating that the firm had undertaken "aggressive deleveraging." Lowitt concluded by reaffirming that the firm remained in a strong capital and liquidity position (Lehman Brothers 2008b).

The third quarter conference call fell on September 10, 2008—five days before Lehman filed for bankruptcy. Fuld stated that the firm would cut its dividend to preserve capital. He also noted that the firm further reduced leverage during the quarter. Lowitt claimed that the firm's capital and leverage ratio were stronger than at the end of the second quarter. Finally, the firm stated that it held $41 billion in liquidity reserves (Lehman Brothers 2008c). These remarkable statements masked the fact that Lehman suffered from severely illiquid assets, high levels of leverage and debt, and insufficient liquidity to avoid bankruptcy five days later.

The Repo 105 transactions profoundly affected liquidity, sufficiency of capital, and, most important, leverage. Lehman's very survival turned on these transactions to mask key elements of its balance sheet. Ordinary investors could not possibly have discerned the degree to which high levels of debt, or leverage, threatened Lehman's survival.

One sophisticated investor suspected some accounting chicanery but could not pinpoint where Lehman was manipulating its balance sheet. David Einhorn, a well-known hedge fund manager, started shorting Lehman stock in 2007, on the basis of its illiquid real estate investments and his suspicions that Lehman's capital position was weaker than disclosed. Einhorn's suspicions turned out to be spot-on, but the market allowed Lehman to stagger along for months longer due to its misrepresentations. Einhorn's suspicions were publicly disclosed in April 2008. He even complained to regulators that Lehman played fast and loose with its financial statements. In the end, Einhorn influenced the price of Lehman's stock with his warnings, but even he was unable to uncover the fraud (Gasparino 2009).

Valukas's report recounts Lehman's intentional deception to manipulate financial reports by abusing an accounting machination. Lehman, knowing that it needed to reduce its reliance on short-term borrowed cash, used Repo 105 to temporarily remove assets (and debt) from its balance sheet just before issuing its quarterly financial statements, reducing leverage and making it appear as if its debt was decreasing. Immediately following the distribution of its quarterly financial statements, the assets would then appear right back where they came from on Lehman's balance sheet. In order to appear healthy on paper and hide its alarmingly high leverage, Lehman took this strategy to the extreme, reaching $50 billion at the end of the second quarter of 2008. In the end, Lehman's machinations proved futile; the firm simply drowned in debt and sought refuge in bankruptcy. Investors could have averted losses if the true level of leverage had been disclosed, but that never occurred until after bankruptcy.

Scienter, Willful Blindness, and Beyond

Valukas found plenty of evidence to support "colorable claims of fraud" relating to the Repo 105 transactions. He also uncovered documents suggesting that the Repo 105 accounting ruse was a matter of common knowledge among Lehman's senior management team. For example, from April to September 2008, Lehman regularly circulated a document called the Daily Balance Sheet and Disclosure Scorecard among its senior managers via email. This report included (among other things) a regular tally of Repo 105 transactions and the benefit provided to Lehman's balance sheet from the transactions.

Internal emails as well as interview statements demonstrate a deliberate deception to make the company appear more liquid and less leveraged than reality. Countless emails between top Lehman officers, discussing their use of Repo 105 specifically for the purpose of manipulating the financial statements, with no other economic substance, show a deliberate intent to mislead Lehman shareholders and other users of the financial statement. Statements from high-level company officers expressed serious ethical and legal concerns about the use of Repo 105. Since intent to defraud, false or fraudulent representations, or willful blindness is necessary to show that any individual committed criminal or civil fraud, this section reviews evidence of scienter in detail.

One unusual complicating fact in any claims of fraud against Lehman would be the role of the government in the months prior to its bankruptcy. Former CEO Richard Fuld testified to Congress that representatives of the SEC and the Fed placed government agents at Lehman's headquarters throughout 2008 to monitor the firm's condition on a real-time basis and asserted those agents had access to Lehman's books and records, claiming "they saw what we saw." This could suggest an innocent state of mind for Lehman employees—perhaps for some Lehman managers the government's presence created an impression of tacit approval (Valukas 2012).

Nevertheless, the Valukas report portrays both the Fed and SEC as essentially clueless regarding the Repo 105 transactions. Valukas found no evidence that Lehman disclosed any facts about the transactions to either agency. Valukas interviewed key Fed and SEC representatives, and none recalled any discussion of Repo 105. These representatives also noted that such transactions would have raised regulatory concerns (Valukas 2010). Thus, any argument that these regulators tacitly approved the Repo 105 transactions could backfire to demonstrate that Lehman worked to keep the accounting gimmick well concealed from government regulators. Moreover, at the same congressional hearing, Fuld maintained that he was unaware of Repo 105 and the scheme to use accounting machinations to shift liabilities off the financial statements. If Fuld's claim of ignorance is believed (and Valukas maintains there is some evidence to the contrary), then one would not expect outside agents, such as the Fed or the SEC, to detect from those same documents that which is undetectable by the CEO.

Fuld told the bankruptcy examiner as well as Congress that he had no knowledge of the Repo 105 transactions. Yet, the president and chief operating officer of Lehman, Bart McDade, told the examiner a completely different story. In April 2008, McDade wrote in an email that the Repo 105 transactions "are another drug we r on" (McDade 2008). McDade's equating the transactions with drug use would support a grand jury finding that he knew the transactions were dubious.

McDade also recalled a detailed discussion of Repo 105 transactions with Fuld in June 2008, shortly after McDade became president and COO. They discussed the size of the transactions and agreed they should cut the volume of such transactions in half by year-end. Fuld stated that if reducing Repo 105 transactions was "doable" then "go do it." McDade specifically "walked Fuld through [a] presentation" on the firm's balance sheet and leverage ratio and the impact of Repo 105 transactions. McDade concluded that Fuld did know about the Repo 105 transactions and was familiar with Lehman's use of the accounting gimmick to reduce its balance sheet and project less leverage to the investing public.

The presentation that McDade claims he discussed with Fuld involved a document titled Balance Sheet and Key Disclosures. That document specified the total amount of Repo 105 transactions that Lehman used to reduce its apparent leverage. It showed a $38 billion reduction in Lehman's balance sheet in the fourth quarter of 2007, a $49 billion reduction in the first quarter of 2008, and a $50 billion reduction in the second quarter of 2008.

CEO Fuld also received an email dated March 27, 2008, which was sent to the entire Lehman Executive Committee and included an attached agenda that referenced Repo 105 transactions and indicated the amount of such transactions for the first quarter of 2008—$49 billion. Fuld's assistant also forwarded this email to other Lehman managers (Valukas 2010). Although Fuld claimed he never opened the attachment, it strains credulity to think a CEO would not be stay abreast of the agenda for an Executive Committee meeting.

Lehman deliberately misled the investing public, and Valukas uncovered documentary evidence that its senior managers knew that its actions were questionable. Matthew Lee, a senior accountant at Lehman in charge of Lehman's global balance sheet, blew the whistle on Lehman's accounting practices in early 2008 when he refused to attest to the accuracy of Lehman's financial statements. Lee thought the Repo 105 transactions sounded like "rat poison." He objected to the accounting treatment of these transactions immediately. On May 16, 2008, he protested in writing, circulating a letter to Lehman's senior management team (including its chief financial officer and chief risk officer) objecting to its accounting practices including the Repo 105 transactions. Lee informed four senior officers that Lehman's accounting practices were "unethical and unlawful." Six days later Lehman discharged him after 14 years of service. Thereafter Lehman's auditors at Ernst & Young interviewed Matthew Lee; Lee specifically referred to the efforts of the firm to move assets off its balance sheet in exchange for short-term cash pursuant to Repo 105 transactions as one basis for his objections. At a minimum, the Lehman executives exercised willful blindness to Lee's written warnings by consciously disregarding his assessment of unlawfulness and dispatching the messenger. Lehman thus continued using Repo 105 transactions to mislead investors until its demise (Valukas 2012).

Other evidence also demonstrates that senior officers at Lehman permitted the Repo 105 transactions to proceed despite apparent knowledge of their dubious nature. Not only did Lehman's global financial controller, Martin Kelly receive the Lee letter, Kelly also told Valukas that he informed both Erin Callan (who was also a recipient of the Lee letter) and Ian Lowitt—the last two chief financial officers at Lehman—of the "reputational risk" of the Repo 105 transactions. More specifically, he told them that he questioned the accounting treatment of the transactions, the lack of economic substance to the transactions, the fact that the volume of transactions spiked right at the end of the quarter, and that it appeared the sole purpose was to shrink the balance sheet.

Callan does not dispute that this conversation occurred and places it in late February or March 2008; she just claims she does not recall the substance of the conversation. In fact, she told bankruptcy examiner Valukas that she could recall little about the entire Repo 105 program. Nevertheless, Callan attended an Executive Committee meeting on March 28, 2008, that listed Repo 105 as an agenda item along with a statement that Repo 105 transactions amounted to nearly $50 billion for the first quarter of 2008. Just 12 days later Callan as CFO signed the Lehman financial statements. Callan also received the Daily Balance Sheet and Disclosure Scorecard from April to the end of June 2008, which referred to the Repo 105 transactions and the impact of the transactions on Lehman's balance sheet.

Ian Lowitt succeeded Callan as Lehman's chief financial officer in June 2008. He too claims to have no recollection of the precise volume or impact of the Repo 105 transactions. However, Lowitt wrote an email in late 2007, when he served as chief administrative officer at Lehman, that proves he was worried about market perceptions of leverage on Lehman's balance sheet even before becoming CFO. Similarly in February 2008, Lowitt emailed other senior managers at Lehman inquiring about the volume of Repo 105 transactions and why they fluctuated from quarter to quarter. Lowitt told the bankruptcy examiner that he sent the email in an effort to gauge the materiality of the Repo 105 transactions.

Lowitt also attended the March 28 special meeting of the Executive Committee requested by McDade. Lowitt received the same documents that listed the $49.1 billion in Repo 105 transactions Lehman had undertaken at the end of the first quarter 2008 and was present when McDade discussed Lehman's use of Repo 105 transactions. Lowitt received the Daily Balance Sheet and Disclosure Scorecard from April to September 2008. Repo 105 transactions and their effect on Lehman's balance sheet figured prominently in these reports.

The motive to gain money or property is another element bearing upon criminal intent in any case against Lehman representatives. Each of the senior officers had a clear motive to perpetuate this long-standing fraud for as long as possible. Their compensation packages created a significant incentive to continue in their positions as long as possible and to boost Lehman's stock price as high as possible for as long as possible. During the period of the accounting machinations, compensation for Lehman employees amounted to about 50 percent of revenues. Moreover, Lehman showered its senior officers with huge stock option compensation that directly motivated those managers to try to pump up the Lehman stock price as high as possible for as long as possible. Coming clean about the actual leverage would not achieve that goal (Valukas 2010). Lehman's managers held a powerful motive to manipulate their financial statements: to fool investors regarding the true value of Lehman's stock so that they could maintain their very high levels of compensation.

Some may argue that because Lehman management held so much stock and vested as well as unvested stock options, they would not commit securities fraud. However, an in-depth study of compensation at Lehman found that overall the senior officers garnered $1 billion in total compensation between 2000 and 2008. The structure of options compensation meant that Lehman's senior managers faced constant incentives to push short-term stock prices as high as possible as their options vested over time. Simply put, the longer they could fool public investors about their financial stability, the more money they could continue to make (Bebchuk et al. 2010). Thus, in keeping Lehman afloat as long as possible and portraying it as financially stable as possible, senior management could continue to sell stock and exercise options as they vested as well as to garner compensation payments, bonuses, and more options. That proved lucrative, if dubious and possibly illegal.

The Valukas report became publicly available in 2010. The investigation into Repo 105 spans 321 pages. Valukas invited counsel for these senior officers to present additional information that could bear on his final conclusions. They each accepted the invitation and met with Valukas. Nevertheless, the Valukas report concluded that "colorable claims," at least insofar as the bankruptcy court was concerned, existed against each of them based upon the information gathered from the investigation and due consideration of the information presented by the senior officers' representatives (Valukas 2010). Had the DOJ presented that information to a grand jury, one could imagine that it could find probable cause to charge several Lehman senior officers with fraud-based crimes. The report offers considerable evidence that Fuld, Callan, and Lowitt each knew that the Repo 105 transactions crossed the threshold of materiality once they reached the high levels of late 2007 and into 2008, when they climbed from $38 billion to $50 billion. At the very least, a grand jury could find they were willfully blind to the existence and impact of the transactions. The investing environment of late 2007 and 2008 caused investors to focus intensively on issues of leverage, and these transactions materially affected Lehman's leverage calculation by its own standards of materiality (as discussed below). At some point, these three senior officers should have insisted upon a full disclosure of the Repo 105 transactions. There is no colorable argument that such disclosure occurred. Each of these senior officers also reassured investors that Lehman's financial reports represented the true nature of its leverage position and benefited from the additional capital pumped into Lehman by investors. Despite ample evidence to present to a grand jury, there is no indication that DOJ followed through with a grand jury investigation against Lehman or its senior officers.

These senior officers also each owed specific obligations under the federal securities laws to certify that Lehman's financial statements "fairly [present], in all material respects, the financial condition and results of operations of the [firm]" (18 USC § 1350). The SEC interprets this requirement to mean that each financial statement "meets a standard of overall accuracy and completeness that is broader than financial reporting requirements under generally accepted accounting principles." The SEC further requires that officers certify they have "designed such disclosure controls and procedures to ensure that material information . . . is made known to them" and that "certifying officers have disclosed . . . to the issuer's auditors and the audit committee of the board of directors . . . [a]ny fraud, whether or not material, that involves management or other employees who have a significant role in the issuer's internal controls" (SEC 2002). Thus, again, compliance with GAAP is explicitly not a defense under law. Furthermore, these certifications essentially impose an affirmative obligation on certifying officers to ensure the disclosure of material facts as well as fraud by any senior accounting officer. Consequently, it is difficult for these officers to proclaim ignorance of the huge Repo 105 transactions given their affirmative obligation to certify the Lehman financial statements.

In fact, a judge has already found in civil litigation brought by private plaintiffs and relying in part on the Valukas report that plaintiffs had pleaded facts giving rise to a strong inference that the senior managers discussed above acted with intent to defraud. While pleaded facts do not constitute a jury finding that the defendants acted with intent to defraud, the denial of a motion to dismiss is a judicial determination that if plaintiffs can prove the facts alleged in their complaint they will have made a strong showing of scienter by demonstrating "strong circumstantial evidence of conscious misbehavior." Under the Private Securities Litigation Reform Act, a judge must find that allegations regarding scienter are more plausible than any innocent explanation. On September 8, 2011, US District Court Judge Lewis A. Kaplan denied motions to dismiss filed by former CEO Fuld, former CFO Callan, and former CFO Lowitt, among others (In re Lehman Bros. Securities and ERISA Litigation 2011). This amounts to a finding that the allegations based upon the Valukas report regarding scienter likely would be sufficient to sway a grand jury that the defendants acted with an intent to defraud or misrepresent.

If the government had pursued criminal charges, an astonishing degree of helpful testimony would have been available to assist in securing a criminal conviction. President and COO McDade readily admitted to the key facts underlying the Repo 105 transactions. Whistleblower and former Senior Vice President for Global Balance Sheet Matthew Lee would also figure as a cooperative insider who sacrificed his job to stem wrongdoing to serve as a persuasive witness. Global Controller Martin Kelly also raised misgivings regarding Repo 105 transactions to successive CFOs. These three senior officers could explain in plain terms how Lehman used these transactions to take in cash, pay down debt, and mask leverage without full disclosure to investors. The Valukas report points to several other witnesses who would likely prove useful if the government pursued a vigorous prosecution.

The Valukas report also provides the government with a virtual documentary roadmap. Documents sent to the defendants would prove helpful to the government's case, as discussed above. The government might also be able to persuade Lehman's auditors through offers of leniency to cooperate in a criminal proceeding against Lehman's senior officers. On the other hand, Ernst & Young remains embroiled in civil litigation for its misconduct in connection with the Repo 105 transactions, as we explain in the next section.

The Case against Ernst & Young

Ernst & Young served as auditors for Lehman and therefore opined to the accuracy of the Lehman financial statements in terms of compliance with GAAP. This means that some Lehman officers could be expected to argue that they relied on the expertise of Ernst & Young with respect to the Lehman Repo 105 transactions. Reliance by Lehman senior officers upon outside accounting expertise as a defense has not been successful in civil litigation thus far, however, in part because even if the transactions were found to be technically lawful or in accordance with GAAP, the quarterly transactions could still be found to be intentionally deceptive and misleading (In re Lehman Bros. Securities and ERISA Litigation 2011).

Consider, for example, the settlements of securities fraud actions already entered into by Ernst & Young. Once Lehman declared bankruptcy, investors victimized by the Repo 105 transactions could look to only Ernst & Young for compensation. Consequently, the firm faced a number of civil lawsuits for securities fraud arising from their audit of Lehman's financial statements. In late 2013, Ernst agreed to pay investors $99 million to settle a class action for securities fraud relating to the Repo 105 transactions (Brown 2013). More recently, Ernst & Young settled similar claims with a number of municipalities, pension funds, and other investors in Lehman securities from around the world for undisclosed sums (Fitzgerald 2015). Ernst & Young continues to maintain that its conduct of the Lehman audits was appropriate, and a 2014 arbitration ruling supported that position to an extent (Goldstein 2014a).

Nevertheless, the Valukas report identified two witnesses to the role Ernst & Young played in addressing the objections of Senior Vice President Matthew Lee. Lee blew the whistle on inappropriate accounting practices in May 2008, and Lehman discharged him shortly thereafter. In June, Ernst & Young representatives interviewed Lee at the request of Lehman's audit committee of the board. The audit committee directed Ernst to report on all of Lee's allegations. The notes of the Lee interview corroborate Lee's own recollection that he discussed the Repo 105 transactions including the precise volume of the transactions and the intent to reduce Lehman's balance sheet. The Ernst representative who conducted the interview claims she returned to Ernst & Young's offices after the interview to meet with the lead partner on the Lehman audit and that they specifically discussed the Repo 105 transactions. The lead partner told Valukas that he did not recall any discussion of the Repo 105 transactions.

In any event, when Ernst & Young met with the audit committee the day following the meeting with Lee, Ernst & Young made no mention of the Repo 105 transactions. A few weeks later Ernst & Young met with the audit committee again about Lehman's second quarter financial statements and again failed to mention the Repo 105 transactions. On July 10, 2008, Ernst & Young signed Lehman's second quarter financial statement, which made no mention of the $50 billion of Repo 105 transactions that masked Lehman's true leverage despite the whistleblowing of Matthew Lee to Ernst & Young in the June interview (Valukas 2010).

Based upon these facts, Judge Kaplan denied the Ernst & Young motion to dismiss and found that it acted with the requisite scienter for the purposes of its statements in connection with the Lehman 10-Q filed on July 10, 2008. Ernst & Young vouched for this document, notwithstanding its knowledge of accounting irregularities with respect to the Repo 105 transactions from its interview of Matthew Lee. Indeed, inexplicably, Ernst & Young failed to follow up on Lee's allegations in any meaningful way and concealed these particular allegations from the audit committee. As such, Judge Kaplan soundly concluded that Ernst & Young acted with the requisite scienter for purposes of a motion to dismiss in connection with the Lee interview (In re Lehman Bros. Securities and ERISA Litigation 2011). In contrast, the SEC and the DOJ backed away from pursuing the Lehman defendants and Ernst & Young. The next section focuses on the government's weak-kneed response to the Lehman fraud. Indeed, given the massive recoveries achieved in private lawsuits, the government's decision to allow these wrongdoers to escape all accountability is inexplicable.

The Government's Response

The failure of Lehman bears a strong resemblance to that of Enron. Like Enron, Lehman attracted more capital for a longer time than would have been the case had the firm truthfully disclosed all material facts. Yet, the government's response to the failure of Lehman could not stand in greater contrast to the response to Enron. Put simply, grounds for a criminal investigation were handed to the government on a silver platter, and yet the government refused to charge even a single person with fraud from the failure of Lehman.

The SEC, in an apparently internally divisive decision, declined to proceed with even civil charges. The SEC needs to show the elements of securities fraud only by a preponderance of evidence. Nevertheless, the SEC enforcement attorneys feared they could not demonstrate materiality by Lehman's actions of routinely moving billions of debt per quarter off the Lehman balance sheet immediately before submitting quarterly reports to the agency during the days following the failure of Bear Stearns. The *New York Times* reported that the enforcement team may have allowed the great wealth of the senior Lehman managers to intimidate them from bringing charges. Given the role of Lehman in triggering the 2008 financial crisis, this outcome is difficult to fathom. SEC Chair Mary Schapiro reportedly was incredulous that her staff recommended no enforcement action (Protess & Craig 2013).

Her reaction is understandable. Sham transactions totaling $50 billion would strike any reasonable investor as material. Lehman engaged in such transactions quarter after quarter for years. If the leadership of

Lehman had thought the impact of these massive sham transactions was immaterial, they would not have so persistently engaged in these transactions and monitored them so closely. Lehman engaged in these transactions specifically to alter perceptions of the degree of leverage. Senior officers knew the Repo 105 transactions operated like a "drug" and sounded like "rat poison." They undertook them out of desperation to influence the price of Lehman shares by deterring investors from flight—the very definition of materiality, as discussed previously. Lehman's senior managers emphasized the strong liquidity and net leverages deliberately in quarter conference calls precisely because of the important role the transactions played in misleading the public with regard to its leverage. In short, it stretches credibility to accept that the SEC shut down its case based upon materiality.

In fact, when hedge fund manager David Einhorn raised mere suspicions of accounting machinations in the spring of 2008, the stock price reacted dramatically. Einhorn argued that Lehman concealed its leverage and overstated its asset values in its financial statements. At a meeting of hedge fund managers, Einhorn reportedly practically accused Lehman of engaging in accounting fraud. These allegations drove Lehman's stock price down, and as Einhorn stepped up his attacks the price fell even lower. Ultimately, Einhorn's attacks led to the dismissal of Erin Callan, the firm's chief financial officer, and Joe Gregory, the firm's chief operating officer (Gasparino 2009). Einhorn's attacks offer further proof that accounting issues involving leverage for investment banks heavily invested in real estate meet the definition of materiality.

Valukas investigated materiality as part of the bankruptcy investigation and interviewed the credit rating agencies. Representatives of each of the three major rating agencies told the bankruptcy examiner that despite detailed communications and meetings with Lehman management they had no knowledge of the Repo 105 transactions. All three agencies would have wanted to know the truth of the Repo 105 transactions. While none of the representatives could state definitively whether truthful disclosure would have influenced their ratings on Lehman securities, each thought the transactions were relevant to their ratings either directly through the leverage ratio or indirectly through other risk metrics.

Lehman Brothers and Ernst & Young themselves supplied another measure of materiality. Specifically, in a walk-through document prepared for Ernst & Young's 2007 fiscal year-end audit of Lehman, they defined "materiality" with respect to the balance as "any item individually, or in the aggregate, that moves net leverage by 0.1 or more (typically $1.8 billion)." Lehman and Ernst essentially agreed that any accounting issue that affected Lehman's "net leverage ratio" by 0.1 one way or another was material. As evidenced by Table 4.1, the Repo 105 transactions affected leverage by nearly 20 times more than the agreed-on threshold (Valukas 2010). This self-definition of materiality provides ready support to satisfy this element of any case brought by the government against the Lehman officers (Valukas 2010).

It appears that the Bush administration acted in complete harmony with historic precedent for such massive scandals. In October 2008, the Bush administration initiated three grand jury proceedings into the bankruptcy of Lehman Brothers, and the press reported that DOJ issued dozens of subpoenas. A grand jury reportedly targeted former CEO Fuld, among others (Siemaszko 2008). We could find no indication of any material activity since then. President Obama was sworn into office in January 2009. Given the Valukas report, it would seem Obama's DOJ either lacked basic prosecutorial competency or held other interests that took priority over enforcing the rule of law upon the most powerful.

The *Wall Street Journal* reported that the US Department of Justice deferred to the determination of the SEC. It also reported that the government thought that Lehman's accounting machinations may not necessarily have violated the law (Eaglesham & Rappaport 2011). Neither the SEC nor the DOJ appears to have revisited the issue of liability even after the release of the Valukas report. In the end, the DOJ holds independent criminal jurisdiction, unbound by the SEC's decisions, and so far the government has offered no good reason for its lack of law enforcement activity with respect to Lehman's manifest misconduct.

While the federal government stood idly by based upon these flimsy justifications, plaintiffs' attorneys pursued civil claims for securities fraud and did not allow concerns regarding materiality to hinder their recovery. Instead, these attorneys recovered $516 million (in addition to the $99 million recovery against Ernst & Young discussed above) against the senior managers of Lehman and the underwriters of certain Lehman securities during the time period of the Repo 105 fraud (Rapaport 2013). Furthermore, the state of New York used the Valukas report to structure its fraud claims against Ernst & Young, which settled with the state for an additional $10 million (Freifeld 2015). Thus, the defendants in these lawsuits failed to raise lack of materiality as an effective defense to these civil actions. Essentially these lawsuits succeeded on the very issue that the federal government declined to pursue civilly or criminally.

Based upon the best primary source documents available, the strongest criminal charges relate to the misconduct of the senior officers as discussed above, yet at least one clear criminal charge is no longer viable because the government permitted the six-year statute of limitations to expire. Specifically, under 18 USC section 1350 every chief executive officer and chief financial officer must certify that any financial statement filed with the SEC "fairly presents, in all material respects, the financial condition and results of operations of the issuer." An officer who makes a knowing false certification can be "fined not more than $1,000,000 or imprisoned not more than 10 years, or both." Any criminal charge against senior officers for knowingly certifying inaccurate financial statements expired on September 10, 2014. Given the documentary support demonstrating the knowledge of these three senior officers regarding the Repo 105 transactions, this may well have been the Department of Justice's clearest shot at criminal convictions. The Sarbanes-Oxley Act of 2002 added this criminal provision to affirmatively highlight the duty of senior management under peril of criminal liability to verify such financial statements fairly present the financial condition of the organization. The failure to bring this obvious claim suggests an abandonment of DOJ prosecutorial responsibility to deter criminality in the financial sector.

The government still can proceed under 18 USC section 3293, which provides a 10-year statute of limitations applicable to bank, wire, or mail fraud affecting a financial institution. Lehman's accounting fraud affected a bank, as Lehman's corporate structure included both a bank and a thrift. It also included a bank holding company in its corporate structure (Lehman Brothers 2007a). If any bank or bank holding company held Lehman securities and lost money from the Lehman fraud, then the government could seek grand jury indictments against the senior officers for bank fraud, which would also trigger the 10-year statute of limitations. Assuming the fraud ended on September 10, 2008, when Lehman last assured the market about its capital and liquidity levels, the statute of limitations under this section would not expire until September 10, 2018.

The Lehman accounting fraud proved costly to the economy in general. Lehman prolonged its existence through aggressive manipulation of its leverage relative to capital. By taking in massive cash and reducing debt without disclosing the repayment obligation, Lehman attracted more investment than it otherwise would have. Once the inevitable crash came, it was much worse than if Lehman had truthfully disclosed its financial condition. It is not possible to know with certainty if an earlier failure of Lehman would have been less destructive than its actual failure on September 15, 2008.

Similarly, we cannot know the alternative reality if Lehman had decided against using Repo 105 transactions, and instead aggressively sold more assets sooner, perhaps even in mid-2007. This would have been the nonfraudulent means of reducing the firm's balance sheet. The only reality we can know with certainty is that Lehman did postpone its market reckoning and survived longer than it otherwise would have, ending in the largest bankruptcy in US history and triggering a massive global financial crisis.

We do know that despite the collapse of Lehman Brothers, the current financial conditions of CEO Fuld and Ernst & Young appear sound. Ernst & Young continues to operate a lucrative auditing and consulting firm. Whether one believes the whistleblower who claims that Fuld took in over $500 million in compensation between 2000 and 2007 or Fuld's testimony before Congress claiming about $300 million, Fuld continues to enjoy a comfortable standard of living (Sterngold 2010). The Center for Public Integrity reported that former Lehman CEO Fuld now operates a financial consulting firm. Moreover, Fuld maintains an $8 million home in Greenwich, Connecticut, and a 40-acre ranch in Idaho. Fuld transferred a $10 million Florida property to his wife in 2008, and the Fulds reportedly sold their Park Avenue apartment for $25 million (Fitzgerald 2013).

The government's decision to affirm Lehman's misconduct essentially tells financiers that accounting manipulation pays. Creating effective deterrence requires that laws be enforced. Also, many senior Lehman managers no doubt continue to work in the financial sector. The SEC should have sought professional disqualification where appropriate in the case of Lehman, as discussed in the introduction. Such regulatory enforcement actions would benefit from a lower burden of proof—preponderance of the evidence.

Certainly, no Lehman senior manager or auditor can be convicted of a crime without a guilty plea or jury finding that any such defendant acted with the requisite criminal intent—at a minimum the government would have to show scienter (an intent to defraud, knowing material false or fraudulent statements, or willful blindness). Criminal cases require proof beyond a reasonable doubt. The tragedy of the Lehman story is no jury heard any evidence that individuals committed crimes, despite the evidence of the manifest misrepresentations perpetrated by Lehman on its creditors and stockholders. The corporation went bankrupt and thereby imposed its own death penalty, so there is no corporation to charge criminally. Nonetheless, a corporation can act only through its agents or employees, and so fraud could have been perpetrated only through the people at Lehman. Yet, Lehman stands as a testament to a disturbing reality in America today: for the most powerful financial elites at the apex of our economic system, crime pays.

5

Joe Cassano and AIG's Derivatives Casino

I think if there's a single episode in this entire 18 months that
has made me more angry, I can't think of one, than AIG. AIG
exploited a huge gap in the regulatory system. There was no
oversight of the financial products division. This was a hedge
fund, basically, that was attached to a large and stable insurance company, [that] made huge numbers of irresponsible
bets [and] took huge losses.
—Federal Reserve Chairman Ben Bernanke, 2009

AIG holds the gold medal for sheer recklessness in the years prior to
the financial collapse. AIG used its relatively high credit rating to turn
pools of subprime mortgages into highly rated debt instruments. The
company offered to pay if billions in subprime debt defaulted or threatened to default. As such, AIG directly encouraged more capital to flow
into the subprime mortgage market than otherwise would have been the
case. While we can never know with certainty, it is likely that billions
and billions in toxic mortgages would not have existed without AIG's
misconduct, as recounted in this chapter.

The key to AIG's recklessness involved hundreds of billions of dollars
in derivatives transactions called credit default swaps (CDSs). AIG agreed
to pay under these CDS contracts if the subprime mortgage market collapsed. While AIG senior managers understood the risks they inflicted
on their company, AIG's investors had no clue because the firm never disclosed the true risks to the investing public as required by law. By the time
AIG came clean about the risks of the CDS transactions in late February 2008, shareholders had suffered huge losses. Ultimately, these undisclosed risks sank AIG and took the global economy down along the way.

Pursuant to these CDS transactions, AIG agreed, in exchange for fees,
to pay if certain subprime mortgage-related debt defaulted. When massive subprime debt defaults occurred during the crash of 2007–2008,

AIG took tens of billions in losses. In fact, the group lost more money than any publicly traded firm in history—shedding $61.7 billion in the fourth quarter of 2008. These losses led directly to a massive federal bailout of $180 billion, which the government determined to be necessary because the counterparties on the CDSs included the largest and most powerful financial institutions around the world (Zuill and Somerville 2009). These institutions ultimately received billions from these CDS contracts with AIG. Goldman Sachs, for example, received $12.9 billion, Bank of America $12 billion (Mamudi & Kennedy 2009). Thus, the AIG bailout trickled down to shield a host of powerful Wall Street firms from severe losses.

AIG's CDS business made Wall Street's structured finance business more lucrative. Structured finance involved the creation of more complicated investment vehicles like collateralized debt obligation (CDO) funds. These funds allowed investment in debt instruments with a twist: investors could select the degree of risk (and accompanying return) based upon their payout priority. The alchemy of structured finance allowed Wall Street to take even the worst of the worst subprime mortgages and bundle them into investment vehicles where investors could get different payout priorities depending on which part—or tranche— they invested in. So the most senior tranche would get top payout priority and would qualify for the highest credit rating, and the tranches with lower priority would receive lower credit ratings. If AIG provided credit protection, the protected tranches would be even safer and could be sold more widely based upon a higher credit rating.

The AIG CDSs also allowed traders to bet that the mortgage market would collapse. Buyers of CDSs need not actually hold exposure to mortgages. This entailed even more risks. Big Wall Street banks assembled the CDOs that AIG insured, meaning they enjoyed an informational advantage about the precise subprime loans underlying the insured CDOs. If AIG did not carefully underwrite the subprime loans underlying the instruments that AIG insured, the temptation would exist for the megabanks to assemble rigged CDOs predestined to fail and pawn off the risk of default onto AIG, making its shareholders the suckers of last resort.

AIG conducted its CDS business in the London office of its affiliate, AIG Financial Products (AIGFP). This location allowed AIG to escape virtually all regulatory review. As such, AIGFP could take exorbitant risks that paid off for employees but ultimately sank the parent company. The CEO of AIGFP, Joseph Cassano, made $280 million in compensation over the eight-year period ending in 2007. His compensation peaked at nearly $44 million in 2006, immediately prior to the subprime meltdown (Frye & Son 2011). In essence, AIG paid its senior managers hundreds of millions of dollars in bonus payments for taking on the excessive risks of the CDS portfolio and sinking the firm. Indeed, the conduct of AIG's reckless CDS business makes sense only when considered in light of the compensation earned by AIG's senior managers.

The CDS transactions carried two major risks. First, if the subprime mortgage market tanked, AIG would have to pay its counterparties to cover the losses on the subprime investments it had insured. Second, as the market for subprime securities declined, or as AIG's credit ratings sagged, AIG would face cash collateral calls from the counterparties. Each of these risks came home to roost and drove AIG deep into insolvency and in need of a massive federal bailout. Neither of these risks was effectively disclosed to shareholders of AIG in any of its periodic reports at any time prior to late February 2008.

Rather, prior to February 2008, AIG's senior management worked to minimize these risks and delayed any effective disclosure of the magnitude of the CDS portfolio until the summer of 2007. Even then, statements by Cassano in August 2007 and by AIG's parent company CEO in December 2007 dismissed the portfolio's risk during earnings calls with investment analysts in August 2007 and again in December 2007. These statements proved manifestly false as the risk on the books at AIG at that time exploded in 2008, resulting in the most massive quarterly loss in history (FCIC 2011).

This chapter relies heavily upon the findings of the Financial Crisis Inquiry Commission (FCIC), the most thorough government investigation of AIG's demise to date, which included witness interviews and the review of a multitude of documents. The facts from the FCIC report are broadly consistent with those from two additional congressional inquiries. The first one revolves around documents submitted and testimony rendered at extensive hearings held by the House Committee on Oversight and Government Reform, on October 7, 2008, and January 27, 2010. The second is a report on the AIG bailout by the Congressio-

nal Oversight Panel, submitted on June 10, 2010. In addition, a plaintiffs' securities fraud action settled for $970 million, and counsel for the
plaintiffs conducted an investigation in connection with that successful civil securities fraud action. The facts therefore are not particularly
controverted.

AIG's CDS Business

AIG was the world's largest insurance company and boasted a pristine
AAA rating from the credit rating agencies before 2005. AIG started to
sell its high credit rating through the derivatives markets by exchanging
fees for agreements to assume the credit risks associated with a variety
of debt instruments, effectively insuring the debt instruments against
losses. These transactions actually swapped the risk of credit default to
AIG—hence the term "credit default swaps." Relying on the AAA rating
of its parent corporation, AIGFP became the dominant dealer in credit
defaults by the cusp of the financial collapse.

AIG's CDS portfolio, consisting of contract obligations to give credit
protection to creditors on a wide array of assets, including those related
to mortgage-backed securities, mushroomed from $20 billion in 2002
to $533 billion in 2007, right before the mortgage market crashed. Much
of this exposure to credit defaults included subprime debt. AIG could
offer such massive protection because it held a relatively high credit rating. Any debt securities guaranteed by AIG through its CDS portfolio
could essentially be converted to investment-grade securities regardless
of quality. Demand for such protection was high.

Normally, a regulated insurance company must set aside reserves
against future insurance payout obligations. With respect to the CDS
transactions, not only did AIG not set aside reserves, it did not post any
collateral to secure its obligations when it wrote these CDS contracts.
Instead, AIGFP agreed to post collateral if the value of the underlying
securities dropped or if the rating agencies downgraded AIG's long-term
debt ratings. Consequently, AIG faced two risks from its CDS portfolio:
first, that the securities it agreed to guarantee against default would in
fact default and trigger a payment obligation; and, second, that the value
of those securities would fall or AIG would suffer a downgrade, forcing
the expenditure of liquid cash if a counterparty made a cash collateral

demand. Due to the fact that many of the CDS transactions guaranteed subprime mortgage debt, AIG consequently faced catastrophic risks of insolvency in the event of a subprime collapse.

AIG understood these subprime risks. Senior executives at AIGFP, including head credit trader Andrew Forster and managing director Gene Park, became concerned about such risks as early as 2005. Park told the FCIC that he checked the extent of subprime exposure being assumed in the CDS portfolio and found it amounted to 80 to 90 percent of the underlying debt instruments. Park concluded then that the CDS business was a "horrendous business" that AIG should exit without any further involvement. In July 2005, Forster emailed other senior managers: "We are taking on a huge amount of subprime mortgage exposure here," with many transactions involving subprime concentrations of 80 percent. This subprime mortgage exposure was not disclosed to AIG's investors, however, until the losses already imperiled AIG's solvency, as we will discuss.

Internal AIG analysts found in February 2006 that many subprime mortgage vehicles were structured to fail, and many mortgage borrowers were dependent upon constantly rising real estate prices to avoid foreclosure. AIG executives decided to pull back on subprime deals because of "deteriorating underwriting standards" and too much concentrated risk tied to residential real estate markets. Despite this bearish outlook, AIG had many subprime deals in the pipeline. They continued to write CDSs on subprime real estate deals through September 2006. One such deal was 93 percent backed by subprime debt. By June 2007, AIG held total exposure of $79 billion of credit instruments tied to subprime mortgages. Nevertheless, AIG never disclosed the risk of massive losses on its subprime investments and instead claimed its risk management function would protect investors from losses.

Yet, according to confidential witness statements recounted in the securities fraud complaint leading to a $970 million settlement with AIG and its senior managers, AIG's risk management function never assessed the AIGFP CDSs. Furthermore, in offering CDSs, AIGFP personnel never bothered to look at the loan-level risks of default and instead simply reviewed the offering documents of the CDOs to assess risk. Of course, such documents are more geared to the marketing of such instruments rather than a true risk disclosure, as discussed in prior chapters. This lack of true risk assessment made AIG an easy target for the megabanks (*In re AIG, Inc. 2008 Securities Fraud Litigation* 2009). Once Wall Street realized that AIG would so freely guarantee subprime-mortgage-related debt, massive risk migrated onto AIG's balance sheet.

The risks did not end with the fact that too much of the CDS portfolio was tied to subprime mortgages. If either the market value of the instruments insured by AIG or AIG itself suffered a ratings downgrade, the firm could be forced to post cash collateral to its CDS counterparties. Regardless of actual losses, AIG could be legally required to post billions in response to collateral calls, and it could therefore face insolvency separate and apart from the value of the investments it guaranteed. The possibility of huge collateral calls posed a potentially lethal liquidity risk to AIG and, combined with valuation losses, could lead directly to the firm's demise. In other words, AIG could face crippling collateral calls in addition to losses in the value of the mortgage pools they insured.

Remarkably, senior AIG executives generally failed to appreciate the risks posed by potential collateral calls. AIG CEO Martin Sullivan, CFO Steven Bensinger, Chief Risk Officer Robert Lewis, Chief Credit Officer Kevin McGinn, and Financial Services Division CFO Elias Habayeb all told the FCIC they did not know about these secondary risks until the collateral calls started draining cash during July 2007. Nor did AIG's primary federal regulator appreciate these risks to liquidity. Alan Frost, the chief CDS salesman at AIGFP, understood the potential for collateral calls, as did Joseph Cassano, CEO of AIGFP. One may question how this risk could be missed by so many senior executives at AIG, but the compensation payments associated with the CDS business could blind anyone (House Committee on Oversight and Government Reform 2010).

Simply stated, these CDS transactions put enormous amounts of cash into the pockets of senior managers at AIGFP. AIG received fees for providing guarantees for a variety of subprime-related debt and other debt instruments. The fees generated amounted to 0.12 percent of the face amount of the CDS. If the face amount of the derivatives and securities that AIG backed amounted to billions, then the fees generated would pile up quickly and lead to immense profits, at little immediate cost and with risks that could be buried for years. The senior managers at AIGFP would get larger bonuses. The bonus pool amounted to 30 percent of earnings achieved. So, using 2007 as an example, the $533 billion in

CDSs written by AIGFP would expand the bonus pool by roughly $200 million.

AIGFP CEO Cassano made bonus determinations at year-end based upon the size of the bonus pool. In the six years prior to the crash, Cassano paid himself no less than $38 million per annum. Some years he made twice as much as the CEO of AIG, the parent company of AIGFP, although both achieved very large compensation payments. The CEO of AIG made tens of millions per annum and was also richly compensated for loading the firm up with illusory profits today at the expense of massive risks down the road. AIG CEO Sullivan made $107 million over a four-year period, including an $18 million severance package. Thus, CDS transactions generated cash that boosted many AIG senior managers' compensation and bonuses.

When the subprime mortgage market collapsed in 2007, the CDS obligations that AIG had assumed required billions in payments to counterparties. If AIG would have sold insurance, regulations would require sufficient capital reserves for all insurance obligations. AIGFP was deliberately structured to evade any requirement to set capital reserves aside. Instead AIG sold protection it could not pay for when the subprime market collapsed. AIG's total CDS exposure reached $500 billion, with no capital reserves accumulated to defray the obligations it had assumed. The government ultimately committed more than $180 billion to cover the shortfall. The government concluded that AIG's failure would trigger cascading losses throughout global financial markets. The bailout of AIG constituted nothing less than a bailout of global finance (FCIC 2011).

The Crash

The unraveling of AIG's CDS portfolio started in early summer of 2007. The breakdown in the subprime mortgage market caused one senior manager at AIGFP, Andrew Forster, to confide in another senior manager that he was starting to feel "suicidal." On July 11, 2007, Forster stated in a recorded phone call that AIG was "f***ed basically." The immediate trigger to such despondency was the announcement of massive downgrades on subprime-related debt on July 10, 2007, by the major credit rating agencies. Real estate prices had started to decline, causing the rating agencies to review all real-estate-related debt.

Shortly thereafter, on July 26, 2007, Goldman Sachs invoiced AIG for $1.8 billion, the first of many collateral calls relating to the CDS portfolio. Inside AIG, the size of the collateral call shocked many. AIG had not prepared for such large demands. Vice President of Accounting Policy Joseph St. Denis told the FCIC that he was so "stunned" that he "had to sit down" upon hearing the news (FCIC 2011). The problem, according to St. Denis, was that there should never be any losses on the CDS portfolio. "The mantra at [AIGFP] had always been . . . that there could never be losses." This collateral call belied that mantra (FCIC 2011). St. Denis continued to raise concerns throughout 2007, and ultimately resigned in protest of the management of the CDS portfolio, on October 1, 2007 (Pleven & Efreti 2008).

Throughout the fall of 2007, AIG's problems multiplied. On August 10, AIG met the first collateral call, paying Goldman $450 million. Goldman's call was followed by more calls from Société Générale, UBS, and Merrill Lynch. Goldman increased its demands by $300 million, and by November 2 Goldman's demand reached $2.8 billion. On November 6, AIGFP informed AIG's Audit Committee that five counterparties demanded cash collateral from AIG. By late November, payments to Goldman totaled $2 billion. During this time, AIG's auditor became increasingly concerned that AIGFP had no means of monitoring its collateral call obligations, depending instead on counterparties to notify it of AIG's exposure.

All of these problems with the CDS portfolio greatly aggravated other sources of subprime risk within AIG. Most notably, AIG suffered huge losses in its securities lending business, which also invested heavily in subprime-related debt. In its securities lending business, AIG would loan marketable securities to other firms in exchange for cash from borrowers. This cash needed to be reinvested pending repayment of the securities. AIG used this cash to invest in mortgage-related debt. By June 2008, these investments totaled $75 billion, and the total value of these investments stood at only about $59 billion. AIG lost $16 billion in additional subprime exposure as a result of its securities lending business. Yet, AIG still owed the cash upon the return of the securities it had lent. Counterparties were demanding $24 billion to offset the shortfall on cash owed. Thus, AIG's exposure to the risks of subprime mortgages was multilayered.

AIG's auditor, PricewaterhouseCoopers (PwC), initially thought that relying on counterparties to determine collateral call obligations could compensate for flaws in AIG's risk management systems applicable to the CDS portfolio, and collateral call obligations in particular. Needless to say this posed huge risks. As the FCIC described it, "[O]ne of AIG's risk management tools was to learn of its own problems from counterparties who did have the ability to mark their own positions to market prices and then demand collateral from AIG." Once PwC came to understand the magnitude of liquidity risk arising from the collateral calls, it raised serious concerns with AIG's senior management. PwC prompted AIG to develop its own model for tracking the valuations and obligations arising from the CDS portfolio. PwC, however, then questioned AIG's model because AIG did not validate it in advance of its earnings releases, and it neglected important structural information about the underlying CDS portfolios that AIG insured. Moreover, there were questions about the quality of the data that AIG inputted into the model.

During a meeting on November 29 with senior managers of AIG, PwC laid out its concerns in detail. According to notes obtained by the FCIC, these concerns included risk management flaws involving the CDS portfolio, with a particular unease regarding policies and procedures for meeting collateral calls and the lack of involvement of the parent company's Enterprise Risk Management group in these issues. Furthermore, PwC noted that AIG had not managed its subprime mortgage risk across the entire consolidated enterprise. Specifically, while AIGFP sought to limit its exposure starting in early 2006, the securities lending subsidiary increased its subprime exposure from $69 billion to $88 billion from late 2006 through September 2007. This lack of coordination of risk management meant that AIG held great exposure to the fate of the subprime mortgage market and could not survive a subprime crash. PwC concluded that "these items together raised control concerns around risk management which could be a material weakness." This fact was never disclosed to AIG's investors until it was too late.

The most serious concern PwC raised, however, emerged in late 2007. AIG botched the valuation of its CDS portfolio just as it had botched tracking its obligation to pay cash collateral. So when it came time to calculate the loss on the underlying CDS portfolio, AIG botched the calculation. A senior executive at AIG came up with something called

a "negative basis adjustment," which greatly reduced the loss AIG recognized on the CDS portfolio but lacked any basis in reality. Ultimately,
PwC met with AIG Chair Robert Willumstad on February 6, 2008.

PwC told him that the "negative basis adjustment" was improper
and unsupported. This meant that PwC essentially would restate the
loss numbers provided to investors on a December 7 investor call (discussed below). PwC further stated that "controls over the AIG Financial
Products [credit] default swap portfolio valuation process and oversight
thereof were not effective." PwC concluded that "this deficiency was a
material weakness as of December 31, 2007." The next day, PwC repeated
its presentation before the entire audit committee of the board (FCIC
2011).

PwC also told the audit committee that the risk management function had been ineffective at AIGFP. Minutes from an audit committee
meeting reveal that PwC told the committee that the "root cause" of
AIG's problems was that risk managers did not enjoy "appropriate access" to AIGFP (House Committee on Oversight and Government Reform 2010). As we demonstrate below, these findings of AIG's auditor
and financial accountant directly contradict AIG's public disclosures
regarding the role of superior risk management of the CDS portfolio in
eliminating possible losses.

The upshot of all of this demonstrates that senior managers within
AIG understood the massive risks of the CDS portfolio as early as 2005.
They knew early on inside AIG that the CDS portfolio held concentrated subprime mortgage risks. Furthermore, management did not control the risks appropriately. It failed to track its subprime exposure and
obligations under the CDS transactions and to coordinate the subprime
mortgage risks across the AIG business enterprise. By 2007, AIG was in
fact highly exposed to lethal risks in the event of a subprime collapse.

This stands in stark contrast to what AIG told its investors in its investor conference calls and SEC filings. The next section reviews those
disclosures in detail starting with its earliest deficient disclosures from
its 2005 annual report or SEC Form 10-K.

AIG's Investor Disclosures

In each of AIG's 2005 and 2006 Form 10-K filings with the SEC, AIG did little to disclose to the investing public that the CDS and subprime time bomb was already on its balance sheet. For example, neither annual report even mentioned the term "subprime." Nor did the forms declare that AIG wrote transactions called "credit default swaps." Instead, AIG gave a short summary of its derivatives activities such as this statement from its 2005 Form 10-K: "AIGFP participates . . . in the derivatives markets conducting, primarily as principal, an interest rate, currency, equity, commodity, and credit products business." Nowhere did AIG describe the types of CDOs being insured or that a significant portion of the CDOs included subprime debt. Similarly, AIG's discussion of the securities lending business disclosed only investments in "floating rate debt securities." Finally, AIG's annual SEC filings to investors for 2005 and 2006 mentioned the risk of collateral calls only if AIG were downgraded, and no mention was made of the liquidity risk posed by downgrades to insured debt instruments (AIG 2006 & 2007).

The 2006 annual report included more details regarding transactions that appear to refer to the CDS transactions. AIG stated that it essentially insured payment on senior tranches of CDOs, stating, "The majority of AIGFP's credit derivatives require AIGFP to provide credit protection on a designated portfolio of loans or debt securities." But even this discussion made no mention of the need to provide cash in response to collateral calls, nor gave any indication that the portfolios insured included subprime mortgage debt. Also AIG suggested that it would monitor its exposures to these transactions and hedge its obligations in the event any portfolio presented a risk of loss. Consequently, these more detailed 2006 disclosures still did not outline the manifest risk of serious economic losses (AIG 2007).

On August 9, 2007, AIG first publicly disclosed the $79 billion subprime exposure arising from its CDS transactions during its second quarter earnings call. AIGFP CEO Cassano told AIG's shareholders and investors, "It is hard for us, without being flippant, to even see a scenario within any kind of realm or reason that would see us losing $1 in any of those transactions." He concluded, "Any reasonable scenario that anyone can draw, and when I say reasonable, I mean a severe recession scenario that you can draw out for the life of the securities" (FCIC 2011). Senior Vice President and Chief Risk Officer Robert Lewis affirmed the point: "We believe that it would take declines in housing values to reach depression proportions, along with default frequencies never experienced, before our AAA and AA investments would be impaired." AIG CEO Sullivan assured the audience that AIG was "a very safe haven in stormy times." All of these disclosures quickly circulated throughout investment media (e.g., Kuykendall 2007). Cassano did not disclose in that call that Goldman had already demanded $1.8 billion, and the next day, August 10, Cassano made a long-negotiated payment to Goldman of $450 million (FCIC 2011). One investor analyst stated in a note authored that day to investors, "The bottom line on subprime is that AIG disclosed no ticking time bomb as many had feared."

On November 7, 2007, AIG reported its third quarter earnings. It disclosed $900 million in charges against earnings "related to its super senior credit default swap portfolio." Despite this disclosure, CEO Sullivan refused to acknowledge the tip of the iceberg threatening to sink AIG, telling investors, "AIG continues to believe that it is highly unlikely that AIGFP will be required to make payments with respect to these derivatives." Cassano added that AIG had "more than enough resources to meet any of the collateral calls that might come in." Essentially, the company remained adamant that there would be no realized economic losses from the CDSs, despite a deteriorating mortgage market and the parade of collateral calls that were draining AIG of cash throughout the second half of 2007.

On December 5, AIG CEO Sullivan told investors that AIG's risk management systems had managed its firm-wide subprime exposure: "The risk we have taken in the U.S. residential housing sector is supported by sound analysis and a risk management structure." Sullivan added, "we believe the probability that it will sustain an economic loss is close to zero." An analyst asked about collateral disputes with counterparties. Cassano replied, "We have from time to time gotten collateral calls from people and then we say to them, well we don't agree with your numbers. And they go, oh, and they go away. And you say well what was that? It's like a drive-by in a way. And the other times they sat down with us, and none of this is hostile or anything, it's all very cordial, and we sit down and we try and find the middle ground and compare where we are."

AIG finally disclosed to the investing public the manifest problems in the CDS portfolio in its Form 8-K filed on February 11, 2008. Specifically, in that SEC filing AIG admitted that its auditor had identified the material weakness in its internal controls over the valuation of the CDS portfolio and AIG's payment obligations under the cash collateral calls. It also finally admitted that it had suffered more serious losses on the valuation of the CDS portfolio in 2007 than prior disclosures had indicated. More specifically, AIG disclosed greater valuation losses of as much as $3.6 billion as of November 30, 2007. AIG finally admitted that the negative basis adjustment lacked any support and would no longer apply any such adjustment in estimating the valuation losses in the CDS portfolio (AIG 2008a). The rating agencies immediately announced downgrades. AIG's stock dropped 12 percent in immediate reaction (FCIC 2011). The mantra that there could never be any economic losses finally met its demise.

On February 28, 2008, AIG made even more dismal disclosures when it filed its 2007 Form 10-K. It reported a net loss of $5.92 billion and valuation losses related to the super-senior CDS portfolio of more than $11.16 billion. It also disclosed its subprime losses in its securities lending business of $2.6 billion. Given that AIG held about $95 billion in capital, these staggering losses threatened its continuing financial viability (AIG 2008b). The truth finally emerged: AIG had taken potentially lethal subprime risks onto its balance sheet.

Securities Fraud Settlements

AIG's misconduct led to a series of securities fraud actions and an enormous settlement payment of $960 million. According to AIG's SEC Form 10-Q for the quarter ended June 30, 2014, "Between May 21, 2008 and January 15, 2009, eight . . . class action complaints were filed against AIG and certain directors and officers of AIG and AIGFP . . . and the underwriters of various securities offerings in the United States District Court for the Southern District of New York . . . alleging [securities fraud]." These actions ultimately proceeded as a consolidated action.

"The consolidated complaint alleges that defendants made statements during the class period in press releases, AIG's quarterly and year-end filings, during conference calls, and in various registration statements and prospectuses in connection with the various offerings that were materially false and misleading and that artificially inflated the price of AIG Common Stock. The alleged false and misleading statements relate to, among other things, the Subprime Exposure Issues."

After much procedural rankling, "[o]n July 15, 2014, the parties accepted a mediator's proposal to settle the Consolidated 2008 Securities Litigation for a cash payment by AIG of $960 million." This settlement did not resolve all securities fraud actions pending against AIG, just the broadest class actions alleging the misrepresentation of the risks of AIG's CDS portfolio. As the company disclosed, "Between November 18, 2011 and September 16, 2013, nine separate, though similar, securities actions were filed asserting claims substantially similar to those in the Consolidated 2008 Securities Litigation against AIG and certain directors and officers of AIG and AIGFP" (AIG 2014).

Under the Private Securities Litigation Reform Act, a private action under the federal securities laws cannot go forward without a finding that the plaintiffs allege facts give rise to a strong inference that defendants acted with an intent to defraud, or scienter. In the AIG securities fraud action, US District Court Judge Laura Taylor Swain ruled that the plaintiffs did plead sufficient facts to support a strong inference that the AIG senior officers acted with an intent to defraud. Judge Swain ruled that "[a]ccording to the Complaint, AIG and the Section 10(b) Defendants knew, beginning in 2005, that the Company had acquired billions of dollars' worth of exposure to RMBS through the CDS portfolio, and knew that, while their model could not properly evaluate the extent of the related risk, the portfolio carried considerable valuation risk and collateral risk as well as credit risk." Despite this knowledge, "Defendants deliberately declined, nonetheless, to disclose these risks to the marketplace, and they similarly declined to disclose the risk presented by the Company's aggressive expansion into RMBS through the securities lending program" *(In re AIG, Inc. 2008 Securities Litigation 2010)*.

Judge Swain recognized that these failures to disclose came at a time of heightened market concerns over subprime exposure. Yet AIG "continued to proclaim—through their public filings, conference calls with the investment community, and press releases—their confidence that the CDS portfolio only presented 'remote risk' and that the Company's controls were adequate to evaluate that risk." Furthermore, "AIG and the Section 10(b) Defendants did so despite various internal indicators to the contrary, including the Company's recognition of the weakness of the [valuation] model; the resignation of St. Denis; PwC's warning of a potential material weakness; and the multi-billion dollar collateral calls received from AIGFP's CDS counterparties." Thus, on the key element of intent to defraud, Judge Swain has already ruled that if the above facts can be proven there is a strong inference that the defendants in the securities fraud action acted with an intent to defraud.

The claim against AIGFP CEO Cassano seems particularly compelling. As Judge Swain stated, the complaint alleged that "when St. Denis became concerned about the valuation of AIGFP's CDS portfolio, Cassano told him, 'I deliberately excluded you from the valuation of the [CDS portfolio] because I was concerned you would pollute the process.'" St. Denis repeated this widely reported statement in his written testimony to Congress in the fall of 2008 (House Committee on Oversight and Government Reform 2010). St. Denis would no doubt provide valuable evidence should the government proceed to investigate criminal or regulatory sanctions.

Cassano also tried to silence PwC from disclosing important facts to investors. PwC first alerted AIG senior management of serious auditing concerns on November 29. According to the FCIC, on February 6, 2008, PwC met with the entire audit committee of the AIG board and the auditors informed the audit committee that while they could complete AIG's audit, AIG needed to make sure Cassano "did not interfere in the process." Furthermore, while Cassano's continued employment was a "management judgment . . . the culture needed to change at FP" (FCIC 2011).

The entire culture at AIG discouraged whistleblowing. One former AIG executive blew the whistle on potential accounting-related fraud in connection with the valuation of its bond portfolio in 2007. Gordon Massie was the head of the Leveraged Finance Group at AIG and supervised 60 investment professionals. His group managed $20 billion in investments, including high-yield bonds, a variety of other debt instruments, and distressed/bankrupt debt. Massie exposed AIG's accounting machinations in a corporate-wide memo. He was demoted, transferred, isolated, and ultimately terminated (Massie 2010). This sort of treatment of whistleblowers demonstrates precisely the willful blindness needed to support a criminal conviction.

Another problem for all of the AIG senior managers arises from two deferred prosecution agreements with government authorities for securities fraud crimes committed at AIG from 2006 and 2004. These deferred prosecution agreements bear upon the state of mind of senior managers at AIG. After these agreements AIG senior officers should have been on heightened alert for potential fraud and misrepresentations at AIG. Instead, they seemed utterly unconcerned about ensuring that all material facts were disclosed to the investing public. These prior deferred prosecution agreements undermine any claim of an innocent state of mind. Indeed, much of the criminal misconduct the government authorities found underlying those deferred prosecution agreements related to securities fraud at AIGFP (Lattman 2009).

There is little doubt that the senior managers at AIG and AIGFP had powerful motives to keep the true exposure of the CDS portfolio concealed from investors. The longer they could hide the true risks, the more compensation and bonuses they could collect. Indeed, even after the government rescued AIG and even after the staggering CDS losses materialized, the AIGFP senior management team still paid themselves handsome bonuses. On March 19, 2009, New York Attorney General Andrew Cuomo announced that AIGFP had paid 73 employees more than $1 million each in bonus payments despite the huge losses the unit realized. Fifteen individuals garnered payments of over $2 million. Cuomo subpoenaed AIG to obtain the details of the bonus compensation after AIG announced that it was paying bonuses amounting to $160 million to AIGFP personnel (Story 2009). These bonus payments were in addition to over $200 million in bonuses paid to AIG employees (Andrews & Baker 2009). Judge Swain's findings on scienter therefore enjoy very strong factual support.

The complaint in the AIG securities fraud class action also refers to the cooperation of several confidential witnesses. One such witness stated that essentially AIGFP gave CDS counterparties (such as Goldman Sachs) a loaded gun that could be used to bankrupt AIG. According to one confidential witness, "an unusual feature of many of the CDS contracts written by AIGFP was that the counterparty bank was designated as the calculation agent for determining the valuation of the referenced CDO for purposes of determining when collateral had to be posted." Thus, from a contract point of view, once Goldman demanded cash collateral it enjoyed a huge, even unfathomable, bargaining advantage. It had final say under the terms of the contract. This fact was never disclosed to investors in AIG securities (*In re AIG, Inc. 2008 Securities Fraud Litigation* 2009). These confidential witnesses do not enjoy any attorney-client privilege, so the government could easily determine their identity.

Reuters reported that attorneys representing the plaintiffs claim that this settlement, amounting to about $960 million, represents the largest shareholder payout in a class action in which the government brought no parallel criminal or regulatory enforcement actions (Raymond & Pierson 2015). The plaintiffs' recovery, the statements of confidential witnesses, and the order of Judge Swain regarding scienter suggest that the allegations of that private action had some degree of validity. Indeed, we argue that the government easily could present enough evidence to a grand jury to indict AIGFP CEO Cassano and AIG CEO Sullivan, among others. The next section critiques the government's inaction in the face of such potential fraud.

The Government Stands Down on AIG

It is difficult to assess the government's response to the AIG fiasco because it has failed to prosecute all financial frauds emerging from the Great Financial Crisis (and beyond). If that broad policy explains the nonprosecution of AIG and its senior managers, then the United States is in fact in the midst of new and outrageous breakdown in the rule of law. On the other hand, at least with respect to AIG, the government may harbor other concerns about pursuing criminal actions. Specifically, it recently came to light that the government itself may ultimately look rather lawless if it pursues criminal charges against any AIG senior managers.

In litigation revolving around the government's conduct during the AIG bailout, a federal judge ruled that AIG's attorneys waived the attorney-client privilege with respect to events following the government's takeover of AIG. The otherwise privileged communications of attorneys representing the government do not depict the government in a positive light. One attorney for the government stated, with respect to the government's authority to bail out AIG, "there is no express authority, which is one of the reasons Treasury and the Fed discussed their actions with congressional leaders of both parties." Instead, this attorney stated that the government "is on thin ice and they know it" (Kessler 2015).

This recent revelation compounds another problem the government would face if it pursued criminal charges. Specifically, defendants could argue that the government itself caused the massive losses on the CDS portfolio. Cassano maintains, for example, that AIG could never suffer losses on the swaps because the CDS contracts were written only on the super-senior tranches of CDOs and consequently AIG was exposed only to defaults on top-rated securities within the CDOs at issue. Lower rated tranches would have to default in order for losses to reach the AIG-insured tranches, which enjoyed payment priority. Also, much of AIG's subprime exposure came from loans made before 2006, before underwriting standards significantly deteriorated (FCIC 2011). Cassano told the FCIC, "As I look at the performance of some of these same CDOs in Maiden Lane III, I think there would have been few, if any, realized losses on the CDS contracts had they not been unwound in the bailout." In other words, Cassano still refuses to acknowledge the losses associated with AIG's CDS portfolio.

Yet, once again Cassano simply has the numbers wrong. A document disclosed at congressional hearings on the AIG bailout shows losses on underlying securities and debt instruments far beyond Cassano's position. One lost 77 percent of its face value, and many others lost around 70 percent; the vast majority lost over 50 percent. These enormous losses mean the government held a very weak hand in trying to keep AIG afloat and that Cassano loaded up AIG with a host of very risky securities and debt obligations without effective disclosure to shareholders and other securities holders. Any argument by Cassano that the government caused the losses would therefore fail (Teitelbaum 2010). Although Cassano disclaims the riskiness of these instruments acquired by AIGFP, these huge losses show that AIG had taken on enormous risks.

This document, however, does raise a possible "empty chair" defense—whereby any AIG defendants attempt to show that the crimes at issue were committed by some other parties not before the court. Specifically the document shows that many of the primary recipients of bailout funds paid to counterparties also acted as underwriters on the very CDO deals that were the subject of the CDS transactions. Given the deep losses on the supposed "super-senior" tranches, government investigators would need to consider if these underwriters/counterparties defrauded AIGFP. The disclosures made to AIGFP at the time of sale would need to be carefully scrutinized. Nevertheless, AIG's failure to employ proper risk management, its assurances to investors regarding the strength of its oversight, and AIGFP's dismissal of employees who called attention to the risks could fill the chair with a willful blindness jury instruction. Under this approach, it is not the poor quality of the investments at issue but rather AIG and AIGFP senior management's cover-up of the risks once they were understood.

Another potential problem for any criminal prosecution against AIG or its senior managers would be the role of the credit rating agencies. AIG insured super-senior tranches with high ratings. As the rating agencies downgraded those securities, the downgrades made AIG subject to collateral calls. As AIG hemorrhaged cash, the credit rating agencies downgraded AIG. That caused yet another round of collateral calls. Therefore the rating agencies played a central role in the fall of AIG. Arguably, AIG relied in good faith on the rating agencies.

This argument will not succeed. First, credit rating agencies frequently downgrade prior ratings, and AIG itself suffered such a downgrade in 2005. Second, the would-be defendants all operated as seasoned financial professionals with high compensation, supposedly reflecting that ability. Third, the material risk of downgrades and their impact on AIG's financial structure went undisclosed. Downgrades happen and credit ratings are not permanent, which investment professionals know. The possible losses associated with the CDS portfolio from downgrades represent the very risk that AIG consistently told its investors did not exist (Congressional Oversight Panel 2010).

The government apparently leaked its supposed justification for nonprosecution of AIG and its senior managers to the *Wall Street Journal*, which reported that the following statement in an auditor's scrawled notes exonerated Cassano: "Cash/CDS spread differential . . . need to quantify . . . could be 10 points on $75 billion." These notes reflect a meeting that occurred in early December 2007, prior to the investor conference call discussed above. According to the *Journal*, "Along with other documents, they could be used by the defense to support its contention that Mr. Cassano had in fact disclosed the size of the accounting adjustments to both his bosses and external auditors" (Catan & Efreti 2010). This argument makes no sense. If Cassano knew that the losses already existed in the CDS portfolio, he should have disclosed that to investors in August 2007, certainly in December 2007. Instead he allowed the AIG mantra that there could be no loss to stand in both investor conference calls despite his clear knowledge that losses were already accumulating. In fact, rather than exonerating Cassano, these notes demonstrate his knowing misstatements in the conference call of December 2007. At no point did Cassano take steps to correct his prior misstatements or to otherwise ensure disclosure to investors of the key risks of the CDS portfolio.

The government would enjoy strong evidence on the issue of the criminal state of mind needed to support a fraud conviction. Judge Swain already found that if certain facts could be proved that a strong inference of scienter is justified. Her findings rested on facts already shown in the FCIC report, the most comprehensive government investigation to date. Once again, we see willing whistleblowers retaliated against and silenced at AIG, showing a willful blindness to fraud. The fact that the senior managers at AIG and AIGFP profited so handsomely while they concealed the true risks AIG had taken on board shows they had a powerful motive to commit fraud and collect millions and millions in compensation and bonus payments. These profits, combined with the retaliation against whistleblowers, support an intent to defraud.

The statute of limitations on this fraud will not expire until February 2018, 10 years after AIG finally told investors the truth about its lethal subprime risks. AIG held a federal savings and loan in its corporate structure, making it a savings and loan holding company. Therefore, this fraud certainly affected a financial institution under 18 USC section 3293, which triggers that statute's longer 10-year limitations period. Moreover, if any banks or bank holding companies owned or purchased any AIG securities (stocks, bonds, or even commercial paper), that would also trigger the longer 10-year statute of limitations applicable to frauds affecting a financial institution. This longer statute of limitations means that the government continues to have no excuse for not bringing criminal charges based upon facts now known about AIG.

On the other hand, if the aim is to protect the megabanks, then non-prosecution makes sense. At the very least, any criminal prosecution of AIG may well cast the megabanks that both underwrote the CDOs and entered into the CDSs in a negative light. At worst, it could lead to more civil litigation against the megabanks and increase political pressure for criminal prosecutions. The case against the most senior officers, Sullivan and Cassano, who knowingly misled shareholders, rests on a solid foundation. Others, such as Frost and Forster, could well provide helpful testimony if the government sought their cooperation through a plea agreement or an immunity deal. Given the success of the private civil case, which rested virtually upon the same facts established by the FCIC's investigation supported by subpoena power and witness testimony, there is certainly sufficient evidence to support presenting the case to a grand jury seeking a probable cause finding to pursue criminal charges.

The politics of criminally prosecuting AIG or its senior managers could provide a possible explanation for DOJ's lack of prosecution. The board of AIG featured many well-known public figures with strong political connections. No fewer than four AIG directors held powerful government posts prior to the AIG crash: Carla Hills acted as US Trade Representative, Martin Feldstein as chair of the Council of Economic Advisors, Richard Holbrook as UN Ambassador, and William Cohen as Secretary of Defense. According to the Center for Public Integrity, "Between 1993 and 2008, AIG contributed $8,526,940 [to political candidates]. In the 2008 election cycle, as the company was nearing the precipice of its dramatic fall, it gave $854,905 to 100 different candidates. . . . Barack Obama, the top recipient in the 2008 election cycle, collected more than $100,000 from AIG" (Aaron 2009). Joe Cassano gave $22,000 in campaign contributions and urged his fellow workers at AIG to contribute too. President Obama collected $6,900 from Cassano in 2008 (Beckel 2011). AIG and its senior managers enjoyed powerful political connections.

Nevertheless, the political connections of all of the Wall Street megabanks may pose an even more insurmountable barrier. These huge Wall Street institutions made billions from the failure of AIG. Any criminal prosecution would necessarily entail a thorough criminal investigation into the degree to which the megabanks that purchased CDS protection knew the CDOs were constructed to fail. More simply, did the megabanks tell AIG the truth about the risks of the mortgages in the CDOs? Did they intentionally sell mortgages to AIG that were sure to default? These questions, in turn, raise more questions regarding criminal culpability at AIG. In the end, a criminal prosecution at AIG could well become a Pandora's box, releasing the potential for more criminal prosecutions against more politically connected and economically powerful individuals and institutions.

This analysis however returns us to our essential point: failure to pursue obvious lawlessness through criminal prosecution suggests the government is so beholden to the megabanks and their senior managers that it will tolerate all kinds of lawlessness, including financial fraud. The government's nonprosecution of the megabanks creates a moral hazard that seems destined to spread not just to the senior managers and employees of the megabanks but to any number of firms that do business with the megabanks. AIG was a recidivist company whose management blatantly lied to investors, on the record. Perhaps AIG and its management were spared because the CDO business conducted by the megabanks is simply too toxic to touch. This possibility is discussed in the next chapter.

In any event, no criminal prosecutions resulted from this epic misrepresentation of risks. AIG was not broken up, and no single individual suffered any industry disqualification. The government never even attempted to justify this reality. The flimsy justification for a lack of prosecution of Joe Cassano offered through the *Wall Street Journal* is the only word from our government. AIG senior managers remain free to work in the financial sector, and AIG itself remains a major financial institution. The $970 million settlement for securities fraud achieved by private plaintiff attorneys stands as the only accountability exacted against AIG and makes a mockery of the government's law enforcement inaction.

Notably, the FCIC conducted one of the most thorough investigations to date. The FCIC made criminal referrals to the DOJ with respect to its disclosures of the risks of the CDS portfolio (Viswanatha & Tracy 2016). The DOJ apparently never pursued these referrals.

6

Goldman's Abacus

Goldman acknowledges that the marketing materials for the
[Abacus] transaction contained incomplete information. In
particular, it was a mistake for the Goldman marketing ma-
terials to state that the reference portfolio was "selected by"
ACA Management LLC without disclosing the role of Paul-
son & Co. Inc. in the portfolio selection process and that
Paulson's economic interests were adverse to CDO investors.
—Goldman Sachs 2010

The Goldman Sachs Abacus deal from early 2007 symbolizes massive
fraud in connection with the sales of mortgage-backed securities in a
wide variety of collateralized debt obligation (CDO) funds through a
fiendishly simple fraud wrapped in complexity. The Abacus fraud was
simple because it involved lies about an investment in subprime mortgages and the concealed interest of the sponsor of the CDO to sink the
investment for profit. It was wrapped in complexity because the mechanism by which the Wall Street banks took in capital (hundreds of billions
of dollars worth) involved a newfangled investment fund called a CDO.
Such a fund holds debt instruments (or collateral) such as subprime
mortgage debt or is otherwise tied to such debt. Notwithstanding Goldman's above acknowledgment that it mislead investors and a civil jury
finding of fraud in connection with the sale of securities, the Department of Justice declined to enforce the law against anyone for this fraud,
as did the FDIC, the Fed, and the SEC. The Abacus deal metastasized on
Wall Street like an aggressive cancer and was replicated over and over,
infecting hundreds of billions of dollars of toxic mortgages.

In the Abacus deal, Goldman offered to sell $1 billion of interests
in residential-mortgage-backed securities to investors in the form of a
CDO. Such CDOs are divided into "tranches" that offer investors different payout priorities depending upon which tranche (or part) the in-

vestor buys. The tranches are typically rated by credit rating agencies. Senior tranches receive top priority for payouts, whereas the unrated "equity" tranches are the riskiest portions of the CDO and the first to lose if the underlying collateral defaults. Goldman did not disclose to investors that the underlying collateral for the CDO had been selected by a hedge fund manager who was planning to short the CDO, that is, to bet against the CDO's success. That hedge fund manager made huge profits when the deal failed. In other words, unbeknownst to investors, the investment was assembled and sold by parties who made money if it failed (FCIC 2011). This material fact went totally undisclosed to the fund's investors (FCIC CDO Library 2011). Goldman knew of this fact, the investors did not. Predictably, the investors other than the sponsor took huge losses.

Goldman settled allegations of securities fraud with the SEC on the Abacus deal for $550 million, a record SEC settlement against a Wall Street firm. As part of the settlement the SEC insisted that Goldman acknowledge that it made material misrepresentations in connection with the sale of investment interests in the Abacus deal. The huge investment bank further agreed to reeducate its employees regarding their legal obligations under the federal securities laws and to impose an enhanced review process on its securities offerings (SEC 2010b). The SEC brought a civil case pursuing securities fraud claims against Fabrice Tourre, a vice president at Goldman in structured finance, and the registered representative principally responsible for creating and marketing the Abacus deal (SEC 2010d).

The claims against Tourre ended up before a jury, which found that Tourre committed securities fraud in connection with the Abacus deal. Put simply, a jury has already found that Tourre (and by extension Goldman) committed securities fraud by the preponderance of evidence after a full-blown jury trial. More specifically, on August 1, 2013, a jury returned a verdict against defendant Tourre for violating various provisions of the federal securities laws, including Rule 10b-5, the broadest federal prohibition against securities fraud. The jury verdict was the culmination of three years of litigation and an 11-day trial. Tourre moved to set aside the jury verdict, but the judge denied that motion (SDNY 2014). Tourre did not pursue any appeal. The jury finding seemingly provided the federal government a solid evidentiary basis for seeking criminal indictments against at least Tourre and Goldman for securities fraud in connection with the Abacus deal, and likely others at Goldman. As discussed below, the facts also support indictment of certain Goldman senior executives who supervised and approved Tourre's fraud. Even so, no indictments have been handed down, nor has either the Fed or the FDIC exercised its enforcement powers to impose any corporate death penalty or career death penalty.

Goldman's fraud in connection with the sale of the Abacus CDO from 2007 is only the tip of the iceberg of the megabank's fraud on this particular front. Goldman offered interests in many similar CDO funds. Other Wall Street banks also engaged in similar transactions. JPMorgan Chase, Citigroup, and others settled similar charges. Furthermore, the FCIC found that these deals—often termed the Magnetar Trade— were systemic in 2006 and 2007 and that much of the worst subprime lending during the end of the bubble could be attributed to this kind of deal (FCIC 2011). Wall Street demanded mortgages that would default quickly pursuant these deals. In other words, the worst subprime lending occurred because Wall Street affirmatively sought rotten loans that could be bundled into investments that were structured to fail (Eisinger & Bernstein 2010).

This chapter first explains the term "Magnetar Trade," as these deals came to be known, and the manner of their operation and contribution to the financial crisis. This type of trade became prominent on Wall Street especially in 2006 and 2007, and we provide a detailed summary of the Goldman Sachs Abacus deal that went to a jury trial that resulted in a civil finding of securities fraud. This discussion includes an overview of many other similar Goldman deals. Next, the chapter discusses other SEC settlements of the same tenor. Then, the chapter examines the degree to which this type of transaction drove the financial crisis. The chapter closes with an assessment of the government's lack of any criminal prosecution or regulatory enforcement action to break up criminal megabanks and terminate the careers of miscreant bankers on these deals.

The Magnitude of the Magnetar Trade

The FCIC conducted perhaps the most comprehensive inquiry regarding the so-called Magnetar Trade. Magnetar was a hedge fund that pioneered this type of deal, which enticed investors to pay money into a CDO fund without any disclosure of a short interest in their investment by persons with the ability to ensure the failure of the fund. In other words, the deals were structured to fail by firms that reaped billions in profits when the subprime collapse came. The FCIC surveyed more than 170 hedge funds with over $1 trillion in assets to learn more about the Magnetar Trade. More than half of all the CDOs issued by these firms in the second half of 2006 featured equity tranches that were purchased by hedge funds that also shorted other more senior tranches. These short positions would pay off handsomely if the subprime mortgage market collapsed. These CDO deals were not the only way to bet on the collapse of the subprime mortgage market, just one common scheme. The FCIC found that the same trading scheme occurred with respect to the mortgage-backed securities market in general.

While precise information on the total amount of capital diverted into financial instruments designed to fail is unavailable, the FCIC's survey found that "by June 2007, the largest hedge funds held $25 billion in equity and other lower-rated tranches of mortgage-backed securities [and] these [positions] were more than offset by $45 billion in short positions." Thus, these funds made money by betting on a subprime meltdown. The magnitude of these bets implies a tremendous amount of diverted capital. The riskiest and lowest rated tranches typically constitute a small portion of the total amount of money invested in CDOs. For example, under the terms of the Abacus deal, discussed below, the unrated tranches consisted of only 10 percent of the total offering (FCIC CDO Library 2011). Thus, the $25 billion invested in equity tranches could support $250 billion in total CDO investments. That in turn suggests an enormous demand for very low-quality loans that would not only fail, but fail quickly.

The FCIC also concluded that the ability to short a CDO while holding a smaller interest in the riskiest tranche fundamentally changed the market for CDO investors: "These types of trades changed the structured finance market. Investors in the equity and most junior tranches of CDOs and mortgage-backed securities traditionally had the greatest incentive to monitor the credit risk of an underlying portfolio. With the advent of credit default swaps, it was no longer clear who—if anyone—had that incentive." The Magnetar Trade explains the worst of the worst subprime mortgages during the peak of the bubble. No investor in a CDO held sufficient incentive to monitor loan quality, except for the investor with the interest in the CDO crashing fast. It fed the demand for ultra low-quality mortgage loans.

Author Yves Smith argues that the Magnetar Trade drove the subprime debacle: "Our studies indicate that Magnetar alone accounted for between 35% and 60% of demand for subprime mortgages in the year 2006." According to Smith, "Magnetar's true objective was not to invest in this toxic waste, which its role as funder of the CDO would lead most to believe. While Magnetar paid roughly 5% of the CDO total deal value for its equity stake, it took a much bigger short position" through credit default swaps (CDSs) sold by the originators of these same CDOs. These CDS transactions offered many investors protection against the risk of default.

Here, the CDSs were a tool with which to bet on and profit from a subprime collapse: "This [CDS] insurance in turn was artificially cheap because over 80% of the deal was rated AAA. Most investors did not understand what Magnetar recognized: [because these CDOs] concentrated exposure to the very riskiest type of bond associated with risky mortgage borrowers, each of these CDOs was a binary bet. It would either work out (in which case Magnetar would still show a thin profit) or it would fail completely, giving Magnetar an enormous profit [from the CDS] and wiping out even the AAA investors who mistakenly believed they were protected by having other investors sit below them and take losses first" (Smith 2010). The risk of loss was not left to chance. Smith explains that "[a]s the equity investor, Magnetar could stack the deck in its favor through the influence it gained over the deals' parameters. It was able to ensure that the CDOs held particularly dubious risky exposures" (Smith 2010).

Smith argues that without "Magnetar-inspired appetite, it is hard to find an explanation for the widely-discussed phenomenon of 2006 and 2007, of the mortgage securitization pipeline screaming for more subprime product, precisely when Federal Reserve interest rate increases should have stanched demand for risky loans above all others" (Smith 2010). If the government investigated these deals in depth, as would occur in a criminal proceeding or a serious regulatory action to break up the megabanks, a central question of the subprime debacle might finally find an answer: who actually profited from the worst mortgage underwriting in our nation's history? As Smith highlights, and as this chapter shows in great detail, the best answer appears to be certain megabanks and their managers.

Some claim that many of the Magnetar Trade deals were not actually very dangerous because they often involved so-called synthetic CDOs: those that did not actually buy mortgage-backed securities but simply referenced such assets in determining payouts for investors. This really changes very little and arguably makes matters more dangerous. First, as Wall Street banks cranked up these Magnetar deals, synthetic or otherwise, they sent the market a signal that investors demanded subprime loans and stood ready to invest in even the worst such loans. So long as investors could be lulled into the apparent safety of these deals and ambushed by truly horrendous loans, Wall Street would furnish demand for even the worst of the worst mortgages. Thus, the Magnetar Trade, with a disclosed long interest and concealed short interest, encouraged and depended upon generating the worst loans in the history of mortgage lending. Second, because more and more investors were tied to the performance of the referenced securities, even synthetic CDOs posed great danger because they amplified the financial losses associated with subprime defaults. Thus, synthetic CDOs both inflated the bubble by encouraging investment in really awful mortgage loans that would default and default quickly and accelerated the bust by multiplying losses.

As we demonstrate below, Goldman's Abacus CDO program was very similar in structure to the Magnetar Trade, in that it involved a long equity tranche investor with a net short position. The only difference is that Goldman "went short on various real estate exposures by effectively dumping the risk on customers," placing its own risky mortgage assets into the CDOs that were then shorted. On the other hand, the Magnetar Trades in total were much larger than Goldman's Abacus deals, and therefore did much more systemic damage (Smith 2010). Nevertheless, the Abacus deal is one of the few to end up before a jury, as we explain below. The fact that a jury found the Abacus deal to constitute civil fraud suggests that government investigators would meet with much success if they decided to enforce the law more aggressively against those responsible for these rigged deals.

Abacus and the Jury Finding of Securities Fraud

The 2007 Abacus deal that led a jury to find securities fraud was part of a series of similar deals that Goldman sold to investors. Abacus arose from a broad-based strategy that Goldman pursued that is referred to in its own internal documents as "the big short." The big short meant that Goldman would sell as much subprime exposure as possible as quickly as possible. By mid-2006, senior managers at Goldman Sachs had concluded that the subprime mortgage bubble was "going to have a very unhappy ending." At that time, Goldman owned substantial amounts of subprime mortgages (that is, it held a significant long position in subprime mortgages) and was exposed to losses from subprime defaults (US Senate 2011).

From a pure business and economic perspective, much more so than Countrywide or AIG, Goldman used hard-headed business sense to see the obvious unsustainability of subprime lending and armed itself accordingly by selling off subprime mortgages and shorting the market at the same time. Nevertheless, the federal securities laws clearly mandate that sellers of securities disclose all material facts to potential buyers and that marketing materials be free of half-truths as well as material omissions. This created a fundamental problem for Goldman: how to unload its toxic subprime exposure without disclosing that it was selling toxic subprime exposure to its clients and to the investors to which it peddled its investment products. The jury verdict in *SEC v. Tourre* illustrates this legal problem well.

Essentially the jury found that Tourre lied in order to dump toxic securities on Goldman clients. Tourre tried to blame higher-ups, but jurors rejected this defense (Van Voris & Hurtado 2013). This suggests that Tourre might be a willing witness in a plea deal if the government pursued charges against Tourre and his supervisors. The basis of the jury's findings that Tourre committed securities fraud is the SEC's allegations in a complaint filed in that action in 2010 against Goldman Sachs and Tourre (SEC 2010d). The following is a summary of that complaint, as supplemented by the key orders of US District Court Judge Katherine B. Forrest, as well as the findings of a US Senate investigation into Goldman's CDO business.

Goldman offered interests in this Abacus deal to investors for $1 billion. The Abacus CDO involved various tranches with different payout priorities and hence different credit risks and ratings. Paulson & Co. Inc., a large hedge fund, sponsored the fund by taking the riskiest tranche—the equity tranche that got paid only after all other investors. This structure naturally encouraged the more senior investors to assume that the most junior investor had carefully underwritten the risks of the underlying mortgage debt or collateral for the deal.

Undisclosed in the Abacus marketing materials and unbeknownst to investors, Paulson assumed a short position in the CDO, meaning it had held an economic position directly adverse to the investors in the more senior tranches of the Abacus CDO. As such, Paulson's investment interest was that Abacus would fail under the weight of massive defaults. Due to Paulson's short position, the greater the losses for the other investors, the more Paulson made. Paulson's short position did not operate to automatically sink the other investors, but the nondisclosures did not end there.

Goldman also did not disclose that Paulson played a significant role in the portfolio selection process. The portfolio consisted of specific referenced residential-mortgage-backed securities (RMBS) investments. With the power to select the portfolio, Paulson could cause the very losses to the other investors that Paulson was betting on through its short position. Paulson effectively shorted the RMBS portfolio it helped select by entering into CDS transactions through Goldman Sachs to buy protection on specific more senior tranches of the Abacus capital structure. Given its financial short interest, Paulson had an economic incentive to choose RMBS interests that it expected to experience defaults in the near future. Goldman did not disclose Paulson's adverse economic interests or Paulson's role in the portfolio selection process in the offering memorandum or other marketing materials provided to investors.

Goldman created this investment scheme at the behest of Paulson and arranged the transactions at Paulson's request and to further Paulson's profits interests. The other investors were unknowing pawns in this effort. Paulson heavily influenced the selection of the portfolio to suit its economic interests, but Goldman failed to disclose this to investors. If these facts had been disclosed, no investor would have invested willingly in a financial instrument rigged in favor of Paulson at the expense of the other investors. In short, this deal was a financial death trap for the duped investors.

Tourre devised the transaction, prepared the marketing materials and communicated directly with investors. Tourre knew of Paulson's undisclosed short interest and its role in the collateral selection process. Tourre also misled the deal's collateral manager, ACA, into believing that because Paulson invested approximately $200 million in the equity tranche of Abacus (a long position), Paulson's interests in the collateral section process were aligned with those of the other investors in the deal when in reality Paulson's interests were sharply conflicting. ACA had also invested in Abacus and lost money.

Paulson paid Goldman approximately $15 million for structuring and marketing fees for Abacus. The deal closed on April 26, 2007. By October 24, 2007, 83 percent of the RMBS in the Abacus portfolio had been downgraded and 17 percent were on negative watch. By January 29, 2008, 99 percent of the portfolio had been downgraded. As a result, investors in Abacus lost over $1 billion. Paulson's opposite CDS positions yielded a profit of approximately $1 billion. The deal failed, just as Goldman and Paulson structured it to fail and fail quickly.

Tourre's misconduct occurred with the full knowledge of his supervisors at Goldman. The US Senate uncovered a number of important facts that demonstrate that Tourre acted with the approval and authority of his supervisors and more senior managers at Goldman. Specifically, Tourre sent an email to the head of the Goldman Mortgage Department, Daniel Sparks, stating quite openly, "Gerstie and I are finishing up engagement letters . . . for the large . . . Abacus trade that will help Paulson short senior tranches off a reference portfolio of Baa2 subprime RMBS risk selected by ACA." Tourre also openly testified to the Senate that Paulson's involvement in selecting collateral while holding a short position was not disclosed to investors. In another email discussing a portfolio selection agent for Abacus, a Goldman employee wrote to a colleague that Mr. Tourre "suggested Faxtor was a potential portfolio selection agent [for Paulson] since they are relatively inexpensive and easy to work with." The colleague seemed more concerned with using that firm on another Goldman deal: "We already have a portfolio in front of Faxtor; they probably will be willing to structure a short that I believe we would want to keep for ourselves." In other words, not only was Goldman aware of these fraudulent transactions, but also the culture at Goldman evidenced more interest in keeping cooperative collateral agents for Goldman's own fraudulent shorts instead of disclosing this securities fraud to investors (US Senate 2011).

Subsequently, Mr. Tourre reported to his colleagues that one firm, GSC, declined to act as portfolio selection agent due to its negative views of the assets Paulson wanted to put in the Abacus CDO: "As you know, a couple of weeks ago we had approached GSC to ask them to act as portfolio selection agent for that Paulson-sponsored trade, and GSC declined given their negative views on most of the credits that Paulson had selected." Later, when Goldman started selling the Abacus securities, a senior trader at GSC, Edward Steffelin, emailed Peter Ostrem, the head of Goldman's CDO desk, stating, "I do not have to say how bad it is that you guys are pushing this thing." When asked by the Senate Permanent Subcommittee on Investigations why he sent this email, Mr. Steffelin testified that he was concerned that this particular Abacus CDO created "reputational risk" for his firm as the collateral manager as well as for the whole securities market. Yet, Goldman went forward with the sordid deal (US Senate 2011).

The key point is that Tourre worked with others at Goldman specifically to find a collateral manager who would go ahead with the transaction proposed by Paulson, notwithstanding the low-quality collateral he sought to place in the CDO. Contemporaneous internal correspondence reflects that Goldman recognized that not every collateral manager would "agree to the type of names [of RMBS] Paulson want[s] to use" and put its "name at risk . . . on a weak quality portfolio." The collateral manager is a third-party contractor who is responsible for selecting collateral to reference in the CDO and managing the trust. On February 2, 2007, Paulson, Tourre, and ACA met at ACA's offices in New York City to discuss the reference portfolio. Unbeknownst to ACA at the time, Paulson intended to effectively short the RMBS portfolio it helped select by entering into a CDS with Goldman to buy protection on specific layers of the CDO's capital structure. Tourre and Goldman, of course, were fully aware that Paulson's economic interests with respect to the quality of the reference portfolio were directly adverse to CDO investors. During the meeting, Tourre sent an email to another Goldman Sachs supervisor stating, "I am at this aca paulson meeting, this is surreal" (SEC 2010d).

Later the same day, ACA emailed Paulson, Tourre, and others at Goldman a list of 82 RMBS on which Paulson and ACA concurred, plus a list of 21 "replacement" RMBS. ACA sought Paulson's approval of the revised list, asking, "Let me know if these work for you at the Baa2 level." On February 5, 2007, Paulson sent an email to ACA, with a copy to Tourre, deleting eight RMBS recommended by ACA, leaving the rest, and stating that Tourre agreed that 92 bonds were a sufficient portfolio (SEC 2010d).

Paulson's role in selecting collateral was as hidden from investors as its interest in seeing the CDO default quickly. For example, a nine-page term sheet from February 2007 for the Abacus deal identified ACA as the "Portfolio Selection Agent" and stated in bold print that the portfolio of referenced RMBS had been "selected by ACA." This document contained no mention of Paulson, its economic interests in the transaction, or its role in selecting the reference portfolio (SEC 2010d). The final term sheet from July 2007 also fails to mention Paulson or its role in selected the portfolio. Instead, both of these documents highlight only ACA's role in selecting the portfolio.

Similarly, a 65-page offering booklet for the Abacus deal stated on its cover page that the underlying referenced assets were "Selected by ACA Management, LLC." The booklet discussed ACA extensively (including its ownership, history, and board structure) and provided great detail into its credit selection process and biographical information on key ACA employees. Furthermore, the booklet reassured investors that ACA possessed an "alignment of economic interest" with investors. This document contained no mention of Paulson or its short interests in the transaction (FCIC CDO Library 2011).

Internal Goldman documents clearly identified Paulson, its economic interests, and its role in the transaction. For example, a March 12, 2007, Mortgage Capital Committee (which supervised Tourre) memorandum stated, "Goldman is effectively working an order for Paulson to buy protection on specific layers of the [Abacus] capital structure." Essentially, Goldman favored one client, Paulson, at the expense of those clients to whom it was selling securities, without disclosure of material facts regarding Paulson's or Goldman's role and objectives.

Goldman also misled ACA. On January 10, 2007, Tourre emailed ACA a "Transaction Summary" that included a description of Paulson as the "Transaction Sponsor" and referenced a "Contemplated Capital Structure" with a "first loss" equity tranche that supposedly represented the Paulson investment in the CDO, as sponsor. The description of this tranche at the bottom of the capital structure made it appear that Paulson wanted the CDO it sponsored to succeed economically. ACA reasonably could conclude that is was protected by that interest and that the sponsor would select strong collateral for the CDO to perform as disclosed. In fact, Goldman knew there would be no substantial investment in the equity tranche in this transaction due to the undisclosed short interest of Paulson.

Consequently, the misconduct at Goldman transcends Tourre and implicates Goldman on an organization-wide level, up to and including senior managers. Given the scope of the fraud, the explicit emails used as evidence in the civil cases, and the jury finding by the preponderance of the evidence of fraud in connection with the sale of Goldman's Abacus deal, the DOJ's prosecutorial inaction with respect to Tourre, his supervisors, and Goldman itself is puzzling. In particular, the emails Tourre sent to his Goldman colleagues and supervisors highlight the firm's involvement in such transactions, and the record SEC settlement payment by Goldman supports this conclusion. Goldman's exposure to criminal sanctions arises from the fact that Tourre acted at all times in the scope of his employment and for the benefit of Goldman. Goldman senior managers approved of the transaction, and there is no evidence that he acted other than to enhance profits at Goldman. Thus, as discussed in prior chapters, Goldman could be held accountable for the criminality of its vice president if Tourre were found to have engaged in crimes. These conclusions are consistent with long-standing white-collar crime principles (Podgor et al. 2013). Again, the jury verdict was rendered in a civil rather than criminal case; nevertheless, it certainly supplies a strong factual foundation for criminal charges.

Andrew Ceresney, co-director of the SEC's Division of Enforcement, said in a statement after the verdict, "As shown by this verdict, we proved that Mr. Tourre, as a Goldman Sachs vice president, put together a complicated financial product that was secretly designed to maximize the likelihood that it would fail, and marketed and sold it to investors without appropriate disclosure" (SEC 2013d). This statement encapsulates the thesis of this book. The government enjoys plenty of evidence of criminal securities fraud (among other crimes) but has steadfastly refused to proceed with criminal investigations and charges despite widespread fraud in the industry yielding tremendous returns to the fraudfeasors while devastating investors and markets.

Within months of closing, the senior tranches of the Abacus deal plunged in value, with several banks suffering losses. One bank, among other investors, lost virtually all of its $150 million investment. Furthermore, shortly after the Abacus deal closed, a bank sold protection on the $909 million super senior tranche of Abacus CDO, meaning that it assumed the credit risk associated through a CDS in exchange for premium payments. ACA and Goldman also contracted with ABN bank, a global financial services behemoth, to pay if the underlying collateral could not. Thus, many banks ultimately lost money on this Abacus transaction (US Senate 2011).

In sum, the Goldman Abacus deal spawned a massive securities fraud. Unfortunately, this kind of fraud, through the use of complex and opaque CDOs that could be sold and shorted and sabotaged for investors, became systemically important in 2006 and 2007 and inflated the subprime bubble to the breaking point. While Goldman's Abacus deal led to a civil finding of securities fraud, the SEC entered into a series of huge securities fraud settlements with other megabanks that followed the same basic pattern of the Abacus deal. The sad truth is that virtually all of Wall Street was in on these scams. Goldman's activities in connection with a strategy it developed, called the "big short," illustrate the same pattern as many of these deals. Wall Street banks simply off-loaded massive risk through material nondisclosures to investors regarding short interests and deals that were structured to fail.

The Big Short

Goldman structured many different Abacus deals. Sometimes Goldman would assume a short position directly. One example dates from 2004 when Goldman launched its first major CDO, Abacus 2004–1, worth $2 billion. About one-third of the referenced assets consisted of RMBS, another third referenced other CDOs, and the remainder consisted primarily of commercial-mortgage-backed securities. Goldman was short the entire deal. The other investors—including banks—bought nearly

$200 million of more senior tranches of the deal. Goldman entered into CDS transactions with AIG. This made AIG the largest investor in the super-senior tranches of the Abacus deal. Goldman stood to make almost $2 billion if the assets failed (FCIC 2011). Ultimately, this transaction, combined with similar Abacus transactions, yielded Goldman billions in federal bailout funds from the government bailout of AIG.

In December 2006 Goldman's most senior executives hatched a plan to reduce the risk posed by its position in subprime mortgages. They decided upon a "game plan" to aggressively reduce Goldman's exposure by, among other things, shifting its subprime risks to customers, particularly buyers of CDOs underwritten and sold by Goldman. This game plan was approved at the highest levels of management at Goldman. In fact, by early 2007, CEO Lloyd Blankfein himself inquired as to the progress in reducing subprime risk.

By the beginning of 2007, Goldman knew the financial system was blinking red under the weight of billions in rotten subprime mortgages as reflected in the internal emails of Goldman representatives: "More and more leverage in the system, [t]he whole building is about to collapse anytime now." Another Goldman executive statement reflected the same sentiment: "the cdo biz is dead we don't have a lot of time left." At this same point, Tourre termed the CDOs he ushered into the financial system monstrosities (or as he put it in an email "monstruosities!!!"). Around this time, Paulson discussed with Goldman the creation of a CDO that would allow Paulson to participate in selecting a portfolio of referenced obligations and then effectively short the RMBS portfolio it helped select by entering into CDS with Goldman Sachs to buy protection on specific layers of the CDO's capital structure.

By 2007, in direct response to the above directives, the Goldman Sachs's Mortgage Department decided to go "VERY short" on subprime exposure. This meant massive off-loading of subprime risk and taking as many opportunities as possible to enter into CDS transactions on subprime interests so that if the subprime market tanked Goldman would mitigate losses or even prosper. By February 2007, the net short position reached $10 billion. Ultimately it reached as high as $13 billion (US Senate 2011). These short positions meant Goldman was investing in a subprime bust.

In the last chapter we described how AIG exposed itself to huge amounts of subprime risks that it did not disclose to investors. A major unanswered question regarding that exposure is whether Goldman appropriately disclosed its role in sabotaging many CDOs that ended up on AIG's balance sheet through its CDSs with Goldman. More specifically, according to the *New York Times*, an anonymous Goldman salesperson stated that "[AIG] probably did not know it, but [it] was working with the bears of Goldman. [It] was signing . . . up to insure trades made by people with really very negative views" of mortgage debt. Furthermore, Goldman bought more short positions from AIG through Société Générale, according to a former AIG executive with "direct knowledge" of these particular deals. In fact, an internal AIG email demonstrates that Joe Cassano believed that Goldman pushed Société Générale to aggressively pursue cash collateral from AIG (Morgenson & Story 2010). Obviously, if Goldman had effectively disclosed all material facts to AIG, there would be no claim of securities fraud. But given the jury verdict in the civil securities fraud trial against Goldman executive Tourre, there certainly is sufficient basis for a thorough grand jury investigation.

According to documents Goldman provided to the FCIC, it received billions from the US government in AIG bailout funds, much of it for its own proprietary trades. The FCIC found that these trades were "largely relating to Goldman's Abacus CDOs." It is impossible to trace the toxic CDOs from there, however Goldman received more of the federal AIG bailout money than any other counterparty to the AIG CDOs.

AIG shareholders were not the only victims. The US Senate over a two-year period conducted an exhaustive investigation of the financial crisis. That investigation included an in-depth case study of the Goldman CDO machine. The Senate found that Goldman peddled about $100 billion in mortgage-backed securities and CDO securities in 2006 and 2007. Goldman knew that defaults of subprime mortgage securities were soaring. In response Goldman built a massive short position in mortgage securities while at the same time selling these CDOs to investors worldwide.

When the collapse came in 2007, Goldman held a net short position of $13.9 billion. Goldman CFO David Viniar termed this massive bet against the US housing market "the big short." CEO Lloyd Blankfein stated to his colleagues in November 2007, "Of course we didn't dodge the mortgage mess. We lost money, then made more than we lost because of shorts." This big short represented a massive capital commitment but enabled

Goldman to generate a $3.7 billion in profit in 2007 in just its Structured Products Group alone (US Senate 2011). In the high-stakes game of securities peddling, Goldman's ruthlessness stands above the rest. Its huge profits contrast to the massive losses suffered at other banks.

The Senate found that Goldman sold interests in mortgage securities to its clients without notifying them of its short position, often against the same product. The case study revealed that Goldman even dumped risky assets from its inventory into many CDOs, transferring the risky assets into the securities so they could be sold off to unsuspecting investors. It knowingly included high-risk instruments in three of the CDOs, effectively shifting Goldman's toxic assets to its clients. One such CDO lost 80 percent of its value within five months and ultimately became worthless.

Goldman frequently filled these CDOs with CDSs that referenced portfolios of mortgage-backed securities, making them synthetic CDOs (US Senate 2011). As discussed above, this did not change the economic substance of the transaction. If the mortgage-backed securities referenced by the CDSs performed well, then investors retained the income from them. If they did not perform well, investors in the CDO lost their investment and could be wiped out. Furthermore, the fact that CDO investors were willing to absorb the risk of loss on pools of mortgages in exchange for fees encouraged Wall Street's mortgage machine to continue to originate subprime mortgages.

Goldman ultimately packaged and sold $66 billion in CDOs in the three years prior to the financial collapse. It also originated billions more in mortgage-backed securities. It earned millions in underwriting fees on these deals, in addition to gains from other short interests it held in the deals. On others, it would profit by facilitating the transaction between the buyer and the seller of CDS protection. These profits are problematic unless accompanied by full disclosure. Senator Levin stated that his investigation found "overwhelming evidence" that investment banks "deceived their clients and deceived the public, and they were aided and abetted by deferential regulators and credit ratings agencies who had conflicts of interest" (US Senate 2011). This conclusion strongly suggests that the DOJ and financial regulators should meet this misconduct with sterner sanctions, including criminal prosecutions and the corporate and career death penalty.

Other SEC Settlements

Citigroup also settled securities fraud claims with the SEC on October 19, 2011, for $285 million in connection with a CDO it underwrote and sold. Citigroup held an undisclosed short position in the very securities it was selling to investors. Citigroup also allegedly exercised "significant influence" in selecting the collateral underlying the portfolio. According to the SEC, "One experienced CDO trader characterized the . . . portfolio in an e-mail as 'dogsh!t' and 'possibly the best short EVER!'" An experienced collateral manager commented that "the portfolio is horrible." Of course, if Citi had shared these conclusions with investors, they would have been unable to sell these investments and garner their prodigious fees.

As with Goldman, Citi sold securities that it wanted to default and therefore sought the riskiest loans possible from mortgage originators. Perhaps this explains why private subprime loans from 2006 and 2007 failed at such high rates. Banks like Citi wanted loans that would default quickly. In fact, the portfolio at issue in the SEC action closed in February 2007 and defaulted by November, in synch with the subprime collapse. Citi made $160 million on this sordid deal. Notably, the SEC pursued charges in this case against a midlevel executive at Citigroup and lost (SEC 2011a).

JPMorgan Chase paid the SEC $153.6 million for its misconduct in subprime lending. According to an SEC official, "What J.P. Morgan failed to tell investors was that a prominent hedge fund that would financially profit from the failure of CDO portfolio assets heavily influenced the CDO portfolio selection. With today's settlement, harmed investors receive a full return of the losses they suffered." The SEC also alleged that when the deal closed in May 2007, the hedge fund—called Magnetar—held a $600 million short position that dwarfed its $8.9 million long position in the portfolio. "In an internal e-mail, a J.P. Morgan employee noted, 'We all know [Magnetar] wants to print as many deals as possible before everything completely falls apart.'" The SEC further found that Chase frantically sold interests in the portfolio because it knew how bad it was and knew the market was starting to come unglued (SEC 2011b).

Merrill Lynch also faced significant regulatory sanction for the undisclosed influence of an equity investor with short positions in 2006. The

SEC co-director of the Division of Enforcement stated, "Merrill Lynch marketed complex CDO investments using misleading materials that portrayed an independent process for collateral selection that was in the best interests of long-term debt investors. Investors did not have the benefit of knowing that a prominent hedge fund firm with its own interests was heavily involved behind the scenes in selecting the underlying portfolios." Merrill Lynch settled the SEC's claims for $131.8 million (SEC 2013c).

The SEC also pursued administrative sanctions against an investment adviser registered with the commission relating to Magnetar deals. The adviser, Harding Advisory LLC, has no apparent link to any megabank, so the SEC actually enforced the law. In that case, an administrative law judge found that the investment advisor and its employee acted in a manner that was "shockingly oblivious to their fiduciary duties." The judge found that the adviser had given Magnetar Capital LLC undisclosed rights to veto assets placed in Octans I, a roughly $1 billion CDO that imploded in April 2008. Magnetar bet against the deal with undisclosed short positions and profited when the deal crashed. The judge ordered disgorgement of more than $1 million in profits and civil penalties of over $2 million after an administrative trial on the merits. The investment adviser was also stripped of its registration and the employee was barred from the securities industry. This appears to be the only case where any of the financial regulators assessed both the corporate death penalty and the career death penalty arising from the subprime crisis.

The administrative law judge found, "Respondents committed multiple violations in 2006 and 2007, involving multiple distinct violative acts, including misrepresentations, failure to follow the standard of care, and selling securities by fraud; the violations were plainly recurrent" (SEC 2015b). This finding could conceivably support criminal charges because any violation of the federal securities laws is also a violation of criminal law under 15 USC section 78. An appeal of this administrative decision is now pending before the SEC, and the DOJ failed to pursue any criminal charges at all arising from this case, as in the Abacus and Magnetar Trade deals in general. It is odd that the SEC seemingly reserves administrative sanctions for a firm and individual not associated with a megabank. This fact directly supports the thesis of this book that economic and political power accounts for the cease-fire of the government regarding misconduct arising from the subprime collapse.

Notably, all the deals underlying the SEC securities fraud actions discussed above hail from 2006 and 2007. The four megabank settlements above already total in excess of $1 billion but cover just a sliver of the total trades of this nature. Thus, billions and billions of dollars worth of subprime mortgages were initiated due to this demand for loans that would default. And the only individual or firm to suffer the ultimate civil penalty is not affiliated with a megabank. The next section assesses the political power of those most central to the misconduct discussed in this chapter.

The Government's Response

Magnetar's founder contributed significant money to former Obama Chief of Staff Rahm Emanuel and political action committees associated with Emanuel during the very time period it engaged in the Magnetar Trade. These contributions totaled nearly $70,000, including $51,700 to the Democratic Congressional Campaign Committee. On some levels these political contributions seem an integral part of the Magnetar Trade, given that this apparent effort at risk management also paid off (Smith 2010). Despite SEC investigations of Magnetar deals, no criminal sanctions have been imposed against it or its agents.

Magnetar further benefitted greatly from outstanding legal representation in connection with the SEC's investigation into its role in the Magnetar Trade. One attorney representing Magnetar in the SEC investigation previously served as the acting general counsel of the SEC as well as deputy general counsel from 2006 to 2008. Magnetar also hired the former head of the SEC Enforcement Division who served from 1989 to 1998. While there may well have been no violation of law in this legal representation, it highlights the revolving door between the regulated and the regulators at the SEC (Stendahl 2014). It also illustrates the new challenge of holding financial elites to a rule of law when they can afford such specific expertise.

Goldman Sachs's influence extends far beyond that of Magnetar. Former Goldman managers have populated key government posts of both the Bush and Obama administrations. For example, the Secretary of the

Treasury during the Bush administration, Hank Paulson, who served during the height of the financial crisis and who personally helped engineer the AIG bailout that led to billions in payouts to Goldman, previously led Goldman. The Obama administration also includes senior policy makers who hailed from Goldman, including Dina Farrell, Deputy Director of the National Economic Council; Randall M. Fort, Assistant Secretary of State for Intelligence and Research; Gary Gensler, Chairman of the US Commodity Futures Trading Commission; Robert D. Hormats, Under Secretary of State for Economic, Energy, and Agricultural Affairs; Mark Patterson, Treasury Department Chief of Staff; Sonal Shah, Director, Office of Social Innovation and Civic Participation; and Adam Storch, COO, SEC Enforcement Division. In many ways Goldman Sachs epitomizes the revolving door between government and the private-sector interests with the most intensive stakes in government regulation (*CBS Nightly News* 2010).

Goldman's influence over the government only begins with the revolving door. It is also a bipartisan source of campaign contributions. In 2008, no firm bundled more contributions for President Obama's campaign than Goldman. In 2012, Goldman strongly supported fellow financial sector executive Mitt Romney. But, like any good Wall Street trader, Goldman always hedges its political positions and ultimately enjoys leverage within parties and over any eventual winner (Rappaport & Mullins 2012).

The jury verdict against Fabrice Tourre highlights another important fact. The case involved a CDO fund where the equity investor shorted the more senior tranches through CDSs. The government's case by necessity required explaining much jargon to an ordinary jury with no particular training in complex financial terms and instruments. Nevertheless, the jury saw right through the complexity to the simplicity of how Goldman's vice president lied to investors in exchange for money. As one juror told reporters after the trial, "Here is a man who was in charge of the deal, a highly-paid specialist working in a highly specialized area, asking people to invest billions of dollars in a product he created. In those circumstances, it's not a defense to say, 'I'm only 28 years old and that's why I didn't tell these people the truth.'" Lying for money is the essence of fraud, and this case illustrates that juries can plainly see the essential simplicity of financial frauds.

Investor advocates argue that "[t]he SEC must stop chasing minnows while letting the whales of Wall Street go free. That only rewards and incentivizes more crime" (Van Voris & Hurtado 2013). The government's response to these big shorts on subprime mortgages lies at the heart of this criticism. Goldman paid $550 million to the SEC in connection with the 2007 Abacus deal. Whatever benefit Tourre received from this single deal, it pales in comparison to the big short strategy that not only directly led to that deal but also yielded Goldman billions in profits. And the megabanks certainly racked up more profits from the Magnetar Trade deals than did Harding Advisory—yet it is the one involved firm to have suffered the corporate death penalty at the hands of the SEC.

Furthermore, Goldman senior managers did not candidly disclose the extent of their big short position in testimony to the US Senate. CEO Blankfein told the Senate, "Much has been said about the supposedly massive short Goldman Sachs had on the U.S. housing market. The fact is, we were not consistently or significantly net short . . . the market in residential mortgage-related products in 2007 and 2008." CFO Viniar echoed this in his Senate testimony: "Across 2007, we were primarily, although not consistently short, and it was not a large short." The Senate Permanent Subcommittee on Investigations found that "Goldman's denials of its net short positions in the subprime mortgage market, and the large profits produced by those net short positions, are directly contradicted by its own financial records and internal communications, as well as its own public statements in 2007, and are not credible" (US Senate 2011). Apparently having taken in billions on its short bets, Goldman did not want the public to perceive that it contributed to the financial crisis through the practice. Despite documentary evidence contradicting their testimony, no prosecutorial effort has been made to hold these managers accountable for their efforts to mislead Congress.

The Senate as well as the SEC made criminal referrals to the Department of Justice with respect to its findings. As is normal, news of a criminal investigation relating to Goldman's activities in mortgage-backed securities emerged. The inquiries into Goldman's actions reportedly drove its stock price down 20 percent (Goldfarb & Markon 2010). Yet, in a highly unusual move, the DOJ affirmatively announced that "there is not a viable basis to bring a criminal prosecution with respect to Goldman Sachs or its employees in regard to the allegations set forth" in the

Senate's report, but allowing that it was not prevented from reviewing new "evidence and making a different determination, if warranted" (Ingram 2012). The decision of the jury that Tourre participated in fraud while selling securities at Goldman can only be termed evidence that is inconsistent with DOJ's failure to pursue criminal charges.

The statute of limitations on the Abacus deal will not expire until July 2017, 10 years after the date of the final term sheet on the deal (FCIC CDO Library 2011). Goldman is a bank holding company, and the $550 million it paid the SEC to settle securities fraud charges therefore clearly affected a financial institution for purposes of 18 USC section 3293. An additional basis for the application of the extended 10-year statute of limitations exists because Goldman also sold its CDOs to banks and affiliates of banks. If Abacus is properly viewed as just one part of a broader fraudulent scheme to short subprime securities at the expense of buyers to whom Goldman did not disclose material facts, then the limitations period would not expire before December 2017, or 10 years after it recognized billions in profits from its big short strategy.

Goldman's short positions totaled $10 billion in February 2007 and $13.9 billion in June 2007. These concealed positions led to massive profits at Goldman, far exceeding any losses attributable to subprime exposures. According to the Senate Permanent Subcommittee on Investigations, "The $3.7 billion in net revenues from the SPG's short positions helped to offset other mortgage related losses, and, at year's end, at a time when mortgage departments at other large financial institutions were reporting record losses, Goldman's Mortgage Department reported overall net revenues of $1.1 billion" (US Senate 2011). In 2008, billions more flowed, including the massive $12.9 billion resulting from the government's massive bailout of AIG.

These outsized profits from the schemes make the SEC look like a toll collector on the road home from bankster fraud. Furthermore, the cost of settlements arising from the frauds landed squarely on the shoulders of innocent Goldman shareholders, not the executives at Goldman who tolerated or even encouraged the fraud. The message once again is that fraud pays. One could argue that by pursuing one case against each of the megabanks, Goldman Sachs, Citigroup, JPMorgan Chase, and Merrill Lynch, the SEC was sending the message that this type of fraud is unlawful under the US securities laws. Nevertheless, those who gained financially but continue to manage these banks, and perhaps other banks, are unlikely to be dissuaded from further schemes because they suffered no loss and no harm. This message can lead only to more fraud in the financial sector with potentially exponentially devastating consequences exceeding those seen in 2008. More pointedly, given the magnitude of the Magnetar Trade and Goldman's big short, the government's failure to prosecute anyone amounts to acquiescing to more frauds of the same type regardless of the costs imposed on US homeowners and taxpayers and the global economy.

7

The Dimensions of Lawlessness

It's perplexing at best . . . it's deeply troubling at worst.
—Phil Angelides, chair, Financial Crisis Inquiry
Commission, May 2012

As former chair of the FCIC, Phil Angelides knows more than almost anyone about the causes (and potential criminality) of the financial crisis of 2008. Yet, with financial fraud prosecutions hitting a 20-year low and DOJ ignoring manifest frauds and other serious financial crimes, he finds himself unable to explain the Obama administration's approach to Wall Street fraud. The FCIC like the SEC and the US Senate made criminal referrals to the DOJ (Boyer 2012). According to Angelides these referrals included documented and widespread fraud and corruption (Angelides 2016a). No prosecution ensued. In this chapter, we attempt to decode the DOJ's approach to financial frauds involving the most powerful and wealthiest Wall Street bankers. Due to the fact that DOJ and the administration offered only the most incoherent explanations, this chapter seeks to probe deeper into exactly what the DOJ's policy means.

Thus far, this book has demonstrated a series of Department of Justice decisions to decline prosecution in white-collar crime cases involving the financial crisis. It also has spotlighted regulatory inaction at the FDIC, the Fed, and the SEC. These agencies failed to use law enforcement powers to impose the corporate death penalty on criminal megabanks and the career death penalty on criminal bankers at the megabanks. We argue that these decisions enjoy little support from an evidentiary view—that is, the crisis produced plenty of evidence of costly criminality. Furthermore, these decisions to decline prosecution stand in stark contrast to the history of white-collar prosecutions of recent decades. The government has failed to offer any coherent explanation for its conduct on this score. As such, the United States faces a crisis in the rule of law because a small class of powerful individuals successfully evaded the reach of traditional white-collar law and accountability in the wake of the financial collapse of 2008.

The pattern that has emerged in prior chapters is one of powerful evidence of crimes committed by persons affiliated with major Wall Street banks but no ensuing criminal actions initiated by the Department of Justice against any single person or bank, nor any regulatory actions to terminate careers or break up the megabanks under current law. That serves to only partially define the problem. All of the prior chapters have primarily addressed misconduct at very large Wall Street Banks and misconduct arising directly from the crisis of 2007 to 2009. Based upon the foregoing chapters one could conclude that this new criminal immunity for financial crimes applied due to the unique circumstances of the crisis and only to the most fragile and systemically important banks.

In this chapter, we attempt to forge a better understanding of the contours of the government's inaction by offering an overview of criminality in the financial sector that includes misconduct after the financial crisis ended and that appears unrelated to the causes of the financial crisis. This requires an assessment of the pattern of criminality emerging in our financial sector rather than just focusing on the criminality of specific firms or fraudulent schemes that arose during the financial crisis as we did in prior chapters. The pattern proves far more disturbing than the individual cases. It is possible, for example, that in any given criminal scheme discussed in past chapters, the government may have knowledge we lack that justifies nonprosecution. Nevertheless, as this chapter demonstrates, it simply defies logic, reason, known facts, history, and experience to conclude that any appropriate justification can explain the *pattern* of criminality and nonprosecution, and this pattern persists today.

In order to understand this crisis in the rule of law, the dimensions of the problem must be well defined. Unfortunately, the lawlessness that emerged in the wake of the financial crisis has now spread beyond that crisis and the very large banks that threatened the American economy. Four cases in particular illustrate the spread of implied criminal immunity for powerful financial elites: (1) the foreclosure frauds revealed shortly after the crisis, (2) the failure of MF Global and the disappearance of customer funds, (3) the megabanks' misconduct in connection with the manipulation of LIBOR (a key global interest rate) as well global currency markets, and (4) extensive money laundering at HSBC. The meaning of these instances of the government failing to enforce the law support the notion that the new criminal immunity for financial elites appears to be all about power and not any putative policy basis. Simply stated, there is no economic or legal justification for nonprosecution of these crimes and for allowing lawlessness to spread in the financial sector.

Instead, the lack of criminal charges in these cases seems better explained by economic and political power rather than any supposed interest in repairing the financial sector after the Great Financial Crisis of 2008 or protecting frail banks. These cases illustrate the new frontiers of the new criminal immunity for financial crimes on Wall Street. That immunity transcends both the financial crisis as well as the largest banking entities. The common factor that seems to trigger criminal immunity for financial criminals is the political and economic power of the chieftains of these firms. Their control of the vast resources of a megabank and their personal political power cannot be ignored (Boyer 2012).

At the same time, these more recent cases create an ideal opportunity for a new administration to change the approach of the Department of Justice to financial crimes and frauds and resume criminal enforcement of the laws, as intended by Congress. The statute of limitations would not operate to bar the prosecution of any crimes discussed in this chapter.

Robo-Fraud

After the financial crisis and the urgently enacted bailouts, one might have expected the megabankers to be on their best behavior, having been the beneficiaries of taxpayer largess. Moreover, given the massive losses pervasive in the industry, one would expect bankers to worry about perp walks and prosecutions similar to those experienced by CEOs of major corporations that went bankrupt during the accounting fraud scandals earlier that same decade. Yet, the failure to swiftly address the rampant frauds described in earlier chapters of this book seems to have emboldened the bankers to double down on fraudulent activity.

A severe contraction in credit and the economy following the crisis hit consumers hard, particularly those homeowners duped into predatory mortgages. Loan defaults soared predictably, necessitating millions of home foreclosures. The banks moved rapidly to collect the fees that foreclosures generated while concurrently disregarding the law or treating distressed homeowners fairly. In the run-up to the financial crisis, mortgages had been granted, then sold, then bundled into securities so rapidly that banks and mortgage lenders had not recorded the transfers consistent with well-established property and commercial paper laws, and instead relied upon a newly created independent private electronic system intended to track transfers in ownership. In the shift from fevered lending to zealous foreclosing, banks soon realized records required by law for foreclosure claims were absent or deficient. Agents or loan servicers were enlisted to create the supporting documentation and generate sworn affidavits to confirm ownership and the right to foreclose (Paltrow & Brown 2011). The magnitude and systematic nature of the fraud that followed are difficult to overstate. One whistleblower admitted that she notarized "tens of thousands of false documents in a massive foreclosure scam before blowing the whistle on the scandal" (*NBC News* 2011). The robotic nature of the frauds gave rise to the term "robo-signing."

On February 9, 2012, the US Department of Justice announced that the five largest mortgage servicers (including Bank of America, Citi, JPMorgan Chase, and Wells Fargo) agreed to a historic settlement with the federal government and 49 states. The settlement required the banks to extend $25 billion in mortgage relief to distressed homeowners and in direct payments to the states and federal government. According to the DOJ, "The joint federal-state agreement requires [the banks] to commit $25 billion to resolve violations of state and federal law. These violations include servicers' use of 'robo-signed' affidavits in foreclosure proceedings; deceptive practices in the offering of loan modifications; failures to offer non-foreclosure alternatives before foreclosing on borrowers with federally insured mortgages; and filing improper documentation in federal bankruptcy court" (DOJ 2012a). This type of massive fraud on our judicial system and homeowners finds no precedent in US history. Once again the DOJ's own website reveals a massive pattern of violations of law, yet no criminal charges were filed and instead the banks used innocent shareholder money from corporate coffers to sweep bank executives' criminality under the rug.

The Office of the Comptroller of the Currency (OCC) and the Fed also imposed sanctions on the megabanks for their role in the "robo-signing" scandal. Federal bank examiners found massive foreclosure frauds, including the submission of fraudulent documents in state and federal courts across the nation (e.g., OCC 2011a, 2011b). During 2011 and 2012, the OCC and the Federal Reserve signed enforcement orders with virtually all of the megabanks (including Bank of America, NA; Citibank, NA; Goldman Sachs; HSBC Bank, USA, NA; JPMorgan Chase, NA; Morgan Stanley; and Wells Fargo Bank, NA) that required them to hire independent consultants to review foreclosure files for irregularities and remedy harm to borrowers. In 2013, the regulators amended the orders and ended the independent reviews. The banks agreed to provide $10 billion in cash payments to about 4.4 million borrowers. The Government Accountability Office found a lack of transparency at the Fed and the OCC and that the decision to cut short the review left regulators with limited information about actual harm to borrowers when they negotiated the $10 billion settlement (Government Accountability Office 2014).

One member of Congress found this disturbing. Representative Elijah E. Cummings (D-MD and ranking member of the House Committee on Oversight and Government Reform) expressed dismay with the process: "I am deeply disappointed that the OCC and the Federal Reserve finalized this settlement and effectively terminated the Independent Foreclosure Review process before providing Congress answers to serious questions about how this settlement amount was determined, who these funds will go to, and what will happen to other families who were abused by these mortgage servicing companies but have not yet had their cases reviewed. I do not know what the rush was to make this settlement without answering these key questions" (Puzzanghera 2013).

More generally, according to some commentators the government's response borders on complicity in the highly damaging foreclosure frauds. One commentator stated, "In this instance, the underlying ownership on potentially millions of loans has been permanently confused, and the resulting disarray will cause chaos for decades into the future, harming homeowners, investors and the broader economy. Holder's corrupt bargain, to let Wall Street walk, comes at the cost of permanent damage to the largest market in the world, the U.S. residential housing market" (Dayen 2014b). Other commentators argue that government silence in the face of massive foreclosure fraud amounts to a partnership with the fraudfeasors: "We believe that only the government can stop fraud from growing to catastrophic levels and that among the government's highest responsibilities is to provide the regulatory 'cops on the beat' with the competence, resources, courage, and integrity to take on our most elite frauds. We believe that anything less is a travesty that causes tens of millions of Americans to be defrauded and poses a grave threat to our economy and democracy" (Black & Wray 2010).

Amazingly, the "robo-signing" scandal has given rise to numerous whistleblowers who would give DOJ strong testimony if it chose to pursue criminal charges. For example, Lynn Szymoniak helped uncover this fraud while facing foreclosure proceedings on her home in Florida. Her bank served her with suspicious-looking documentation. Szymoniak worked as a lawyer and fraud investigator and started investigating further. She found tens of thousands of similarly suspicious documents in many foreclosure proceedings. In particular, she discovered that many different banks employed a fictitious name—Linda Green—to execute fraudulent foreclosure documents. Ultimately her findings helped the government achieve its multibillion-dollar settlement, and she was paid $18 million for her assistance as a whistleblower (Eichler 2012).

More recently, six whistleblowers have emerged with respect to Bank of America's foreclosure practices. Bank of America induced its representatives to lie to homeowners and fraudulently deny mortgage relief applications and paid staff bonuses for generating more foreclosures. This kind of pervasive misrepresentation was pursuant to the policies of the bank, meaning senior management directed this misconduct. One commentator sums up a prevalent view: "Past experience shows that our top regulatory and law enforcement officials are primarily interested in covering for Wall Street's crimes. These well-sourced allegations amount to an accusation of Bank of America stealing thousands of homes, and lying to the government about it. Homeowners who did everything asked of them were nevertheless pushed into foreclosure, all to fortify profits on Wall Street. There's a clear path to punish Bank of America for this conduct. If it doesn't result in prosecutions, it will once again confirm the sorry excuse for justice we have in America" (Dayen 2013a).

Three years later no prosecutions or corporate death penalty against any bank or bank executive for foreclosure fraud have followed in the wake of these whistleblower allegations. In terms of criminal accountability, there is no question that robo-signing fraud occurred in connection with foreclosures on a widespread scale as the federal banking regulators and DOJ found. The megabanks can afford the best legal representation available, and they do not cut multibillion-dollar checks unless their hand is forced. But the American people will never know which bank managers at which banks approved of the practice or allowed it to proceed with full knowledge of what robo-signing entailed. Those faced with foreclosures supported by false documents or those signing false documents to support banks claim well understand the law would not permit them to engage in such open and massive fraud for their own personal gain without punishment. Yet so many persons were enlisted into this criminality without retribution. This fraud stands as a travesty of justice, and there is no historic precedent for such a wide-ranging fraud with so many victims leading to zero criminal accountability.

One need only follow the money to understand where the interests lie in the robo-signing scheme to understand that if pursued criminally, given the large number of megabanks involved, the administration would be forced to indict scores of bankers and employees. These employees work at the very megabanks that contributed so generously to President Obama's presidential campaigns (Boyer 2012). Any prosecution would surely lead directly to senior managers, given the systemic nature and extended duration of the fraud. This racketeering-like behavior resulted from managerial direction.

MF Global

MF Global was a large commodities brokerage firm that aspired to the status of Goldman Sachs. A commodities broker—also called a futures commission merchant—often offers depository services for customers with cash balances not currently needed to support trading activities. In a bank, deposits are backed by federally guaranteed deposit insurance. Cash held in a commodities brokerage account enjoys a different kind of protection: customer funds must be strictly segregated by the commodities brokerage firm in order to be safe vouched by the firm until needed or withdrawn by the customer. The commodities broker may invest the funds only in conservative and safe instruments like US Treasury obligations.

This obligation to strictly segregate customer funds is enforced by the Commodity Futures Trading Commission (CFTC) as well as the commodities exchange (also known as a self-regulatory organization) where the firm primarily trades. In the case of MF Global, that exchange was the CME Group—a long-standing and reputable Chicago commodities exchange. These two entities audit compliance with customer segregation rules through periodic examinations of every commodities broker under their supervision. Furthermore, firms are required to self-report any violation of customer segregation requirements. Under law, any firm violating these customer segregation requirements faces criminal sanctions. Furthermore, any controlling person of a firm that violates these customer segregation requirements also faces criminal penalties. Any person who "willfully" (or with criminal intent) violates the customer segregation rules faces criminal sanctions. As discussed in the introduction, the CFTC also holds the power to terminate careers in the commodities industry and revoke the registration of any firm that violates financial laws.

For many decades this legal and regulatory framework secured customer funds. In fact, self-regulatory organizations (SROs) like the Chicago Mercantile Exchange highlighted that no customer had ever lost any deposits with a commodities broker. Customers could leave cash deposits with their commodities broker with confidence that the funds were safe. This confidence in the sanctity of customer deposits benefited the entire commodities brokerage industry and facilitated the ability of customers to manage risks of commodity price volatility. Then came along Jon Corzine and MF Global (Roe & Koutoulas 2011).

Corzine formerly sat as the governor of New Jersey as well as a US senator from New Jersey. He also served as co-chair of the Obama for President Committee in 2008. He was one of Obama's most successful "bundlers," meaning not only that he personally supported the future president, but also that many of his contacts, cronies, and friends forked over cash to get Obama elected (Dwyer 2011). Prior to entering politics Corzine led Goldman Sachs and made $400 million from taking that iconic firm public (Farzad 2011). Corzine also enjoyed membership in the prestigious and somewhat secretive Bilderberg Group (Bilderberg Group 2015). Corzine therefore epitomizes a well-connected politician combined with tremendous economic resources.

Corzine wanted to turn MF Global into a new Goldman Sachs. More than anything else that would require trading profits. Ultimately, Corzine bet huge money on Eurozone debt. The bet went south and loses mounted quickly. To the extent Corzine undertook to trade positions in Eurozone debt on exchanges, he needed cash to meet margin calls. To the extent Corzine traded derivatives, he needed cash to meet calls for collateral to secure his obligation to derivatives counterparties. The liquidity demands to maintain the Eurozone positions overwhelmed MF Global and led to its bankruptcy on October 31, 2011. MF Global now admits that it funded these bets with customer segregated funds.

Soon after the bankruptcy, customers learned that their cash deposits with MF Global were frozen while the bankruptcy trustee tried to untangle the trades and retrieve cash that rightfully belonged to customers of MF Global. Liquid cash deposits that farmers and ranchers relied upon to hedge the risks of future movements in commodity prices disappeared, exposing customers to unforeseen risks and liquidity challenges. In all, $1.2 billion in customer funds fell into a black hole of margin calls and collateral demands from counterparties. It took years for the bankruptcy trustee to sort out the MF Global mess and return cash to its rightful owners (Protess 2014).

MF Global admitted it broke the law and violated the customer segregation rules in a civil action brought by the CFTC (SDNY 2013). The CFTC pursued MF Global for a variety of legal violations including violations of its rules arising from its failures to maintain segregation of customer funds. CEO Corzine and Treasurer Edith O'Brien also face the same charges. They contest the CFTC allegations (CFTC 2013a).

In terms of their criminal culpability, Corzine and O'Brien can face criminal conviction and prison only based upon a jury finding that they acted willfully or with criminal intent in causing MF Global to violate the customer segregation requirements, the Commodity Exchange Act, or any CFTC rule under that act. The CFTC's investigation turned up some important facts regarding the lost customer funds and the role Corzine and O'Brien played in directing MF Global's violation of the customer segregation rules, and their state of mind. The CFTC, like the

SEC, holds subpoena power to investigate claims of wrongdoing prior to filing a civil complaint. Thus, the CFTC's civil complaint relating to the failure of MF Global benefits from an in-depth investigation that ordinary civil litigants cannot match.

According to that complaint, in the fall of 2010, near the beginning of the Eurozone bond investments, the chief risk officer of MF Global's parent company warned Corzine and the board of directors that the Eurozone bond investment strategy could result in liquidity demands including margin calls that could threaten the liquidity of the firm and recommended that the board limit the cash invested in Eurozone bonds. Thereafter, Corzine decided to replace the chief risk officer, who in March 2011 left the firm. By October 2011, MF Global's investment in Eurozone bonds had increased to $6.4 billion, which represented more than 4.5 times MF Global's equity. Corzine seemingly ignored the risks that the bonds posed to liquidity requirements.

For example, in its civil complaint, the CFTC refers to recorded phone conversations involving Corzine and O'Brien. In one such conversation the CFTC quotes Corzine on October 6, 2011, as telling an MF Global employee in the firm's treasury department that he would rather "go negative" on customer accounts than draw cash from the firm's revolving line of credit. Furthermore, by October 18, Corzine learned that his use of excess cash from the commodities brokerage violated firm policy and that the global treasurer banned the use of excess cash from the commodities firm to fund the liquidity needs generated by the Eurozone bond positions. The recorded phone calls show that by October 19, CEO Corzine was well aware that the firm was suffering a severe liquidity crunch and that there was little to no buffer available at the commodities brokerage to fund the Eurozone investments.

MF Global's problems quickly worsened from there. On the following Monday, Moody's downgraded the parent company's debt. On October 25, 2011, the parent company announced a $191 million loss for the third quarter of 2011. The parent as well as the commodities brokerage unit now suffered a full-blown bank run, as customers withdrew their funds, counterparties demanded more collateral to cover MF Global's debts, and credit dried up.

By Wednesday, October 26, 2011, according to the CFTC, MF Global's brokerage unit fell short of customer segregated funds by $298 million. On that day, O'Brien and her staff transferred $500 million from MF Global's customer segregation accounts to the firm's proprietary accounts. By that evening, O'Brien knew that she faced customer segregation problems to the tune of hundreds of millions of dollars. The problem worsened the next day—according to the CFTC, on Thursday, October 27, 2011, MF Global was short $413 million in customer segregated funds.

Yet O'Brien transferred about $450 million more on October 28, leading to an increase in the shortfall of customer segregated funds to $900 million by close of business. The major problem that day for MF Global was a $200 million margin call related to the Eurozone bonds. Another problem arose from $134 million in overdrafts from firm accounts held at JPMorgan. Corzine contacted O'Brien at 9:00 that morning to demand cash to meet these liquidity demands. According to the CFTC, Corzine told O'Brien that was the "most important" task of the day. By 9:26 O'Brien had moved $200 million from customer segregated funds at JPMorgan to proprietary accounts at JPMorgan. In an email unearthed by a congressional inquiry, O'Brien stated that this transfer was done "per the direct instructions of JC."

At this point JPMorgan balked. On the afternoon of October 28, JPMorgan demanded written assurances from Jon Corzine that the transfers complied with CFTC regulations and sent a letter to Corzine for signature by an MF Global representative. No MF Global representative ever signed the letter. The next day, October 29, O'Brien told an MF Global attorney she did not want to sign the letter and she thought MF Global was "underseg." Corzine never took any steps to ensure the transfers were not from customer segregated funds or compliant with CFTC regulations (CFTC 2013b).

In his congressional testimony, former CEO Corzine stated that he "never intended to break any rules" while serving as MF Global's CEO (Corzine 2011). But a jury can find a criminal violation with or without a specific intent to knowingly violate a specific statute or regulation. For example, a willful blindness to the risk that one's conduct constitutes a criminal act may suffice to show criminal intent for a criminal conviction—particularly if one is on notice of the likelihood that criminal violations may be occurring and that one's conduct is contributing to the violation. As one court states, "defendants cannot escape the reach of [criminal] statutes by deliberately shielding themselves from clear evidence of critical facts that are strongly suggested by the circumstances." Or another formulation reads, "The willful blindness instruction allows the jury to impute the element of knowledge to the defendant if the evidence indicates that he purposely closed his eyes to avoid knowing what was taking place around him" (*Global-Tech Appliances, Inc. v. SEB S.A.* 2011).

Certainly there is sufficient evidence for a grand jury investigation to determine if Corzine had sufficient warning that the Eurozone bond positions were draining enough cash out of MF Global that customer funds must have been at risk.

Of course this misconduct is not the only potential criminal act that a jury could find was committed by Jon Corzine and Edith O'Brien if a criminal indictment was pursued by the DOJ. Along with the primary customer segregation violations, MF Global disregarded its reporting obligations and reported false information regarding its customer segregation problems. As supervisors, Corzine and O'Brien owed duties to comply with these requirements, and the CFTC is already pursuing such violations in a civil action. In addition, MF Global's parent company was a publicly held firm and therefore owed obligations to its investors to disclose material facts under the federal securities laws. MF Global's parent company also appears to have violated these obligations. Corzine acted as CEO of the parent company as well as the commodities brokerage unit. Consequently, if prosecutors presented the violations of customer segregation requirements to a jury, they could also enhance their probability of success considerably with other related charges.

Another mechanism for enhanced success involves negotiating with O'Brien. Underlings do not usually wish to go to prison in order to protect their bosses. Prosecutors routinely reach agreements with lower level employees to secure their testimony against their supervisors. The federal government did this quite effectively when investigating the fraud at Enron, as discussed in the introduction. This is neither a new nor untested prosecutorial tactic.

Given the strong evidence above that O'Brien acted unlawfully, she would be best advised to explore such an arrangement. O'Brien also invoked her right against self-incrimination when called to testify before Congress regarding the MF Global fiasco. If prosecutors agreed to immunize her from criminal prosecution, she could be compelled to testify truthfully against CEO Jon Corzine. Either a negotiated plea or immunity would represent a worst-case scenario for Corzine's defense team. These traditional prosecutorial tools inexplicably lay unused in this case.

From a policy perspective, it is difficult to overstate the case for more vigorous government enforcement action in the MF Global fiasco. As a congressional inquiry found as of February 10, 2012, the shortfall in customer accounts amounted to $1.2 billion—a historically unprecedented shortfall in the futures industry. This amount represents a crippling loss of cash and liquidity for a variety of commodities traders—including family farmers and ranchers throughout the United States. Essentially MF Global converted these customer funds to its own use in order to maintain its Eurozone debt exposure, which amounted to an astounding $7.687 billion as of October 24, 2011. It is difficult to imagine a more brazen conversion of customer funds by a regulated futures commission merchant.

The futures industry seems to have suffered a major loss of trust. "Trading on the futures market was down 8.9 percent in the first six months of 2012 compared with the first six months of 2011. Options trading was down 11.5 percent for the same period. The Chicago Board of Trade's net income declined 17 percent in the same period." Commentators and market experts attribute this decline in business to a "lack of trust" rooted in the MF Global scandal, as the natural consequence of the massive number of victims of the MF Global crime spree: 38,000 commodities traders, farmers, small investors, and hedge funds (Bialosky 2013).

The decision to decline to prosecute the manifest violations of law arising from MF Global has nothing to do with Too-Big-to-Fail. MF Global failed, filing for bankruptcy, yet the economy hardly noticed. Notwithstanding the lack of macroeconomic significance, the government remained totally passive in terms of criminal prosecutions. So it seems like MF Global has called the government's bluff: allowing criminals to go unpunished is not about the economy, but about the political power of a small group of wealthy and connected financial elites who today enjoy a criminal immunity that the vast majority of the population does not. The upshot is that while many Americans face prison for often innocuous crimes that do not materially harm society, one powerful group of individuals escapes criminal sanction even for conduct that causes massive economic pain. That is the hallmark of a corrupted criminal justice system.

In the final analysis, MF Global represents yet another unprecedented breakdown in the rule of law. There is no coherent explanation for not pursuing this case just like similar cases throughout history. In thinking about MF Global, it is extremely difficult to imagine any other person other than one of Corzine's political power escaping prosecution. The government could admittedly lose a criminal prosecution against Corzine (or even O'Brien), but in this case the rules governing the segregation of funds are clear, the actors understood those rules as central to their business, and the unlawful transfer of the funds was readily traced. Indeed, JPMorgan recognized quickly the suspicious nature of the transfers and demanded written assurances, which neither Corzine nor O'Brien was willing to supply. So while the prospect of defeat looms in every decision DOJ makes to pursue criminal sanctions, it seems less likely here. In the end, it is impossible to ignore the wealth and political power of Jon Corzine in trying to understand the government's conduct. Corzine appears to reside above the law, and apparently the government is so committed to that travesty that it grants implicit immunity from prosecution to O'Brien in order to protect Corzine.

Pervasive Financial Market Manipulation

Since the end of the financial crisis, many megabanks have also manipulated financial markets on an unprecedented scale. Specifically, the DOJ found that Wall Street banks manipulated a benchmark interest rate known as LIBOR—the London Interbank Offered Rate. Subsequently, DOJ found that Wall Street banks also manipulated global currency markets. Notwithstanding the enormous scale of these market manipulations and frauds, DOJ declined to criminally prosecute any individual banker and gave the megabanks a free pass too by relieving them of the consequences of their criminality. Once again, the financial regulators followed DOJ's lead and expelled no person or firm from the financial services industry.

For example, five global megabanks (Citicorp, JPMorgan Chase, Barclays, Royal Bank of Scotland, and UBS) pleaded guilty to felony charges arising from their manipulation of currency exchange markets. The criminal megabanks also paid over $2.5 billion of shareholder money to the government. According to the defendant bank plea agreements, over a six-year period, euro-dollar traders at Citicorp, JPMorgan, Barclays, and RBS used an exclusive electronic chat room and coded language to manipulate benchmark exchange rates. The traders even referred to themselves as "The Cartel" and "The Mafia." The Cartel traders conspired to trade US dollars and euros and to manipulate and fix benchmark rates set at the 1:15 PM and 4:00 PM fixes (DOJ 2015b). Despite this powerful evidence of criminal intent, the government failed to charge any individual megabanker with any crime.

In fact, the government affirmatively acted to ensure that the megabanks pleading guilty to crimes could continue their criminal operations unimpeded by law. Specifically, the SEC exempted these banks from automatic disqualifications applicable to crooks for certain securities activities and businesses. In other words, the government shielded the crooks from the full reach of the law. SEC Commissioner Kara Stein voiced strong objections: "I am troubled by repeated instances of noncompliance at these global financial institutions, which may be indicative of a continuing culture that does not adequately support legal and ethical behavior. Further, I am concerned that the latest series of actions has effectively rendered criminal convictions of financial institutions largely symbolic. Firms and institutions increasingly rely on the Commission's repeated issuance of waivers to remove the consequences of a criminal conviction, consequences that may actually positively contribute to a firm's compliance and conduct going forward." Commissioner Stein noted that commission had already granted the megabank defendants at least 23 prior waivers from automatic disqualifications. "Allowing these institutions to continue business as usual, after multiple and serious regulatory and criminal violations, poses risks to investors and the American public that are being ignored" (SEC 2015a).

The government also accommodated the megabanks when it found massive market manipulation of LIBOR. To its credit, the DOJ sought criminal charges against 12 low-level traders with respect to this manifest market manipulation. It also extracted large fines from the megabanks and criminal guilty pleas from foreign subsidiaries of the megabanks. DOJ did nothing, however, to go after senior bankers individually or to change the basic business models of the megabanks. Instead, it preserved the ability of the banks to continue their fundamentally criminally inclined businesses. No senior banker suffered indictment, and no firm suffered the corporate death penalty.

The government cannot claim that this massive manipulation and fraud would be difficult to prove. DOJ already has emails and text messages in hand that establish the illegal market manipulation and fraud. In one example, a Deutsche Bank trader told a crony, "if you need something in particular in the libors i.e. you have an interest in a high or a low fix let me know and there's a high chance i'll be able to go in a different level. Just give me a shout the day before or send an email from your blackberry first thing" (DOJ 2015a). One trader, at UBS, asked another banker to move the six-month LIBOR rate up due to a "gigantic" position he had taken. The other banker responded by moving his bank's bid submission by 0.06 percent, for which the UBS trader thanked him (DOJ 2012f). These emails approach an electronic confession to criminality.

The damage wrought from this scam justified a harsher response. Behind the manipulation lay potentially millions of victimized people who had no way of knowing they were being defrauded into participating in rigged markets. For example, about $350 trillion in derivatives transactions are pegged to LIBOR. LIBOR manipulation, however, affected not just financial market traders. Up to $10 trillion in debt obligations—ranging from car loans to mortgage debt—is indexed to LIBOR. Furthermore, investors also hold debt obligations tied to LIBOR. Thus this market manipulation affected unsuspecting consumers and investors around the world. By manipulating LIBOR, the traders at the megabanks stole small amounts of money from unsuspecting investors and consumers to fatten their own profits by billions of dollars. MIT economist Andrew Lo stated that the LIBOR scandal "dwarfs by orders of magnitude any financial scams in the history of markets" (O'Toole 2012).

Nevertheless, the government specifically sought to preserve the business operations of the megabanks. The UBS case is instructive. According to the DOJ, UBS bankers caused "UBS and other financial institutions to spread false and misleading information about LIBOR [and] manipulated the benchmark interest rate upon which many transactions and consumer financial products are based. They defrauded the company's counterparties of millions of dollars. And they did so primarily to reap increased profits, and secure bigger bonuses, for themselves" (DOJ 2012f). Nevertheless, the guilty plea by UBS's Japanese subsidiary, and only that subsidiary, was specifically structured to shield the company from the legal fallout of its criminality. If the parent company suffered a criminal conviction, its US banking and securities operations could be put in jeopardy, as discussed in the introduction (Henning 2012). At some point, the government's efforts to protect the business of the megabanks and keep their megabank friends out of jail (and the political patronage flowing) shades into complicity.

While the LIBOR scandal has led to a few scattered criminal indictments of individual bank employees, no senior manager at any megabank has faced criminal charges. This despite the fact that evidence emerged that the LIBOR market rigging went on for years and that senior managers knew of its essential elements. Indeed, at one trial in London, a senior banker told a low-level trader to be "careful" when rigging markets, but never told the trader to stop (Black 2015). The scale, the profits, and the duration of the LIBOR rigging scam all strongly suggest that plentiful evidence existed for DOJ to indict senior bankers.

HSBC

HSBC illustrates the power and lawlessness of international megabanks to an extent that previously did not exist, during the years prior to the Great Financial Crisis. HSBC engaged in intensive money laundering on behalf of drug cartels and rogue states such as Iran for years, even though regulators repeatedly raised red flags. Despite evidence of a specific intent to knowingly violate anti-money-laundering laws at the highest levels of HSBC, no individual faced any criminal prosecution. Furthermore, even though criminal convictions seemed easily attainable at US-regulated affiliates of this megabank, which could have forced divestments of subsidiaries (thereby mitigating Too-Big-to-Fail problems), the government bent over backward to avoid this outcome and instead preserved the outlaw megabank. At some level, these efforts to facilitate megabank criminality make the US government a partner in the crimes of the megabanks. Even today, the news is filled with reports that HSBC continues to engage in money laundering (Ensign and

Colchester 2016). Given the approach of the Department of Justice, one might conclude that crime pays.

On December 11, 2012, the Department of Justice announced that HSBC admitted it broke the law, entered into a deferred prosecution agreement with the government, and paid over $1.9 billion in fines and civil penalties. The corporation, not any senior manager, paid the fine. This agreement resolved a wide array of criminal allegations against the megabank and afforded protection to employees, officers, and directors, who knowingly and willfully "engaged in the transactions during the period set forth in the statement of facts" disclosed to the United States as a part of the deferred prosecution agreement (DPA) (DOJ 2012g).

As part of that deferred prosecution agreement, HSBC admitted the following facts: (1) from 2006 to 2010, HSBC Bank USA violated the Bank Secrecy Act (BSA) and federal regulations thereunder; (2) HSBC Bank USA ignored the money laundering risks associated with doing business with certain Mexican customers and failed to implement an anti-money-laundering program as required under the BSA; (3) as a result of these violations, at least $881 million in drug cartel proceeds were laundered through HSBC Bank USA without being detected; (4) HSBC knowingly and willfully processed $660 million worth of transactions with rogue states such as Cuba, Iran, Libya, Sudan, and Burma, in violation of Office of Foreign Assets Control sanctions; and (5) HSBC Group was aware of the significant anti-money-laundering compliance problems at HSBC Mexico yet did not inform HSBC Bank USA of these problems and their potential impact on HSBC Bank USA's anti-money-laundering program. In short, HSBC admitted to facilitating and participating in a pattern of severe criminal misconduct with some of the most reprehensible criminals and outlaw regimes worldwide. Despite the severity of this admittedly criminal conduct, the DOJ agreed to defer prosecution, allowing HSBC off with fines, other civil sanctions, and promises to comply with the law (DOJ 2012g).

The HSBC case provides an excellent example of criminality within a bank pursuant to policies and practices known at the highest levels of the organization. In 2003, the Federal Reserve issued an enforcement order to HSBC demanding that HSBC USA take immediate action to impose policies and procedures to ensure that the bank did not launder money for terrorists and criminals. The president and CEO of HSBC

USA executed that agreement, which the board of directors authorized by board resolution. All communications and notifications under the enforcement agreement went through the senior executive vice president and general counsel (Federal Reserve 2003). The OCC cited HSBC USA in its 2009–2010 bank examination for essentially the same violations and deficient anti-money-laundering policies, and entered into a consent order with the bank mandating that these deficiencies be addressed. The entire board of directors of HSBC executed that consent order (OCC 2010). Thus, senior managers as well as the bank and bank holding company should face criminal accountability, perhaps even reaching into the boardroom. Yet the entity and its managers were penalized very lightly, if at all.

According to the Department of Justice, "[F]rom 2006 to 2010, HSBC Bank USA severely understaffed its AML [anti-money-laundering] compliance function and failed to implement an anti-money laundering program capable of adequately monitoring suspicious transactions and activities from . . . HSBC Mexico. . . . This included a failure to monitor billions of dollars in purchases of physical U.S. dollars, or 'banknotes,' from these affiliates. . . . As a result, HSBC Bank USA failed to monitor over \$670 billion in wire transfers and over \$9.4 billion in purchases of physical U.S. dollars from HSBC Mexico during this period." This made HSBC the preferred mechanism of money laundering for drug cartels (DOJ 2012h). The drug merchants in Mexico moved such huge volumes of cash into HSBC that they came to use specially sized cash boxes that fit the precise dimensions of the teller windows. HSBC willingly cooperated in this profitable if sordid and bloody business (DOJ 2012b).

At the press conference announcing the HSBC settlement, in explaining the agreement to defer prosecution, Assistant Attorney General Lanny Breuer stated that the DOJ was concerned that criminal charges would lead to undesirable "collateral consequences" (Viswanatha & Wolf 2012). Breuer had previously stated, "[T]he decision of whether to indict a corporation . . . is not one I, or anyone in the Criminal Division, take lightly. We are frequently on the receiving end of presentations from defense counsel, CEOs, and economists who argue that the collateral consequences of an indictment would be devastating for their client. In my conference room, over the years, I have heard sober predictions that a company or bank might fail if we indict, that innocent employees could lose their jobs, that entire industries may be affected, and even that global markets will feel the effects" (Breuer 2012). Of course, removing managers and incarcerating them would not possibly harm the global economy, as we explained in the introduction and show in more detail in the conclusion. Employees similarly would not suffer if the firm is spun off to shareholders. The bank need not fail under these sanctions.

HSBC can hardly be termed systemically important to the US financial sector. The HSBC megabank is a global banking empire consisting of a large group of companies with 6,900 branch offices in 80 countries. The ultimate parent firm, HSBC Holdings PLC, is headquartered in the United Kingdom. An affiliate, HSBC North America Holdings, Inc., holds HSBC Bank USA, NA, a federally chartered bank. As mentioned in the introduction, the US government could have forced HSBC to spin-off these units to shareholders, with new noncriminal management and little to no harm to shareholders, innocent workers, and the financial system.

In fact, according to the *Wall Street Journal* HSBC is only the ninth largest bank in the United States. It is a fraction of the size of most Wall Street megabanks, a least insofar as the US financial sector is concerned. Its assets amount to only 11.5 percent of those of JPMorgan, the nation's most husky megabank (Chaudheri 2014b). Furthermore, the megabank's US operations constitute only about 10 percent of its worldwide operations (Tor & Sarfaz 2013). As a result it is difficult to see how spinning off 10 percent of HSBC's global operations would cause the firm to fail or to create any global financial instability. The demons in Breuer's mind that caused him to forgo criminal charges in the HSBC case are simply nonsensical.

Yet Breuer deemed this relatively minor player in the US financial sector worthy of special treatment. Perhaps having left a lucrative white-collar crime defense practice to become the assistant attorney general, and then having returned to that practice after he left the DOJ, Breuer has a special place in his heart for megabankers. Breuer seemed to think that if he deemed a bank worthy of special treatment, then it is appropriate to effectively bestow immunity by refusing to pursue criminal prosecutions. Whatever presentation is made to Breuer is therefore dispositive, without the transparency of a trial, without cross-examination of witnesses, and without a jury to hear and weigh the evidence. This power Breuer so fully appropriated as an emolument of his office is the very definition of lawlessness. It matters not what Congress intended nor what any adversarial system in public might conclude. Only Breuer should be entrusted to make these decisions behind closed doors with no public participation and regardless of what the governing statutes provide. Breuer thereby transformed his prosecutorial discretion into power and lawlessness run riot.

Senators Sherrod Brown and Charles Grassley quoted Holder and Breuer on this point and inquired about whom DOJ prosecutors consult with regarding the external costs of prosecuting a bank (Brown & Grassley 2013). The DOJ responded with a backpedaling statement that it is not currently aware of any consultations with private third-party experts regarding the collateral consequences of prosecutorial actions against the megabanks. But the department claimed that it contacted relevant government agencies, including foreign regulators, to discuss such issues. Notably, the DOJ declined to identify which regulators it consulted with. The senators deemed this response to be "aggressively evasive" (Hamilton & Hopkins 2013).

HSBC, unfortunately, constitutes only the most brazen and persistent money launderer. DOJ signed similar agreements with other megabanks including Lloyds Banking Group, Credit Suisse, Barclays, and Standard Chartered. Each of these megabanks admitted to serious criminal offenses. As a former US Customs agent stated, "all were handed the equivalent of traffic tickets—pay a fine on your way out the door" (Mazur 2013). Given that the fine HSBC paid ultimately consisted of innocent shareholder wealth, the actual criminals within HSBC and these other megabanks faced not even the equivalent of a parking ticket. Any fraudulent compensation garnered by financial elites essentially constitutes risk-free profits, as the risk of fines for discovered illegality falls just on shareholders.

In fairness, the government did pursue innovative and imaginative civil sanctions. First, the government deserves credit for its cooperative use of possible criminal sanctions alongside with regulatory sanctions. Second, on the same day that DOJ announced its criminal deferred prosecution agreement, both the Fed and the OCC announced parallel regulatory actions. The OCC, for example, mandated a compliance committee of the board to ensure future regulatory compliance. Third, under the DPA with the DOJ, HSBC replaced senior management, clawed back deferred compensation bonuses from its most senior compliance officers, and agreed to partially defer bonus compensation for its most senior executives during the period of the five-year DPA. HSBC also made significant changes to its management structure to increase the accountability of its most senior executives for money laundering compliance failures. Once again, the government failed to find any criminals to charge in connection with this heinously criminal misconduct. It is as if crimes simply fall from the sky like pennies from heaven, with no human intervention at all, when DOJ finds criminality at the megabanks. No individual ever actively commits a crime.

All of this alarms those concerned with the rule of law. Senators Brown and Grassley wrote Attorney General Holder, "The nature of these settlements has fostered concerns that too big to fail Wall Street banks enjoy a favored status [which] undermines the public's confidence in our institutions and in the principal that the law is applied equally in all cases" (Brown & Grassley 2013). Consider, for example, the plight of a relatively petty money launderer at about the same time, named Jimmie Goodgame. Goodgame made the mistake of not working for a megabank. According to DOJ, Goodgame laundered over $1.5 million of drug money over a two-year period through front businesses and bank accounts. Unlike the money launderers at HSBC, Goodgame was sentenced to 70 months in federal prison (DOJ 2012c). The bottom-line message: better to work at a megabank that launders hundreds of millions in dirty money than to launder small sums as a petty criminal entrepreneur. Only the megabanks hold charters for criminal profits, and those charters extend to the most nasty financial crimes possible. When Goodgame is released from prison, he would be well advised to send his resume to every Wall Street bank.

In mid-2016, a congressional report disclosed the findings of a comprehensive inquiry into the DOJ's decision to decline criminal prosecution in the HSBC matter. The report revealed that DOJ declined to prosecute notwithstanding an internal recommendation to pursue criminal charges. This decision followed claims from HSBC managers that an indictment would lead to financial disruptions. These claims occurred in an extraordinary meeting at DOJ's offices and were not backed up by any expert or officials from the US Treasury. Holder appears to have unilaterally decided during the meeting to decline any criminal prosecution no matter how structured (Staff Report, US House of Representatives 2016). British officials learned of this outcome well before Congress and lobbied the US government at the highest levels to decline prosecution. In fact, DOJ never produced any documents in response to congressional subpoenas. In light of this report, and the accompanying documents produced by the Treasury Department, there is now no doubt that DOJ will decline prosecution against certain large financial institutions. While the report focuses on just HSBC, there is no reason to think this Too-Big-to-Jail (TBTJ) mentality has not operated with respect to larger (and more politically connected) US megabanks (Morgenson 2016).

Discerning a DOJ Policy

There can be no doubt after the HSBC case and Assistant Attorney General Breuer's comments regarding the lack of criminal enforcement that there is a TBTJ policy at work in the Department of Justice today. Those comments make it clear that Breuer's "conference room" is open to entertain arguments from the financial sector that large banks are too important to face criminal accountability for financial crimes. Undefined "collateral consequences" is the ticket for large banks to escape criminal sanctions. This policy permits payments of shareholder funds to the government in exchange for criminal immunity. These basic contours of the DOJ's TBTJ policy now seem certain.

The case of MF Global adds an important additional element: it is not really at all about potential economic consequences. It is certain that criminal violations occurred at this macroeconomically insignificant commodities firm with no criminal charges at all. This suggests that TBTJ really does not concern financial instability or economic harm. The notable fact here is not MF Global's size or financial significance, but the political power and connections of its very wealthy leader Jon Corzine. HSBC itself simply does not warrant the special treatment it received due to its significance in the American economy. The notable fact for HSBC is its massive economic resources, not its role in the US economy.

Similarly, while Breuer and DOJ may claim that undefined "collateral consequences" inhibit them from prosecuting large financial firms, those "collateral consequences" do not pertain to criminal actions against the individuals in the leadership of criminally active megabanks. DOJ has never voiced any putative policy basis for refraining from criminal prosecution of individual financial elites. Even the wealthiest banker can be jailed with only minute impact in America's $17 trillion economy. Yet no senior manager of any large bank has faced criminal indictment for any of the manifest crimes discussed in this book. Thus, the DOJ's open acknowledgment that some firms may be TBTJ does not operate to explain all of its decisions to decline prosecution, particularly individual prosecutions.

DOJ's behavior can be explained only as an exercise of discretion in favor of the most wealthy and powerful individuals in our society. All beneficiaries of the DOJ's nonprosecution policy are very wealthy and powerful financiers. The firms they preside over control tremendous resources that can fund campaigns, dispense lucrative jobs (including board positions) and speaking engagements, and be a source of patronage in plentiful ways, from corporate jet travel to the use of vacation homes to sweetheart mortgages that often lie just below the public eye. These firms, as shown, operate with an inclination toward criminality and therefore make for lucrative client relationships for any future private attorney.

If true, this explains much. For if the point is to protect the megabanks as a source of patronage and ready political networks, then the curious decisions of the SEC to grant waivers from automatic disqualifications make sense, as does the DOJ's decision to indict foreign subsidiaries instead of parent companies, as was the case in the UBS LIBOR settlement. There need not be any grand government conspiracy at work here for this fact to generally take root. Instead, all or most individuals involved in charging decisions need to consider only if their own self-interest is served by pursuing criminal charges against the most powerful individuals in our society, laden as it is with concentrated wealth at the very top. These individuals hold wealth and control wealth (through their power over megabanks) far beyond any other human (other than a handful of other megabankers).

Indeed, this one proposed explanation of DOJ policy—to indulge the most powerful—explains all of the response to the putative criminality discussed in this book. Wall Street and individual wealth has reached such a level of concentration that certain financiers now operate above the criminal law insofar as financial crimes are concerned. The government has no interest in toppling current management or fragmenting these firms regardless of criminality and long-standing law. We explore this further and offer solutions to this problem in the conclusion.

Conclusion

Looking Forward: Reimposing Law

[L]egislators cannot invent too many devices for subdividing property.
—Thomas Jefferson, 1785

Concentrated power threatens the rule of law and therefore individual liberty. If law functions only as an instrument of elite power, then the mass of citizens must suffer from a rigged legal system and economic system. Jefferson and the other founders of our nation recognized this fact and dealt with it in the political realm through a constitution that fragmented political power. Jefferson and others of his generation also recognized, however, the threats posed by the excessive concentration of economic power. When individuals control great wealth, they hold levers of power that other citizens do not and only a sturdy rule of law can ensure those powers do not spawn great social harm. Society should expect that privately wielded power will serve private not public ends. Laws should either strive to control such power to limit the harm or fragment that power, if necessary. The US Constitution both fragments and limits political power. The United States today demonstrates the need for a similar function in the economic arena.

Today the fundamental threat to individual liberty and the rule of law arises from the concentration of economic power in the hands of the very few who exercise dominion over our financial system as well as our government. As Nobel Laureate Joseph Stiglitz bluntly puts it, Wall Street exercised its "enormous influence" and resources to subvert regulation and escape accountability (Stiglitz 2015). We argue that the power of financial elites now reaches a historic watershed, corrupting justice and effecting a broad criminal immunity for financial crimes. Only fragmentation and accountability of economic power can bring it to heel before law.

The United States faces a rule of law crisis. The nation founded on the very concept that it is a nation of laws not men, and that gave meaning to that concept through the fragmentation of sovereignty and the imposition of limits on sovereignty in the form of individual rights, now allows some to act above the law and without accountability for even the most destructive crimes. Meanwhile, to underline the fact that government acts increasingly in response to power rather than any notion of sound policy, millions of young men of color are marched off to prison and ushered into the criminal justice system for petty offenses as a result of the discriminatory war on drugs (Alexander 2010). Incarceration in America today is more about power than social harm.

Identifying the problem as a power dynamic helps highlight potential solutions. We offer a series of legal innovations that could operate to restore criminal accountability in the financial sector. In the end, the problem of concentrated power and its relation to the legal system is a problem of our nation's fading rule of law. Only when the great economic and political power now held in the financial sector is reduced and brought to heel before law can any of these legal innovations take hold. The core problem is not that financial elites evaded jail—that is merely a symptom. The core problem is that financial elites dominate the law and can subvert it for profit.

Why Did the Government Fail to Enforce the Law?

The Obama administration offered two primary reasons why no criminal actions arising from megabank misconduct were ever taken. First, President Obama argued that while reprehensible conduct took place, it was not necessarily illegal. This book has assembled the best evidence available to demonstrate that many laws were broken at many, if not all, of the megabanks. Fraud, money laundering, and invasion of customer funds constitute basic criminal prohibitions that were promulgated decades before the financial crisis. A criminal jury trial would be required for a conviction, and this book certainly is no substitute for that—indeed, a key point of the book is that the public was robbed of jury trials to determine guilt for the misconduct arising from the financial crisis. Today, there simply can be no reasonable doubt that crimes occurred that materially contributed to or amplified the Great

Financial Crisis of 2008. Simply put, the misconduct that drove the crisis amounts to crimes under long-standing laws and regulations. The only remaining question is the identity of the criminals, and only a jury can determine that.

The assistant attorney general for the Criminal Division of the Department of Justice, Lanny Breuer, took the president's statement one step further in an interview with *Frontline*. His statement reveals perhaps the clearest justification yet of the DOJ's inaction: "I am personally offended by much of what I've seen. I think there was a level of greed, a level of excessive risk taking in this situation that I find abominable and I find very upsetting. But that is not what makes a criminal case. What makes a criminal case is that I can prove beyond a reasonable doubt every element of a crime" (PBS 2013b).

Breuer's reference to a legal sufficiency standard stands in contrast to the substantial publicly available evidence of fraud reviewed in this book. The DOJ has the ability to investigate even in instances where there is no criminality just to be sure none is occurring. The publicly available information from the financial crisis early on would have provided sufficient suspicion of criminality to at least open grand jury investigations against a number of the megabanks and their employees. Although at trial the prosecutor must prove the accused committed the charged crime "beyond a reasonable doubt," the standard for indicting is simply "probable cause" (DOJ 2015d). Federal grand jury proceedings are secret, but grand jury witnesses are not subject to the secrecy imposition. Given the size of the frauds and the number of persons who had some role in the financial transactions (whether knowingly fraudulent or not) and would have been called to testify about their actions, the absence of media reports or by whistleblowers of ongoing grand jury investigations suggests a failure under Breuer's leadership to even bother to investigate these transactions to check whether they went beyond personally offending Breuer. After subpoenaing and reviewing documents, hearing testimony from whistleblowers and employees, and consulting experts in the field, the DOJ would have had a full picture of the alleged frauds (or lack thereof) from which to decide whether to seek indictments, even keeping in mind the greater burden of proof required at trial. Yet, the evidence suggests willful blindness on Breuer's part to ignore the well-established available procedures to investigate potential crimes and to send a message to the financial elites that criminal acts will go unpunished and uninvestigated.

Once the grand jury process for investigating white-collar crime and the standards for such an inquiry are understood, Breuer's justification cannot explain inaction in every case involving the megabanks and their managers; it defies historical experience as well as the mountains of evidence of wrongdoing now publicly available and summarized in this book. There can be no doubt today that many prosecutions in the financial sector relating to the Great Financial Crisis of 2008 would probably succeed and lead to federal convictions. Indeed, DOJ's own website establishes that the megabanks (Bank of America, Citigroup, JPMorgan, etc.) materially misled investors in mortgage-backed securities again and again. No corporation can act except through its employees and other agents. Given the huge profits that the megabanks (and their managers) garnered from this misconduct, the likelihood that material misstatements and omissions occurred accidentally is very close to zero. In other words, some person or persons at the megabanks must have acted with the requisite intent to defraud. The DOJ findings, which the megabanks consented to, serve to belie Breuer's claim that DOJ lacked evidence to probably secure criminal convictions that some employees and managers committed these massive frauds. The multibillion-dollar settlements that DOJ obtained were structured to describe the illegal conduct or consequences without identifying the names of the individuals who committed the acts. Thus, the settlements do not amount to any admission of criminal activity by any particular individual, but they almost certainly prove that some person or persons committed criminal frauds at virtually all the megabanks.

Even beyond these multibillion-dollar settlements between DOJ and the megabanks, strong evidence exists that individuals at the megabanks knowingly participated in or acquiesced to fraud or other crimes. Virtually every case discussed herein features smoking-gun emails and other documents that directly provide insight into the state of mind of both the senders. From Richard Bowen at Citigroup to Michael Winston at Countrywide, DOJ held the advantage of willing whistleblowers ready to lay out criminal cases, to provide critical testimony and evidence, and to use as leverage against targets of criminal investigations (Taibbi 2015a).

Yet, as this book recounts, DOJ squandered these heroic individuals and left them incredulous at the government's utter inaction.

Perhaps no whistleblower exemplifies this conclusion better than JPMorgan whistleblower Alayne Fleischmann: "I think the difficulty is the country has been told that this was all an accident or there's no evidence to go forward on this. There is a mountain of evidence. There are emails. There are reports. There are external reports. There's testimony from other employees. . . . How is it possible that you can have this much fraud and not a single person has done anything criminal?" (Fleischmann 2014). While Fleischmann's statements directly arose from the JPMorgan settlement payment of $13 billion for mortgage fraud, her sentiments apply generally to the DOJ's failure to muster evidence and whistleblower testimony, as recounted in the preceding chapters.

The second reason offered for blanket nonprosecutions for crimes committed at the megabanks involves the possibility that such prosecutions could harm the economy. Under law, the DOJ is not empowered to make macroeconomic determinations behind closed doors with virtually zero institutional expertise and independent expert analysis. Looking past that point, however, the position that allowing pervasive and widespread criminality in the financial sector simply defies common sense and economic science. On some levels this point is absurd, but on others it could hold some degree of plausibility, so we address this illegitimate point in more detail.

The primary absurdity arises from the fact that criminally indicting a single individual or small group of individuals for bank or securities fraud cannot possibly harm the economy. As discussed in chapter 1, Ivan Boesky, Michael Milken, Ken Lay, and Jeff Skilling (among others) all faced criminal charges and trials and the economy did not collapse. More recently, a director of Goldman Sachs faced criminal charges for securities fraud, and his conviction and imprisonment did not in any way threaten financial stability (Van Voris 2014). In fact, upholding the rule of law in the financial sector would more likely enhance investor confidence in finance and the economy generally and thereby act to support macroeconomic growth. Thus, focusing indictments on individual actors and especially on the most egregious actors simply will not harm the economy.

On the other hand, indicting a significant number of our financial leaders at the great weight of American financial institutions could impair investor confidence for years. At some undefined point, there is a possibility that the public and the world concludes that the entire American financial sector is corrupt and unworthy of investment capital. Unfortunately, failing to enforce the rule of law and imposing accountability for crimes like bank fraud and securities fraud runs precisely the same risk to investor confidence. Allowing distorted incentives to take root in the financial sector will only amplify this risk because the lawlessness can now persist. Although mathematical proof about which approach—nonenforcement or enforcement of the rule of law—risks investor confidence more and presents a greater danger to the economy is nonexistent, there simply exists no plausible historic or economic basis for concluding that lawlessness is more economically sound. In fact, economists have shown that a sturdier rule of law is strongly associated with superior economic growth (Chen & Deakin 2015).

Furthermore, aside from economic considerations, the rule of law in the United States represents the democratic negotiation of important economic as well as noneconomic values. Congress determined long ago and reaffirmed its determination as recently as 2002, as discussed in the introduction, that criminality in finance would not be tolerated. This determination is backed by democratic outcomes over a period of decades. The law cannot be rewritten or ignored by the executive branch out of economic convenience, much less to issue indulgences to the most powerful. The legislative branch can hold public hearings and debates on changes to be made in law or regulation. That process would allow for public participation and disclosure. Legislators face reelection every two years and represent local constituencies in a manner the president does not. This represents lawmaking under the Constitution. The executive does not hold the power to vary legislative enactments out of political expediency. Congress can be held accountable to voters for any legal indulgences granted to financial elites. It has never approved indulgences of criminal immunity.

The argument that individuals cannot be criminally charged because of potential economic harm that may result is irrational. Economic harm follows from crimes, not from criminal prosecutions. Preserving the rule of law holds its own economic imperative. Arguments to the contrary should be made in the halls of Congress and the voting booth and not behind closed doors to the attorney general. Therefore it is economically, politically, and institutionally inappropriate for the executive branch to make ad hoc determinations about the economic propriety of prosecuting individuals for socially destructive crimes. Congress has already defined criminality in public statutes through a public lawmaking process.

Similar arguments pertain to claims that large financial institutions that break the law should not face criminal accountability. Gregory Gilchrist argues that bringing criminal charges against the largest banks threatens to impose externalities upon innocent and interconnected financial institutions, shareholders, and workers. More specifically, he exhaustively explores the best possible justifications to explain the inaction of the DOJ. He concludes that DOJ rightfully should consider externalities associated with bringing criminal charges that can lead to a bank failure (Gilchrist 2014). When banks fail, unsecured creditors may rush to exit the bank, triggering a bank run with all of its economic and contagion effects. That is perhaps a fair point.

Banks can be criminally prosecuted, however, in a manner that ensures that only criminal managers bear the pain of criminal sanctions. If the DOJ brings criminal sanctions in league with bank regulators, the sanctions can simply mandate the termination of all senior managers of the criminal financial institution and excise the criminal bank (or bank affiliate) from the megabank family of firms. A spin-off to shareholders of a more efficient, non–criminally managed bank would ensure no losses to innocent shareholders. Unsecured creditors would not suffer losses but would maintain their claim against a lawfully managed bank with a greater prospect of profitability. Innocent employees simply punch the clock at a new non–criminally run financial institution. Another benefit to ridding the financial sector of criminal managers and managers that allowed criminality to fester is a serious mitigation of Too-Big-to-Fail insofar as criminal megabanks and affiliates are concerned.

Notably, Gilchrist offers no new justification for nonprosecution of financial elites. Rather, he contends only that there may be some plausible justifications for why such prosecutions have not been brought. We do not differ with him on this point. Instead, we simply maintain that this is exceedingly unlikely given the evidence now available to the public regarding the crimes unearthed thus far in the financial sector, and in particular with regard to the large-scale and wide-ranging criminality that drove the global financial system off the cliff in 2008. The wholesale refusal by the DOJ to pursue criminal investigations and charges against *any* of the banks or other corporations or against *any* of the individual employees or managers who acted, directed, or failed to act belies these justifications. We have established in the prior chapters of this book that there is sufficient evidence to pursue individual indictments, at the very least.

Given the paucity of justifications offered to date for nonprosecution for financial crimes and the implausibility of those justifications applied wholesale, one can only speculate regarding the actual reasons why no prosecutions occurred against the megabanks and their personnel. These speculations run the gamut from the mundane to the alarming. One plausible but unlikely explanation supposes that the Department of Justice lacked the resources and capability to bring these cases. In fact, the DOJ did shift its focus to the war on terror after 9/11, moving 2,000 FBI agents to counterterrorism duties according to the testimony of FBI Deputy Director John Pistole (C-Span 2009). DOJ's Inspector General however found that the FBI received $196 million in additional funding for mortgage fraud. Nevertheless, it also reported that "the Federal Bureau of Investigation (FBI) Criminal Investigative Division ranked mortgage fraud as the lowest ranked criminal threat in its lowest crime category" (DOJ Inspector General 2014).

Anton Valukas offered lack of expertise at DOJ for an absence of criminal prosecutions arising from the failure of Lehman Brothers (Valukas 2012). Yet again, according to the DOJ Inspector General, the DOJ obtained nearly $60 million in additional funding between 2009 and 2011, but hired only two additional attorneys for its Criminal Division. Consequently, if the DOJ lacked the requisite expertise to bring financial fraud cases, it certainly failed to address that weakness through new hiring. Moreover, the accounting fraud prosecutions of the early 2000s wrapped up during the middle of the decade, just about the time that reports of mortgage fraud were reaching noticeable levels. Prosecutors with experience from the accounting fraud cases would have been available to pursue the bank and mortgage fraud cases.

Indeed, the DOJ in the past prosecuted Enron officers for derivatives trading, Ivan Boesky for insider trading, and Michael Milken for securities violations. The cases demanded tremendous capabilities and resources. This crisis erupted in 2008, and the DOJ has had eight years to obtain expertise and shift resources around. Consequently, if the DOJ lacked expertise and resources to try the cases discussed in this book, it is because they wanted to lack them. One need look to only the resources redirected to immigration, where large-scale detention of powerless immigrants is the new norm, over this same period to understand the fluidity of the resource limitations (Preston 2013).

Another excuse used to justify the lack of criminal prosecutions is the failed DOJ prosecution of two Bear Stearns–affiliated hedge fund managers for criminal charges brought under the Bush administration. The Bear Stearns managers were acquitted. It is well understood, however, that white-collar fraud, with its demanding requirement of proof of scienter, is more difficult to prove beyond a reasonable doubt. If the government is going to hold the most powerful and wealthy accountable under the rule of law, it will lose some cases. After all, banks and bankers have the financial resources to hire the most experienced and expensive white-collar criminal defense attorneys, many of whom served as federal prosecutors early in their careers. Unlike poor defendants who are assigned public defenders with limited time and investigative resources, the wealthy and powerful will inevitably have the means to afford top-quality, well-connected legal representation. In the past, the government has lost major cases involving the HealthSouth scandals and prosecutions against some midlevel Enron executives (Bloomberg News 2009).

Yet, these setbacks did not cause the government to close shop and decline to prosecute all well-heeled or well-connected defendants. On the contrary, particularly with respect to Enron, the Bush administration ultimately secured jury verdicts against the two senior managers of Enron—Ken Lay and Jeff Skilling. Skilling remains in prison today. These individuals reached the pinnacle of economic and political power at the turn of the century; nonetheless, they faced criminal prosecutions and convictions for their crimes. Our argument is not that the government will certainly be successful against every firm and banker it indicts. We specifically allow that the jury in a criminal trial has final say in guilt or innocence. We do not argue that any individual will be found guilty by a jury after a criminal trial. We simply argue that measured by history, evidence, and law, the government has had probable cause to indict many megabanks and some senior managers. Indeed, there will be acquittals, and under our Constitution this is appropriate; at the same time, the government would secure many convictions if it sought indictments.

The Mechanisms of Concentrated Wealth and Influence

Economists in centuries past speculated that concentrated wealth would always seek to exercise inappropriate influence over government action. Adam Smith wrote in 1776, "Whenever the legislature attempts to regulate the differences between masters and their workmen, its counsellors are always the masters." Therefore, Smith concluded that whenever the regulation favored the less powerful laborers "it is always just and equitable." On the other hand, Smith was skeptical regarding laws and regulations favoring the masters. While Smith also evinced suspicions that elites would conspire against the public, perhaps with respect to criminal sanctions he simply stands for an early articulation of cognitive capture (Smith 1776). The point is that Smith clearly spoke to the problems of concentrated economic power.

Mancur Olson wrote an influential volume titled *The Logic of Collective Action*, positing that concentrated interests would always prevail over highly diffused interests, meaning that issues relating to the general welfare would lose out to special interests because concentrated interests face fewer challenges to organize. Diffused interests will suffer from free-rider problems as actors with small stakes in an issue will be rationally apathetic. Olson suggested that this means that, in a range of issues such as war and peace or general economic growth and price stability, general benefits will lose out to the ability of more concentrated interests to impose costs on society in general while obtaining concentrated benefits for themselves (Olson 1971). Certainly, the rule of law in the context of prosecuting even the most powerful will generally benefit our entire society while the concentrated benefits of immunity for financial crimes are available only to a concentrated group of perhaps 10 to 15 large financial institutions and a handful of powerful and politically connected financiers like Jon Corzine at smaller financial institutions.

More modern giants of economics today posit that high inequality is bound to lead to a more unjust legal system. Nobel Laureate Joseph Stiglitz maintains that today in America the rule of law suffers to such an extent from inequality that only the wealthiest can use the legal system to protect their rights (Stiglitz 2012). More recently, Stiglitz observed that the legal system suffers gross distortions from the influence of the megabanks, as the banks used their power and money to abuse the legal system (Stiglitz 2015). This book seeks merely to extend that insight to the realm of criminal prosecutions of financial elites within the mega-banks and beyond for the truly politically connected with the financial wherewithal to gain or maintain those connections.

Building upon these key insights, economists have empirically investigated the links between high economic inequality and the rule of law and found that higher inequality leads to a weaker rule of law. Edward L. Glaeser and Andrei Schleifer investigated the transition economies of the former Soviet Bloc in the 1990s and the US economy during the Gilded Age. They also tested their theory transnationally by regressing the effect of inequality on the rule of law. They found that a constructed rule of law index suffered in both instances under the weight of high economic inequality (Glaeser & Schleifer 2003). Since high inequality naturally leads to more resources in fewer hands, this work vindicates Olson's theory that more concentrated wealth leads to more political success at the cost of the general economy.

Whether viewed through the lens of cognitive capture or soaring inequality or both, the facts presented herein suggest that the criminal prosecution function at the federal level has been subverted by elite influence. Perhaps, however, other facts can shed light on the precise mechanisms at work in the government's response to the manifest criminality that drove all aspects of the subprime debacle. Since the crisis subsided, new insights suggest that our theory of elite subversion rests on a sound foundation, separate and apart from the facts reviewed in earlier chapters that tended to show that in particular cases the government should have pursued more criminal indictments.

For example, Ronald Suskind reported in *Confidence Men* that on March 27, 2009, when President Obama met with the CEOs of all the major megabanks, he stated to them that "I'm not out there to go after you. I'm protecting you." This seems to have foreshadowed a commitment by the administration to avoid pursuing criminal actions. Suskind portrays a fundamentally pro–Wall Street attitude within the administration that would further support a lack of interest in criminal prosecutions. Key members of the administration benefited from close connections with Wall Street, particularly its economic team. Chief of Staff Rahm Emanuel, Chair of the Council of Economic Advisers Larry Summers, and Secretary of the Treasury Timothy Geithner each held deep connections to Wall Street, and Summers and Emanuel earned millions directly from big finance. Obama's top source of contributions for his 2008 presidential campaign was the financial sector (Suskind 2011). These connections would logically color the perceptions of the Obama administration.

Furthermore, the wealth and power of the megabanks and their managers also influence the conduct of those in government at all levels. For example, former SEC Senior Trial Attorney James Kidney attributed the agency's often docile conduct to the fact that many SEC staffers wish to ultimately work for Wall Street banks or represent them as attorneys: "The revolving door is a very serious problem. I have had bosses, and bosses of my bosses, whose names we all know, who made little secret that they were here to punch their ticket. They mouthed serious regard for the mission of the Commission, but their actions were tentative and fearful in many instances." Kidney also stated that the SEC spends too much time and money on relatively powerless defendants and is very risk averse when investigating and enforcing the federal securities laws against the most wealthy. According to Kidney, "for the powerful, we are at most a tollbooth on the bankster turnpike" (Kidney 2014).

Kidney's diagnosis of lethargy at the SEC fits well with the facts. The SEC enforcement chief, Robert Khuzami, left and ended up in a $5-million-per-year job at corporate law firm Kirkland & Ellis, which represents Wall Street behemoths such as Morgan Stanley, UBS, American Express, and Bank of America. The problem transcends the SEC.

Lanny Breuer, the head of the Criminal Division of the Department of Justice, left the DOJ to return to his old firm Covington & Burling, where he now makes $4 million a year as the firm's vice chair. Covington also represents many of the Wall Street firms Breuer failed to prosecute. Geithner is now president at Warburg Pincus, a giant Wall Street fund manager. Former SEC Chair Mary Schapiro now sits on the board of industrial and financial giant General Electric, a firm that had been subject to SEC inquiry during her tenure. Virtually every Obama administration senior economic adviser or financial regulator has landed a lucrative Wall Street position, serving the interests of the very firms they supposedly regulated as public servants (Chittum 2013). Of course, the revolving door is not by any means a new problem. But high inequality and consolidation in the financial sector have heightened these influences.

A high-profile example involves former Treasury Secretary Robert Rubin. While working at the Clinton administration he ushered in a brave new world of megabanks by shepherding through the repeal of the Glass-Steagall Act—which since the Great Depression had mandated the separation of investment banking from commercial banking. After leaving the government he joined Citigroup as chair of the Executive Committee, with no operational responsibilities. Citigroup in particular needed the act's repeal to allow it to maintain its otherwise unlawful acquisition of another financial conglomerate that included an investment bank. Rubin also played a key role in championing derivatives deregulation. Ultimately, Rubin became chairman of the board of Citigroup. Over a period of 10 years he raked in $126 million from Citigroup. Meanwhile Citigroup shareholders suffered massive losses in derivative speculation and beyond, and the government expended billions in bailouts as a result of its bid to be the biggest megabank (Schwartz & Dash 2008).

The problem of elite influence and high inequality pervades the American political system and both political parties. Republican Senator Phil Gramm led the charge to deregulate Wall Street and ended up as vice chairman of the board of UBS. Although he retired from UBS in 2012, he remained a consultant to the firm (Tadena 2012). He has stated that he considers Wall Street "a holy place" and subprime lending "the American dream in action." His compensation at UBS is not disclosed publicly, and he declines to discuss it (Lipton & Labaton 2008).

Speaking fees are another notorious source of Wall Street influence. For example, Wall Street firms hired former President Bill Clinton to speak on 102 occasions. Wall Street is Clinton's most frequent patron. According to the *Washington Post* Wall Street banks and other financial services firms paid him a total of $19.6 million (Rucker et al. 2014). Hillary Clinton also garners significant fees, including a $400,000 payment for two speaking engagements funded by Goldman Sachs (Torres 2013). Secretary of the Treasury Lawrence Summers left the government in 2000 and over a period of eight years increased his net worth by a factor of 8. Not only did he garner $5.8 million consulting for a hedge fund, but he also cashed in to the tune of $2.8 million in speaking fees at firms such as Goldman Sachs and Citigroup (Benson 2013). Wall Street elites are unlikely to pay such sums to hear speakers advocating against their interests or in favor of more indictments of bankers.

Many banks under criminal or regulatory cloud also funded President Clinton's foundation and its key project, the Clinton Global Initiative. According to *CNN* at least six banks that were under scrutiny or fined by government agencies and regulators acted as co-sponsors of the annual meeting of the Clinton Global Initiative. Co-sponsorships reportedly require contributions of $250,000 per annum. A few of these banks, including British bank Standard Chartered, Goldman Sachs, and Germany's Deutsche Bank, support the foundation perennially. HSBC signed on for the highest level of support in 2014—while the statute of limitations on its money laundering ticked apace. All of the banks have what *CNN* termed a "pockmarked past." It is unknown if the banks funded the private foundation beyond these expenditures (Jaffe 2015). Given the leadership of the Clinton family in the Democratic Party and Hillary Clinton's presidential campaign in 2016, these expenditures certainly make sense if these banks would like access and influence over the next Democratic administration and its policies on criminal prosecutions.

Campaign contributions and lobbying expenses also must factor into the analysis. According to the Center for Responsive Politics the financial sector outpaced all others (by far) during the 2013–2014 election cycle, giving over $498 million in campaign contributions. The financial sector also spent a mind-boggling $6.4 billion in lobbying our representatives between 1998 and 2014 (Center for Responsive Politics 2015b & 2015c). More recently, Reuters reported that certain megabanks threatened to withhold funding from the entire Democratic caucus of the US Senate due to the antibank rhetoric of Senators Elizabeth Warren and Sherrod Brown (Flitter 2015). Thus, politicians taking on the Wall Street banks, by advocating for example that the DOJ enforce the criminal law against them, risk alienating not only the banks but also their entire party establishment, which is dependent upon large campaign contributions to fund the ever-increasing costs of a federal election campaign.

Consider the totality of methods available to those controlling great wealth if they desire to influence lawmakers and regulators. The Clinton family illustrates this point well, although, to be fair, they simply mastered the game that virtually all politicians play. The Center for Responsive Politics and the *Wall Street Journal* partnered to tally the total amount of money the Clintons had raised since 1992. They tallied (1) speaking fees paid to the former president; (2) contributions to President Clinton's 1992 and 1996 presidential campaigns; (3) contributions to the Democratic National Committee during Mr. Clinton's eight years in the White House; (4) Mrs. Clinton's bids for Senate and president; and (5) payments to the Bill, Hillary and Chelsea Clinton Foundation. They concluded that the Clintons raised somewhere between $2 billion and $3 billion from these sources. The communications industry and the financial services industry vie for the top sources of Clinton family patronage (Mullins et al. 2014). The need for enormous amounts of funding is simply a fact of life for most successful politicians.

In addition, the *Citizens United* decision by the Supreme Court creates another more shadowy channel of influence for the megabanks. In *Citizens United*, the Supreme Court reversed two of its prior decisions and greatly expanded the ability of corporations to influence elections through independent electioneering expenditures. The Court's decision paved the way for CEOs to support their political causes regardless of the views of shareholders and without even disclosing to shareholders the nature and extent of such activities. As a result, this case gave financial elites the ability to contribute "dark money" to favored candidates and against the election of disfavored candidates. It is impossible to know how much dark money emanates from the Wall Street banks. According to election law expert Richard Hasen, "[i]ncreasingly, large sums contributed by the wealthy affect who wins elections and what the winners do once in office" (Hasen 2012).

High inequality means more wealth in fewer hands. That necessarily implies that more opportunities for cost-effective "investments" in campaign contributions, lobbying efforts, and other mechanisms of influence peddling will be fully exploited by wealthy elites. Furthermore, the sheer size of the megabanks means that the CEOs of these firms may enlist shareholder wealth to further the political goals of the CEO even if they are to the long-run detriment of the shareholders. Because the megabanks are larger than ever, this necessarily means that the CEOs command more wealth, which translates into more political power than ever. JPMorgan Chase, for example, holds assets totaling more than $2.5 trillion, up 29 percent since the financial crisis (Cox 2015b). For an entity of this magnitude, hiring former government officials and bankrolling campaigns even to the tune of hundreds of millions of dollars is simply a cost of doing business with little financial impact on the firm's overall business expenses.

Personal fortunes may also fund political patronage. Wealth concentration in the United States now stands at a historic 100-year high. "In 2012, the top 0.01% wealth share (fortunes of more than $110 million dollars belonging to the richest 16,000 families) is 11.2%, as much as in 1916 and more than in 1929." This wealth concentration arises from a recent and historic concentration of income in the United States (Saez 2016). As Thomas Picketty demonstrates in his recent book *Capital in the Twenty-First Century*, the top 0.1 percent of Americans now control more income than ever before, and this group is disproportionately dominated by financial and corporate elites who have exploited weak corporate governance law and regulation to essentially set their own salaries (Picketty 2014). The upshot of this gaping inequality is that more wealth is concentrated in fewer hands than at virtually any other time in recorded US history.

The combination of runaway CEO compensation and expanding megabanks may well best explain the government's disinclination to prosecute financial elites. Proof of this point may never reach certainty. Yet the facts seem compelling. The megabanks have never been larger than today, and America's income has never been more concentrated than today. Economists predict that this economic concentration adversely undermines the rule of law. The facts reviewed in prior chapters show a historic breakdown in the rule of law with respect to manifest criminality in the financial sector. The law now operates to allow more influence peddling and less transparency influence peddling than ever before, given the ability of corporations to influence elections without limitations.

When financial elites hold and control such vast wealth that they can offer multimillion-dollar jobs to policy makers and regulators, the rule of law is bound to suffer. They also hold the power to place the cronies, friends, and business associates of influential government representatives in high government positions. In addition, they can influence campaigns and the legislative process through campaign contributions and lobbying expenditures. Citizens should expect under these conditions that ultimately power will be exercised to undermine criminal accountability for financial crimes. The money flows only in favor of nonprosecution, and regulators and legislators will no doubt be tempted to change their behavior when they perceive that others have cashed in on catering to the interests of the Wall Street powerbrokers. When more wealth becomes more concentrated in fewer hands, politicians will naturally find it easier and more convenient to serve the interests of the wealthy over the general welfare and will actually seek out such interests to serve (McCaffery & Cohen 2004). This book merely catalogues the mechanics of this process in the financial sector with respect to criminal prosecutions.

In our view, the puzzle now appears complete. The perverse incentives in place at the megabanks naturally encourage more risky behavior that bleeds directly into criminality, as discussed in the introduction. Politicians and regulators at some point discovered that the enlarging aggregations of money within the megabanks created favorable opportunities for patronage for themselves and their networks. Highly concentrated wealth lowered transaction costs for political organizations—for an aspiring politician the concentrated wealth of the megabanks created overwhelming temptations for political partnering. Revolving doors between government and the megabanks led to cognitive capture. And so the final puzzle piece is derived: a new economic royalty rose above the criminal law for financial crimes. The megabanks may create havoc on our economy and financial sector without fear of prosecution. This explanation seems far more compelling than the story offered by the government for its unprecedented wholesale inaction to widespread, catastrophic criminality.

We do not purport to explain every exercise of prosecutorial discretion since the financial crisis. Explaining such decisions coast to coast and across agencies would be impossible. Our point is simply that incentives and disincentives now in place on a systemic basis tip the balance of the scales of justice in favor of the financial elites atop the megabanks. Justice is no longer blind on Wall Street, and there is a thumb on the scale with the fingerprint of elite influence.

Economic theory, the experience with respect to criminality during the crisis, and the experience since the crisis all line up to support this central point.

Reimposing Law on Financial Elites

In an area as important as finance, law and regulation must deter the criminal acts of even the most powerful. Society now faces the risk that law and regulation will continue to be distorted so that the richest and most powerful garner outsized compensation payments for fraud and similar misconduct while imposing crushing losses on the economy and their fellow citizens. We offer a series of solutions to the current lawlessness plaguing the financial sector and the US economy today.

A Corporate Fraud Division

First, white-collar criminal prosecutions frequently expose the most powerful individuals in our society to harsh criminal sanctions. Given the power of these individuals, accountability for financial and corporate elites can best be secured through a more independent and politically insulated criminal prosecution function for financial crimes and crimes involving publicly held firms. Today in America the road to power and wealth runs through the financial sector and publicly held firms. Many of our richest and most powerful citizens now command huge megabanks or achieved huge payoffs from acting as stewards of pubic firms. The economic and political might of these firms requires now more than ever that they adhere to basic criminal constraints. The answer to holding such concentrated power criminally accountable is a depoliticized criminal prosecution function for the corporate and financial elites.

The DOJ should create a separate division dedicated to investigating and prosecuting financial crimes committed by large public firms (Ramirez 2010). This independent unit of the DOJ would exercise autonomy over major white-collar cases from the grand jury investigation through appeal to the US Supreme Court. Just as the DOJ has divisions dedicated to identifiable legal specialties such as National Security, Antitrust Law, Environmental Law, and Tax Law, for example, specialization would shift responsibility to attorneys specifically taxed with investigating and prosecuting, as well as overseeing DOJ policy in this sensitive area. The newest division, the National Security Division, was added after the 9/11 attacks to address heightened concerns about legal cases and policy impacting or impacted by national security issues. As the financial crisis demonstrated, financial crimes by multinational publicly held companies can have devastating economic implications in the United States and abroad and can put both the economy as well as national security at risk.

The Corporate Fraud Division (as it might be called) would collect expertise in a single division drawing its litigation team from experienced criminal prosecutors and financial fraud experts, including forensic accountants and tax experts who could aid in both locating fraud and assessing financial information concealing fraud. Over time expertise would strengthen and provide early intervention to investigate newly identified financial threats. The FBI had indications of mortgage fraud as early as 2004 (Frieden 2004). Had such a division been available at that time, criminal investigations and prosecutions could have communicated to others engaging in criminality to abandon such fraudulent schemes, rather than double down to loan under even riskier circumstances in 2006 and 2007.

A Corporate Fraud Division could better coordinate the DOJ's approach to such frauds while centralizing decision making away from political influence. The division would routinely coordinate among investigating agencies, handle cases that straddle more than one jurisdiction, and use its expertise to train prosecutors across the country. Moreover, the division could coordinate with the regulatory agencies overseeing such firms (whether financial institutions or others) to craft meaningful remedies or punishments that would protect the interests of investors, creditors, and employees, while implementing effective changes in corporate leadership, firm structure, and business culture. This division would pull prosecutorial assessments away from the most politically attuned in the DOJ and toward experienced, career DOJ attorneys committed to the rule of law through the pursuit of justice. The division would not have exclusive jurisdiction over such cases, so that a local US attorney's office could still investigate and prosecute such a case.

Eliminating Nonprosecution Agreements

As discussed in chapter 1, the DOJ has come to rely upon deferred prosecution agreements (DPAs) and nonprosecution agreements (NPAs) as a means to avoid the dichotomous choice of either civil or criminal prosecution. Both processes allow the defendant to avoid a full criminal prosecution through a negotiated agreement that will cut off prosecution provided the defendant complies with the agreement. The key distinction between DPAs and NPAs is judicial oversight. With a DPA, criminal charges are filed with a court, as is the related agreement, and the court retains supervisory power over its implementation. Timing is keyed to the court, and at the expiration of the agreement charges are affirmatively dismissed. The agreement is thus given judicial scrutiny and is timed to create a reason to review compliance before dismissal of charges. In contrast, an NPA does not include court oversight because no charges are filed at the outset and no agreement is filed with the court. Charges would be filed only if the DOJ finds noncompliance. Negotiation, agreement, and compliance review all occur behind the scenes. Sheltering the agreement from public review eliminates the opportunity to discourage sweetheart deals for firms that have engaged in substantial criminal conduct or that have already received the benefit of deferred prosecution for crimes identified previously. Eliminating NPAs would bring greater transparency to this alternative to immediate prosecution.

While DPAs typically set terms for reform in addition to agreements for fines and restitution, scheduled reviews of compliance should be made a standard part of the agreements to further transparency. In the HSBC DPA order, the court directed the parties to file quarterly reports keeping it apprised of all significant developments (DOJ 2013b). The DPAs should explicitly mandate 6- to 12-month reviews and reports (depending upon the overall length of the DPA) to inform the court and the public regarding the firm's overall progress, and also remind the firm and its monitor of the DOJ's option to prosecute if reform is unsatisfactory. In many instances monitors are tasked with assisting reform efforts and reviewing reform mechanisms.

Rather than simply dispensing DPAs to favored firms, meaningful reform should be the goal of the DPA. At least a year before the agreed DPA termination date, such a review should require inquiry by any regulatory agencies tasked with overseeing the firm's industry to confirm the company is in good standing. Such inquiry is particularly relevant to areas of activity where the firm has breached the law in the recent past, especially illegality identified in the DPA as justifying the DPA. These measures would ensure the public not only that the court will be informed when the termination date has arrived, but also that the corporate culture has truly been reformed.

An Expanded Corporate Death Penalty for Criminal Financial Institutions

Another means of restoring legal accountability for financial elites would be to break up the megabanks. The great weight of wrongdoing identified in this book has occurred within a handful of the largest banks in the nation. Moreover, aside from the megabanks, the government did pursue criminal wrongdoing at large banks and regional banks. Willingness to forgo prosecution of the megabanks appears to be tied to their control of such vast wealth that they alone apparently hold enough economic power to convince the US attorney general that economic stability requires that they operate above the law.

The Dodd-Frank Act attempted to scale back the Too-Big-to-Fail banks and to address the array of problems they presented at the time President Obama signed the act into law. No lawmaker at that time could have imagined that the banks had grown so powerful and influential that they no longer needed to fear criminal sanctions for financial crimes as demonstrated in this book. The reality that these megabanks now appear too big to jail adds further weight to the policy of breaking up these banks by any means necessary. The lawlessness described in this book is centered nearly entirely in the megabanks, but the tentacles of lawlessness bred corruption.

Congress should amend the Dodd-Frank Act to make it easier and more common to break up large banks and other systemically important firms—especially if regulators or the DOJ finds violations of key financial laws such as money laundering, consumer protection laws and regulations, or securities or bank fraud. These are systemically important laws and regulations. High-profile violations directly undermine investor confidence. Moreover, pervasive violations of such laws contribute to and propagate financial crises and accompanying economic disruptions. The Dodd-Frank Act gave the government the power to break up the megabanks in vary narrow circumstances. As discussed in prior chapters the financial regulators also currently hold power to force the corporate death penalty onto criminal megabanks. The same political realities that infect prosecutorial decisions, however, also hold sway over regulatory decisions.

The powers to break up financial institutions should be greatly expanded with respect to criminal megabanks. Indeed, when a high level of criminality is shown to have occurred within a bank of sufficient size, Congress should *mandate* that it be fragmented into smaller firms. Congress should delegate the power to promulgate regulations for mandated breakups to an appropriate regulatory body. The content of such regulations is beyond the scope of this book. The mandate should be tailored in a manner that captures the most egregious misconduct.

It is important to understand the losers and winners from an expanded corporate death penalty in the financial sector. There is overwhelming evidence that the megabanks are too big to manage and enjoy no operating efficiencies due to their size. They exist as a result not of economic logic but of the significant subsidies a government guarantee against failure gives to the banks in terms of their cost of capital. Basically creditors will lend the banks more money at a lower cost due to the perception that the government will back the banks and not permit them to default on their debts. Our proposal for a corporate death penalty for criminal financial institutions would end this subsidy by fragmenting the banks into smaller constituent firms that would lose the perception of government backing. Loss of this perception would mean that bankers would need to invest more prudently and that less extreme risk taking would occur.

Shareholders would probably suffer little to no loss. The Too-Big-to-Fail banks do not outperform smaller banks. Shareholders would receive shares in the new, more efficient and competitive smaller firms and would also benefit from the lower likelihood of criminality. As shown throughout these pages the megabanks enjoy some degree of implied criminal immunity that naturally diminishes disincentives to follow the law. More criminality follows as a matter of economic logic. Yet, under the current approach the government imposes monetary fines on the banks and not the managers. Those fines are paid from general corporate funds, meaning shareholder wealth.

Managers would lose big. Those directly implicated in fraud or mismanagement would be fired, as would those who failed to act to stop wrongdoing. Others, based upon their performance, could hope to remain employed at a much smaller firm. The government could require their termination and even forfeiture of all deferred compensation. They could also be required to disgorge past compensation rooted in criminal misconduct. Moreover, their reputation would suffer the taint of having steered their firm into dismemberment. Managers could expect to be the major losers from the corporate death penalty.

Employees would also suffer little. Breaking up the firm and terminating its senior managers would create major promotion possibilities for innocent employees. Each new division would need a new management team. Some jobs would be eliminated, but others would require new staffing. In the end, if the broken-up firm is more competitive and efficient than the megabank, employees would enjoy better economic prospects over the long term.

Restoring the Rule of Law through Electoral Engagement

The disruption in the financial sector due to the lawlessness of a narrow group of financial elites and the failure to prosecute the perpetrators has social meaning (M. Ramirez 2013). It conveys government-sponsored premium value attached to the rights and liberties of the elite that can create apathy, stimulate public engagement, or instigate rebellion in the citizens who do not enjoy these endowments. Apathy allows the value gulf to widen as the narrow interests of the elites continue to press their advantage, and rebellion unleashes uncertainty and instability that few would want to impose upon themselves or their children. Engaged citizens exercising their fundamental right to vote, however, can alter the course of a country.

The ultimate solution to the problem of lawlessness in the financial sector lies in the determination of the voting public to prioritize the re-imposition of the rule of law upon even the wealthiest and most power-ful among us. This means setting aside other issues that create partisan divides among voters to vindicate the rule of law, which enjoys almost universal support. Virtually no voter would vote for candidates espous-ing lawlessness in the financial sector. Nevertheless, voters thus far have not demanded that elected representatives focus first and foremost on reimposing the rule of law in the financial sector. In fact, voter apathy on this point essentially facilitates an unspoken, bipartisan consensus that criminal prosecution of financial elites is not required and thus inconvenient.

Of course, voters are typically neither lawyers nor economists. As such, most understandably struggle to fully understand the inner work-ings of the legal system and white-collar crime prosecutions. This book maintains that the government's explanation for the lack of prosecu-tions is incoherent and unprincipled. From a historic point of view, the lack of prosecutions is also inexplicable. Based upon the best evidence summarized in this book, grand juries should have been convened and indictments should have been pursued so that juries could evaluate the evidence under the scope of criminal trials. While it is impossible to pre-dict whether any particular jury would have found any particular indi-vidual guilty of any crime, history strongly suggests that the government could have made the evidence accessible to juries yielding more convic-tions than acquittals, as they did in the aftermath of Enron scandal and the savings and loan scandal. The government's failure to pursue *any* of the manifest criminal misconduct amounts to a historic breakdown in the rule of law without any colorable justification.

Lawlessness always exacts exorbitant costs. Much of the Great Finan-cial Crisis owes its cause to the ability of financial elites to rig our econ-omy in their favor. More than anything else the crisis arose from their ability to use their resources to free themselves from legal and regulatory constraints of laws and achieve windfall compensation payments while imposing massive costs on the economy generally. Prior to the crisis, however, they could not be certain that their power would mean an un-precedented immunity for massive financial crimes. Today elites have precisely that certainty. Consequently, incentives are even more dis-torted than they were prior to the crisis. The postcrisis cases discussed in chapter 7 uncover that distortion.

The message to financial elites is that fraud and other financial crimes pay. After the failure to prosecute crimes, incentives now exert more power than ever to achieve gains through fraud and crime. Given this deterioration in the rule of law, we should expect more costly and more frequent frauds and financial crimes. The megabanks are after all larger than ever, which suggests they can inflict more economic harm than ever before. While the Dodd-Frank Act mitigated some risks in the banking sector, it did not resolve Too-Big-to-Fail nor in any way alter the incentives and disincentives facing a would-be fraudfeasor or white-collar criminal working at a megabank in any meaningful way.

Yet, fraud drove every element of the Great Financial Crisis. And the cost staggers the imagination. The government puts the cost of the crisis at $20 trillion and counting. Even this figure is misleading, as it fails to account for the huge number of foreclosures that followed in its wake or the families forced out of their homes and the children who had to transfer schools. How does one reduce the increased suicides associated with foreclosures to a monetary figure? A similar accounting difficulty arises from the fact that huge profits flowed into the pockets of the richest and most powerful while the most disempowered suffered the greatest losses. A massive transfer of wealth occurred from the middle class and the disempowered to the most powerful. Much wealth was destroyed along the way as dead weight losses accompanied the transfers.

The transfer reallocated wealth from the most needy to the least needy. The crisis pushed childhood poverty in minority communities to nearly 40 percent and wiped out much of the previously meager household wealth in minority communities. The damage from this fiasco to American families and their highest hopes and dreams—from college education to a comfortable retirement—cannot be quantified. Few Americans escaped the losses from the financial crisis that disempowered these families from reaching their full economic potential and will thereby continue to impose losses for years to come.

The winners and losers from the Great Financial Crisis reflect the underlying power imbalances and disparities that drove all elements of the crisis. When one small group of elites dominates law and regulation, they will rationally use that power to entrench and enrich themselves regardless of the costs to society at large. Viewed from this perspective, the failure to pursue criminal charges is symptomatic of a deeper malady—

the fact that now economic and political power is dangerously concentrated in a few hands in America. The lack of criminal accountability in the wake of such a devastating crisis proves the extent of the concentration of power. Just a few short years ago it was unthinkable that a small cadre of elites would enjoy immunity for such massive financial crimes. The financial crisis suggests that the costs of this new lawlessness are tremendous.

In the end, it is up to the voters in the United States to reimpose the rule of law upon financial elites. The election of 2016 should turn on which candidate evidences the greatest commitment to halting the implied immunity for lawlessness and the transfers of wealth and power corresponding to such lawlessness. Despite the lack of an aggressive effort by the DOJ to investigate, we have substantial evidence about the financial crimes perpetrated on the American public and economy. A commitment to prosecute responsible parties who brought about the financial crisis and continue today untouched by the worst of the crisis, without accountability and often in powerful positions, would certainly be a step toward restoring the rule of law for all. If the voting public remains apathetic to the government's response to such massive and destructive criminality at the heart of the economy, then they will suffer the consequences of living in a lawless economy. If on the other hand they demand a rule of law applicable to all economic actors, then proper economic incentives can be restored and power can be fragmented under law as the most lawless megabanks are broken up. The American people will ultimately get the rule of law they demand.

BIBLIOGRAPHY

ABBREVIATIONS

AIG: American International Group

AU: Auditing Standards, American Institute of Certified Public Accountants

CFTC: US Commodity Futures Trading Commission

DOJ: US Department of Justice

FBI: Federal Bureau of Investigation

FCIC: Financial Crisis Inquiry Commission

FDIC: Federal Deposit Insurance Corporation

SEC: Securities and Exchange Commission

SOURCES

60 Minutes. 2011. "Prosecuting Wall Street" (December 5). www.cbsnews.com.

Aaron, Kat. 2009. "Obama Top Recipient of AIG's Hefty Campaign Contributions." Center for Public Integrity (March 30). www.publicintegrity.org.

Abu Dhabi Commercial Bank v. Morgan Stanley & Co. Inc., 888 F. Supp. 2d 431 (SDNY 2012). http://dealbreaker.com.

Alexander, Michelle. 2010. *The New Jim Crow*. New York: New Press.

Ambinder, Marc. 2002. "WorldCom Directed Money to Democrats, GOP." *ABC News* (June 26). http://abcnews.go.com.

American Banker. 2013. "Transcript: Attorney General Eric Holder on 'Too Big to Jail.'" *American Banker* (March 6). www.americanbanker.com.

AIG. 2006. "Form 10-K Fiscal Year Ended December 31, 2005" (March 16). www.aig.com.

———. 2007. "Form 10-K Fiscal Year Ended December 31, 2006" (March 1). www.aig.com.

———. 2008a. "Form 8-K" (February 11). www.sec.gov.

———. 2008b. "Form 10-K" (February 28). www.aig.com.

———. 2014. "Form 10-Q" (August 4). http://services.corporate-ir.net.

Andrews, Edmund & Baker, Peter. 2009. "A.I.G. Planning Huge Bonuses after $170 Billion Bailout." *New York Times* (March 14). www.nytimes.com.

Angelides, Philip. 2016a. "Interview with Ben McLannahan." *Financial Times* (February 9). http://podcast.ft.com.

———. 2016b. "Last Chance for Justice." *Huffington Post* (February 1). www.huffington-post.com.

Armour, Stephanie & Raice, Shayndi. 2014. "Citi Alumni Are Force in Nation's Capital." *Wall Street Journal* (February 25). www.wsj.com.

Arthur Andersen LLP v. United States, 544 U.S. 696, 699 n.2 (2005).

Associated Press. 2002. "Enron Biggest Contributor to Bush." *Enquirer* (January 13). http://enquirer.com/editions/2002/01/13/fin_enron_biggest.html.

Atkinson, Tyler, et al. 2013. "How Bad Was It? The Costs and Consequences of the 2007–09 Financial Crisis." *Dallas Fed Staff Papers* (July). https://dallasfed.org.

AU 411.04. Public Company Accounting Oversight Board. http://pcaobus.org.

AU 431. Public Company Accounting Oversight Board. http://pcaobus.org.

Bair, Sheila. 2012. "Why It's Time to Break Up the 'Too Big to Fail Banks.'" *Fortune* (January 18). http://fortune.com.

Bajaj, Vikas & Eichenwald, Kurt. 2006. "Kenneth L. Lay, 64, Enron Founder and Symbol of Corporate Excess, Dies." *New York Times* (July 6). www.nytimes.com.

Barrett, Devlin & Perez, Evan. 2012. "HSBC to Pay Record U.S. Penalty." *Wall Street Journal* (December 11). http://online.wsj.com.

BBC News. 2006. "Enron Ex-chief Kenneth Lay Dies" (July 5). http://news.bbc.co.uk.

Bebchuk, Lucian, Cohen, Alma, & Spamman, Holger. 2010. "The Wages of Failure: Executive Compensation at Bear Stearns and Lehman 2000–2008." *Yale Journal on Regulation* 27:257–282.

Beckel, Michael. 2011. "Looking Back at the Political Past of Former AIG Executive Joseph Cassano, Financial Crisis' 'Patient Zero.'" Center for Responsive Politics (February 28). www.opensecrets.org.

Benson, Clea. 2013. "Summers after Government Saw Wealth Surge to $7 Million." *Bloomberg* (August 2). www.bloomberg.com.

Bernanke, Ben. 2009. "Testimony: The Federal Budget and the Economy." *C-SPAN* (March 3). www.c-span.org.

———. 2015. "Ben Bernanke: More Execs Should Have Gone to Jail for Causing Great Recession." *USA Today* (November 15). www.usatoday.com.

Bialosky, Bruce. 2013. "How a Top Obama Bundler Broke a Never-Broken Law of Commodities Trading." *National Review* (February 5). www.nationalreview.com.

Bilderberg Group. 2015. "Former Steering Committee Members." www.bilderbergmeet-ings.org.

Black, William. 2005. *The Best Way to Rob a Bank Is to Own One*. Austin: University of Texas Press.

———. 2013a. "Hundreds of Wall Street Execs Went to Prison during the Last Fraud-Fueled Bank Crisis." *Moyers & Company* (September 17). http://billmoy-ers.com.

———. 2013b. "Which Aspect of the FDIC's Litigation Failures Is the Most Embarrassing and Damaging?" *New Economic Perspectives* (March 12). http://neweconom-icperspectives.org.

———. 2014. "AG Holder: The U.S. Announces the Indictment of Citigroup's Senior Officers for Fraud." *New Economic Perspectives* (July 21). http://neweconomicperspectives.org.

———. 2015. "LIBOR: History's Largest Financial Crime that the WSJ and NYT Would Like You to Forget." *New Economic Perspectives* (July 15). http://neweconomicperspectives.org.

———. 2016. "DOJ Ignores Citi's Elite Criminals: Wins Whistleblowers' 4th Lemons Award." *Huffington Post* (April 8). www.huffingtonpost.com.

Black, William & Wray, Randall. 2010. "Foreclose on the Foreclosure Fraudsters, Part 1: Put Bank of America in Receivership." *Huffington Post* (October 22). www.huffingtonpost.com.

Bloomberg News. 2009. "Bear Stearns Acquittals Latest in String of Losses for Feds." *Chron* (November 12). www.chron.com.

Bowen, Richard M., III. 2010. "Testimony of Richard M. Bowen, III, Presented to the Financial Crisis Inquiry Commission Hearing on Subprime Lending and Securitization and Government Sponsored Enterprises." Financial Crisis Inquiry Commission (April 7). http://fcic-static.law.stanford.edu.

Boyer, Peter. 2012. "Why Can't Obama Bring Wall Street to Justice?" *Newsweek* (May 6). www.newsweek.com.

Breuer, Lanny. 2012. "Speech by Assistant Attorney General to the New York City Bar Association." *Justice.gov* (September 13). www.justice.gov.

Brown, Nick. 2013. "Ernst & Young to Pay $99 Million to End Lehman Investor Lawsuit." Reuters (October 18). www.reuters.com.

Brown, Sherrod & Grassley, Charles. 2013. "Letter to Eric Holder, U.S. Attorney General" (January 29). www.grassley.senate.gov.

Buell, Samuel. 2011. "What Is Securities Fraud?" *Duke Law Journal* 61:511–581.Calkins, Laurel. 2013. "Enron's Skilling to Leave Prison in 2017 as Sentence Cut." *Bloomberg* (June 22). www.bloomberg.com.

Carpenter, David H., Murphy, Edward V., Murphy, M. Maureen. 2016. "The Glass-Steagall Act: A Legal and Policy Analysis." Congressional Research Service (January 19). www.fas.org.

Carter, Zach & Nasiripour, Shahien. 2014. "The Fed Just Acknowledged Its Too Big to Jail Policy." *Huffington Post* (November 21). www.huffingtonpost.com.

Cassidy, John. 2014. "Why Didn't Eric Holder Go after the Bankers?" *New Yorker* (September 26). www.newyorker.com.

Catan, Thomas & Efreti, Amir. 2010. "A Set of Scribbled Notes Helped Scuttle AIG Probe." *Wall Street Journal* (July 22). www.wsj.com.

CBS Nightly News. 2010. "Goldman Sachs' Revolving Door" (April 8). www.cbsnews.com.

CCP Research Foundation. 2015. "Conduct Costs Project." conductcosts.ccpresearchfoundation.com.

Center for Public Integrity. 2004. "Who Bankrolls Bush and His Democratic Rivals?" (January 8). www.publicintegrity.org.

———. 2014. "No. 1 of the Subprime 25: Countrywide Financial Corp" (May 19). www. publicintegrity.org.

Center for Responsive Politics. 2015a. "Citigroup Inc.: Profile for 2012 Election Cycle." *OpenSecrets.org*. www.opensecrets.org.

———. 2015b. "Lobbying, Ranked Sectors." *OpenSecrets.org*. www.opensecrets.org.

———. 2015c. "2014 Overview, Totals by Sector." *OpenSecrets.org*. www.opensecrets.org.

———. n.d.-a. "Enron Corp.: Summary." *OpenSecrets.org*. www.opensecrets.org.

———. n.d.-b. "Republican Party: Top Contributors 2000." *OpenSecrets.org*. www. opensecrets.org.

CFTC. 2013a. "CFTC Charges MF Global Inc., MF Global Holdings Ltd., Former CEO Jon S. Corzine, and Former Employee Edith O'Brien for MF Global's Unlawful Misuse of Nearly One Billion Dollars of Customer Funds and Related Violations" (June 13). www.cftc.gov.

———. 2013b. "CFTC v. MF Global et al., 13 Civ. 4463, SDNY, Complaint for Injunctive Relief" (June 27). www.cftc.gov.

Chaudheri, Saabira. 2014a. "J.P. Morgan Whistleblower Gets $64 Million." *Wall Street Journal* (March 7). http://blogs.wsj.com.

———. 2014b. "Ranking the Biggest U.S. Banks: A New Entrant in Top 5." *Wall Street Journal* (September 14). http://blogs.wsj.com.

Chen, Ding & Deakin, Simon. 2015. "On Heaven's Lathe: State, Rule of Law, and Economic Development." *Land & Development Review* 8:123–145. www.degruyter.com.

Chicago Tribune. 2006. "Sizing Up the Enron Era" (May 26). http://articles.chicagotribune.com.

Chittum, Ryan. 2013. "In Obama's Wall Street-Friendly Cabinet, a Clean Sweep for Finance." *Columbia Journalism Review* (November 16). www.cjr.org.

———. 2014. "Going Easy on Eric Holder's Wall Street Inaction." *Columbia Journalism Review* (September 26). www.cjr.org.

Choi, Stephen & Pritchard, Alan. 2008. *Securities Regulation: The Essentials*. New York: Aspen.

CNN. 2002a. "Ashcroft Recuses Himself from Enron Probe" (January 10). http://edition.cnn.com.

———. 2002b. "Bush-Lay Letters Suggest Close Relationship" (February 17). http://edition.cnn.com.

CNN/Money. 2002. "A Chronology of Enron Corp" (January 21). http://money.cnn.com.

Cohan, William. 2015. "High Risk but Little Reward for Whistle-Blowers." *New York Times* (March 26). www.nytimes.com.

Congressional Oversight Panel. 2010. "AIG Rescue, Its Impact on Markets, and the Government's Exit Strategy." Government Printing Office (June 10). www.gpo.gov.

Corporate Fraud Task Force. 2008. "Report to the President." *Justice.gov* (April 2). www.justice.gov/archive/dag/cftf/corporate-fraud2008.pdf.

Corzine, Jon. 2011. "Testimony before the House Committee on Agriculture: MF Global Bankruptcy." *C-SPAN* (December 8). www.c-span.org.

Cox, Jeff. 2015a. "5 Biggest Banks Now Own Almost Half the Industry." *CNBC* (April 15). www.cnbc.com.

———. 2015b. "Too Big to Fail Banks Just Keep Getting Bigger." *CNBC* (March 5). www.cnbc.com.

———. 2016. "Shedding 'Too Big to Fail' Label Was Worth $50 Billion to G.E." *New York Times* (June 29).

C-SPAN. 2009. "The Need for Increased Fraud Enforcement in the Wake of the Economic Downturn" (February 11). www.c-span.org.

Currier, Cora. 2012. "Four Whistleblowers Who Sounded the Alarm on Banks' Mortgage Shenanigans." *ProPublica.org* (March 15). www.propublica.org.

Dayen, David. 2013a. "Bank of America Whistle-Blower's Bombshell: 'We Were Told to Lie.'" *Salon* (June 18). www.salon.com.

———. 2013b. "Wall Street's Greatest Enemy: The Man Who Knows Too Much." *Moyers & Company* (August 30). http://billmoyers.com.

———. 2014a. "Eric Holder Didn't Send a Single Banker to Jail for the Mortgage Crisis. Is That Justice?" *Guardian* (September 25). www.theguardian.com.

———. 2014b. "Massive New Fraud Coverup: How Banks Are Pillaging Homes—While the Government Watches." *Salon* (April 23). www.salon.com.

DealBreaker. 2009. "Opening Bell" (November 12). http://dealbreaker.com.

DOJ. 1997, 2008. "U.S. Attorneys' Manual." *Justice.gov.* www.justice.gov.

———. 1997, 2015. "U.S. Attorneys' Manual." *Justice.gov.* www.justice.gov.

———. 2002a. "Former Enron Chief Financial Officer Andrew S. Fastow Charged with Fraud, Money Laundering and Conspiracy." *Justice.gov* (October 2). www.justice.gov.

———. 2002b. "Former Enron Employee Pleads Guilty to Tax Charge in Kickback Scheme." *Justice.gov* (November 26). www.justice.gov.

———. 2003. "Justice Department Expands Charges Against Former Enron CFO Andrew Fastow, Broadband Executives." *Justice.gov* (May 15). www.justice.gov.

———. 2008. "More Than 400 Defendants Charged for Roles in Mortgage Fraud Schemes as Part of Operation 'Malicious Mortgage.'" *Justice.gov* (June 19). www.justice.gov.

———. 2011a. "Justice Department Reaches $335 Million Settlement to Resolve Allegations of Lending Discrimination by Countrywide Financial Corporation." *Justice.gov* (December). www.justice.gov.

———. 2011b. "United States of America v. Countrywide Financial Corporation et al., Complaint." *Justice.gov* (December 21). www.justice.gov.

———. 2012a. "Federal Government and State Attorneys General Reach $25 Billion Agreement with Five Largest Mortgage Servicers to Address Mortgage Loan Servicing and Foreclosure Abuses." *Justice.gov* (February 9). www.justice.gov.

———. 2012b. "HSBC Holdings Plc. and HSBC Bank USA N.A. Admit to Anti-Money Laundering and Sanctions Violations, Forfeit $1.256 Billion in Deferred Prosecution Agreement." *Justice.gov* (December 11). www.justice.gov.

———. 2012c. "Jimmie Goodgame Was Sentenced to Nearly Six Years in Prison for Laundering More Than $1.5 Million in Drug Proceeds through Numerous Bank

Accounts and the Purchase of More Than 50 Luxury Automobiles." *Justice.gov* (February 2). www.justice.gov.

———. 2012d. "Manhattan U.S. Attorney Files and Simultaneously Settles Fraud Lawsuit Against CitiMortgage, Inc., for Reckless Mortgage Lending Practices." *Justice. gov* (February 15). www.justice.gov.

———. 2012e. "Remarks as Prepared for Delivery by Attorney General Eric Holder at the Distressed Homeowner Initiative Press Conference." *Justice.gov* (October 9). www.justice.gov.

———. 2012f. "UBS Securities Japan Co. Ltd. to Plead Guilty to Felony Wire Fraud for Long-Running Manipulation of LIBOR Benchmark Interest Rates." *Justice.gov* (December 19). www.justice.gov.

———. 2012g. "United States v. HSBC Bank USA, N.A., 2012 WL 6120512 (Deferred Prosecution Agreement)." *Justice.gov* (December 11). www.justice.gov.

———. 2012h. "United States v. HSBC Bank USA, N.A. (E.D.N.Y. Dec. 11, 2012) (Deferred Prosecution Agreement, Attachment A, Statement of Facts)." *Justice.gov* (December 11). www.justice.gov.

———. 2013a. "Justice Department, Federal and State Partners Secure Record $13 Billion Global Settlement with JPMorgan for Misleading Investors about Securities Containing Toxic Mortgages." *Justice.gov* (November 19). www.justice.gov.

———. 2013b. "United States v. HSBC Bank USA, N.A., 2013 WL 3306161." *Justice.gov* (July 1). www.justice.gov.

———. 2014a. "Audit of the Department of Justice's Effort to Address Mortgage Fraud: U.S. Department of Justice Office of the Inspector General Audit Division, Audit Report 14–12." *Justice.gov* (March). https://oig.justice.gov.

———. 2014b. "Bank of America to Pay $16.65 Billion in Historic Justice Department Settlement for Financial Fraud Leading Up to and During the Financial Crisis." *Justice.gov* (August 21). www.justice.gov.

———. 2014c. "JPMorgan Chase to Pay $614 Million for Submitting False Claims for FHA-Insured and VA-Guaranteed Mortgage Loans." *Justice.gov* (February 4). www. justice.gov.

———. 2014d. "Justice Department, Federal and State Partners Secure Record $7 Billion Global Settlement with Citigroup for Misleading Investors about Securities Containing Toxic Mortgages." *Justice.gov* (July 14). www.justice.gov.

———. 2015a. "Deutsche Bank's London Subsidiary Agrees to Plead Guilty in Connection with Long-Running Manipulation of LIBOR." *Justice.gov* (April 23). www. justice.gov.

———. 2015b. "Five Major Banks Agree to Parent-Level Guilty Pleas." *Justice.gov* (May 20). www.justice.gov.

———. 2015c. "Justice Department and State Partners Secure $1.375 Billion Settlement with S&P for Defrauding Investors in the Lead Up to the Financial Crisis." *Justice. gov* (February 3). www.justice.gov.

———. 2015d. "Principles of Federal Prosecution." *Justice.gov*. www.justice.gov.

———. 2016. "New York Investment Fund Managers Plead Guilty for Orchestrating Two Multi-Million Dollar Fraud Schemes." *StopFraud.gov* (February 5). www.stopfraud.gov.

DOJ Inspector General. 2014. "Audit of the Department of Justice Effort's to Address Mortgage Fraud." *Justice.gov* (March). https://oig.justice.gov.

Dugan, John. 2010. "Remarks by John C. Dugan Comptroller of the Currency Before the Exchequer Club Washington, DC, July 21, 2010." *OCC.gov* (July 21). www.occ.gov.

Dwyer, Devin. 2011. "Jon Corzine, Obama 'Partner' and Campaign Financier, Subpoenaed on MF Global Collapse." *ABC News* (December 2). http://abcnews.go.com.

Eaglesham, Jean & Rappaport, Liz. 2011. "Lehman Probe Stalls: Chance of No Charges." *Wall Street Journal* (March 11). www.wsj.com.

Economic Times. 2015. "Five Big Time CEOs Who Are Serving Their Term in Jail" (May 29). http://economictimes.indiatimes.com.

Economist. 2015. "Justice, Interrupted" (May 23). www.economist.com.

Eichenwald, Kurt. 1990. "The Collapse of Drexel Burnham Lambert." *New York Times* (February 14). www.nytimes.com.

———. 2005. "When the Top Seat Is the Hot Seat." *New York Times* (March 15). www.nytimes.com.

Eichler, Alexander. 2012. "Lynn Szymoniak, Foreclosure Victim, Receives $18 Million for Investigating Mortgage Crisis." *Huffington Post* (March 15). www.huffingtonpost.com.

Eisinger, Jesse & Bernstein, Jake. 2010. "The Magnetar Trade: How One Hedge Fund Helped Keep the Bubble Going." *ProPublica.org* (April 9). www.propublica.org.

Elkind, Peter. 2013. "Enron: The Real Story Behind Jeff Skilling's Big Sentence Reduction." *Fortune* (May 15). http://fortune.com.

Emshwiller, John, et al. 2006. "Lay, Skilling Are Convicted of Fraud." *Wall Street Journal* (May 26). www.wsj.com.

Ensign, Rachel Louise & Colchester, Max. 2016. "HSBC Struggles in Battle Against Money Laundering." *Wall Street Journal* (January 12). www.wsj.com.

Farzad, Roben. 2011. "MF Global's Jon Corzine Runs Out of Luck." *Bloomberg* (November 2). www.bloomberg.com.

FBI. 2006. "Crime in the Suites: A Look Back at the Enron Case." *FBI.gov* (December 13). www.fbi.gov.

FCIC. 2011. "The Financial Crisis Inquiry Report" (January). Washington, DC: US Government Printing Office. http://fcic.law.stanford.edu.

FCIC CDO Library. 2011. "Final Term Sheet Abacus 2007-AC-1, July 1, 2007." http://fcic-static.law.stanford.edu.

FDIC. 2014a. "FDIC Announces Settlement with Citi Entities: Settlement of RMBS Claims Totals $208.2 Million." *FDIC.gov* (July 14). www.fdic.gov.

———. 2014b. "FDIC Announces Settlement with JPMorgan Chase & Co. Settlement of RMBS Claims Totals $515.4 million." *FDIC.gov* (November 13). www.fdic.gov.

Federal Housing Finance Authority v. Nomura Holding America, Inc. 2015. Opinion and Order, 11civ6201 (DLC). US District Court for the Southern District of New York (May 11). www.nysd.uscourts.gov.

Federal Reserve. 2003. "Written Agreement by and among HSBC Bank USA Buffalo, New York, Federal Reserve Bank of New York, New York and New York State Banking Department, New York." *FederalReserve.gov* (April 30). www.federalreserve.gov.

Federal Reserve Bank of St. Louis. 2012. "In-Depth: The Big Banks: Too Complex to Manage?" *StLouisFed.org* (Winter). www.stlouisfed.org.

Fetini, Alyssa. 2008. "A Brief History of the Keating Five." *Time* (October 8). http://content.time.com.

Fitzgerald, Alison. 2013. "Ex-Wall Street Chieftains Living Large in Post-meltdown World." Center for Public Integrity (September 10). www.publicintegrity.org.

Fitzgerald, Patrick. 2015. "Ernst & Young Settles Lehman Suits with New Jersey, California Municipalities." *Wall Street Journal* (March 13). www.wsj.com.

Fleischmann, Alayne. 2014. "JPMorgan Settlement Not Enough, Says Whistleblower." *CNBC* (November 12). www.cnbc.com.

Flitter, Emily. 2015. "Exclusive: Upset by Warren, U.S. Banks Debate Halting Some Campaign Donations." Reuters (March 27). www.reuters.com.

Foster, Eileen. 2012. "Obama Administration Needs to Tap, Not Stiff-Arm, Wall Street Whistleblowers." *Rolling Stone* (August 9). www.rollingstone.com.

Freifeld, Karen. 2015. "Ernst & Young Settles with N.Y. for $10 Million over Lehman Auditing." Reuters (April 15). www.reuters.com.

Frieden, Terry. 2004. "FBI Warns of Mortgage 'Epidemic.'" *CNN* (September 17). http://edition.cnn.com.

Frye, Andrew & Son, Hugh. 2011. "Cassano's Pay at AIG Peaked at $44.6 Million in 2003." *Bloomberg* (February 10). www.bloomberg.com.

Garrett, Brandon. 2014. *Too Big to Jail.* Cambridge, MA: Harvard University Press.

Garrett, Brandon & Ashley, Jon. 2016. "Federal Organizational Prosecution Agreements." University of Virginia School of Law. http://lib.law.virginia.edu.

Gasparino, Charles. 2009. *The Sellout: How Three Decades of Wall Street Greed and Government Mismanagement Destroyed the Global Financial System.* New York: HarperCollins.

Gilchrist, Gregory M. 2014. "The Special Problem of Banks and Crime." *Colorado Law Review* 85:1. http://lawreview.colorado.edu.

Glaeser, Edward L. & Schleifer, Andrei. 2003. "The Injustice of Inequality." *Journal of Monetary Economics* 50:199. www.nber.org.

Global-Tech Appliances, Inc. v. SEB S.A., 563 U.S. 754, 151 S.Ct. 2060, 2069–70 (2011). www.supremecourt.gov.

Goldfarb, Zachery & Markon, Jerry. 2010. "Justice Probe of Goldman Goes Beyond Deals Cited by SEC." *Washington Post* (May 1). www.washingtonpost.com.

Goldstein, Matthew. 2014a. "Arbitrators Ease Blame on Ernst & Young for Audits of Lehman Brothers." *New York Times DealBook* (August 11). http://dealbook.nytimes.com.

———. 2014b. "A Second Bank of America Whistle-Blower Is Set to Get $56 Million." *New York Times DealBook* (December 18). http://dealbook.nytimes.com.

Government Accountability Office. 2014. "Foreclosure Review: Regulators Could Strengthen Oversight and Improve Transparency of the Process." *GAO.gov* (April). www.gao.gov.

Green, Stuart. 2007. "The Coverup Paradox." *Boston Globe* (March 8). www.boston.com.

Grim, Ryan & Nasiripour, Shahien. 2013. "Eric Schneiderman Challenges Obama Administration over Mortgage Investigations." *Huffington Post* (April 24). www.huffingtonpost.com.

Hamilton, Jesse & Hopkins, Cheyenne. 2013. "Senators Call Justice Department Response on HSBC Fine 'Evasive.'" *Bloomberg* (March 1). www.bloomberg.com.

Hamilton, Walter & Reckard, E. Scott. 2010. "Angelo Mozilo, Other Former Countrywide Execs Settle Fraud Charges." *Los Angeles Times* (October 16). http://articles.latimes.com.

Hasen, Richard. 2012. "Worse Than Watergate." *Slate* (July 19). www.slate.com.

Hatch, Orrin. 2002. *Square Peg*. New York: Basic Books.

Hayes, Chris. 2014. "'I Couldn't Understand Why They Were Doing This': JPMorgan Whistle-Blower and Matt Taibbi Sound Off on MSNBC." *Salon.com* (November 11). www.salon.com.

Hays, Kristen. 2006. "2 Former Enron Executives Receive Prison Terms." *Houston Chronicle* (November 17). www.chron.com.

Henning, Peter. 2012. "UBS Settlement Minimizes Impact of Guilty Plea." *New York Times DealBook* (December 20). http://dealbook.nytimes.com.

Herz, Robert H. 2010. "Testimony of Robert H. Herz, Chairman Financial Accounting Standards Board before the U.S. House of Representatives Financial Services Subcommittee on Capital Markets, Insurance, and Government Sponsored Entities, Accounting & Auditing Standards: Pending Proposals & Emerging Issues." *FASB.org* (May 21). www.fasb.org.

H.J. Inc. v. Northwestern Bell Telephone Co., 492 U.S. 229 (1989). www.law.cornell.edu.

House Committee on Oversight and Government Reform. 2010. "The Federal Bailout of AIG." *House.gov* (January 27). http://oversight.house.gov.

House Minority Report. 2002. "Bush Administration Contacts with Enron: Prepared for Rep. Henry A. Waxman Minority Staff Special Investigations Division Committee on Government Reform U.S. House of Representatives" (May 2002). www.yuricareport.com.

Houston Chronicle. 2011. "The Defendants of the Enron Era and Their Cases" (November 25). www.chron.com.

Hurtado, Patricia. 2013. "BofA's Countrywide Found Liable for Defrauding Fannie Mae." *Bloomberg* (October 25). www.bloomberg.com.

———. 2016. "Ex-Goldman Director Rajat Gupta Back Home after Prison Stay." *Bloomberg* (January 19). www.bloomberg.com.

Illinois Attorney General. 2008. "Illinois Attorney General Madigan Leads $8.7 Billion Groundbreaking Settlement of Lawsuit Against Mortgage Giant Countrywide." *IllinoisAttorneyGeneral.gov* (October 6). www.illinoisattorneygeneral.gov.

———. 2014. "Madigan Announces Record $300 Million for Illinois' Pension Systems, Consumers in Bank of America Settlement." *IllinoisAttorneyGeneral.gov* (August 21). www.illinoisattorneygeneral.gov.

Ingram, David. 2012. "Justice Department Will Not Prosecute Goldman Sachs, Employees for Abacus Deal." Reuters (August 9). www.reuters.com.

In re AIG, Inc. 2008 Securities Fraud Litigation. 2009. Consolidated Class Action Complaint. *Securities.Stanford.edu* (May 19). http://securities.stanford.edu.

In re AIG, Inc. 2008 Securities Litigation 2010, 741 F. Supp. 2d 511 (SDNY 2010).

In re Citigroup Securities Fraud Litigation, 753 F. Supp. 2d 206, 212 (SDNY 2010).

In re Global Crossing Ltd. Securities Litigation, 322 F. Supp. 2d 319, 331 (SDNY 2004).

In re Lehman Bros. Securities and ERISA Litigation, 799 F.Supp.2d 258 (SDNY 2011).

International Monetary Fund. 2014. "Big Banks Benefit From Government Subsidies." *IMF.org* (March 31). www.imf.org.

Ivry, Bob. 2012. "Woman Who Couldn't Be Intimidated by Citigroup Wins $31 Million." *Bloomberg* (May 30). www.bloomberg.com.

Jaffe, Alexandra. 2015. "Base Wary of Clinton Foundation's Ties to Troubled Banks." *CNN* (March 3). www.cnn.com.

Jefferson, Thomas. 1785/1953. "Letter from Thomas Jefferson to James Madison (Oct. 28, 1785)." In *The Papers of Thomas Jefferson*, ed. Julian P. Boyd et al. Princeton: Princeton University Press. http://press-pubs.uchicago.edu.

———. 1816. "Thomas Jefferson's Note for Destutt de Tracy's Treatise on Political Economy (ca. 6 April 1816)." National Archives, *Founders Online*. http://founders.archives.gov.

Johnson, Carrie. 2005. "Ebbers Gets 25-Year Sentence for Role in WorldCom Fraud." *Washington Post* (July 1). www.washingtonpost.com.

Kaletsky, Anatole. 2010. *Capitalism 4.0*. Philadelphia: Public Affairs.

Kessler, Aaron. 2015. "Newly Released Documents Reveals Advice to Fed in A.I.G. Bailout." *New York Times* (February 20). www.nytimes.com.

Kidney, James. 2014. "Retirement Remarks." *SECUnion.org* (April 14). www.secunion.org.

Kuykendall, Lavonne. 2007. "AIG Comfortable with Mortgage-Market Exposure." *MarketWatch.com* (August 9). www.marketwatch.com.

Lattman, Peter. 2009. "The U.S.'s Fly on the Wall at AIG." *Wall Street Journal* (March 27). www.wsj.com.

Lehman Brothers. 2007a. "Lehman Brothers Company Overview (Third Quarter)." http://web.stanford.edu.

———. 2007b. "Q4 2007 Preliminary Lehman Brothers Holdings Inc. Earnings Conference Call." *Thomson Street Events* (December 13). http://web.stanford.edu.

———. 2008a. "Q1 2008 Preliminary Lehman Brothers Holdings Inc. Earnings Conference Call." *Thomson Street Events* (March 18). http://jenner.com.

——. 2008b. "Q2 2008 Lehman Brothers Holdings Inc. Earnings Conference Call." *Thomson Street Events* (June 16). http://web.stanford.edu.

——. 2008c. "Q3 2008 Preliminary Lehman Brothers Holdings Inc. Earnings Conference Call." *Thomson Street Events* (September 10). http://jenner.com.

Lewis, Mark. 2002. "WorldCom: Is Bernie Still Bulletproof?" *Forbes* (February 6). www.forbes.com.

Lipton, Eric & Labaton, Stephen. 2008. "Deregulator Looks Back, Unswayed." *New York Times* (November 18). www.nytimes.com.

Looney, J. Jefferson, ed. 2012. *The Papers of Thomas Jefferson. Retirement Series, vol. 9, September 1815 to 1816*. Princeton: Princeton University Press.

Lustiger v. United States, 386 F.2d 132, 138 (9th Cir. 1967).

Mamudi, Sam & Kennedy, Simon. 2009. "AIG Details $105 Billion in Payouts." *MarketWatch.com* (March 16). www.marketwatch.com.

Marbury v. Madison, 5 U.S. 137 (1803).

Massie, Gordon. 2010. *The Whistle Blower's Dilemma: Confronting Fraud at AIG*. Houston, TX: Kingsley Literary.

Mazur, Robert. 2013. "How to Halt the Terrorist Money Train." *New York Times* (January 2). www.nytimes.com.

McCaffery, Edward & Cohen, Linda. 2004. "Shakedown at Gucci Gulch: A Tale of Death, Money & Taxes." *North Carolina Law Review* 84:1159–1252.

McDade, Bart. 2008. "E-mail Sent to Hyung S. Lee Regarding Repo 105" (April 3). http://web.stanford.edu.

McDonnell v. United States, 136 S.Ct. 2355, 579 U.S. ___ (2016).

McLannahan, Ben. 2015. "Banks' Post-crisis Legal Costs Hit $300bn." *Financial Times* (June 8). www.ft.com.

Morgenson, Gretchen. 2007. "Inside the Countrywide Lending Spree." *New York Times* (August 25). www.nytimes.com.

——. 2008. "Countrywide to Set Aside $8.4 Billion in Loan Aid." *New York Times* (October 5). www.nytimes.com.

——. 2011. "Case on Mortgage Official Is Said to Be Dropped." *New York Times* (February 19). www.nytimes.com.

——. 2016. "Kid Gloves for a Bank with Clout." *New York Times* (July 17). www.nytimes.com.

Morgenson, Gretchen & Story, Louise. 2010. "Testy Conflict with Goldman Helped Push A.I.G. to Edge." *New York Times* (February 6). www.nytimes.com.

Mullins, Brody, Nicholas, Peter, & Ballhaus, Rebecca. 2014. "The Bill and Hillary Clinton Money Machine Taps Corporate Cash." *Wall Street Journal* (July 1). www.wsj.com.

NBC News. 2011. "Foreclosure Fraud Whistleblower Found Dead" (November 29). http://usnews.nbcnews.com.

Neder v. United States, 527 U.S. 1 (1999).

Neumann, Jeannette. 2013. "Cost of Ratings Suit: $225 Million." *Wall Street Journal* (April 29). www.wsj.com.

New York Central & Hudson River Railroad Company v. United States, 212 U.S. 481, 492, 495–96 (1909).

New York Times. 1993. "Ex-Chief of Centrust Bank Is Convicted on 68 Charges" (November 25). www.nytimes.com.

———. 1994. "11-Year Sentence for Chief of Failed S. & L." (December 2). www.nytimes.com.

———. 2011. "Two Financial Crises Compared: The Savings and Loan Debacle and the Mortgage Mess" (April 13). www.nytimes.com.

———. 2012a. "Friends of Angelo, Part 2" (January 21). www.nytimes.com.

———. 2012b. "No Crime, No Punishment" (August 25). www.nytimes.com.

———. 2012c. "Too Big to Indict" (December 11). www.nytimes.com.

Office of the Comptroller of the Currency. 2010. "In the Matter of: HSBC Bank USA, N.A. McLean, Virginia." *OCC.gov* (September 24). www.occ.gov.

———. 2011a. "In the Matter of: Citibank, N.A., Las Vegas, Nevada." *OCC.gov* (March 29). www.occ.gov.

———. 2011b. "In the Matter of: JPMorgan Chase Bank, N.A., New York, NY." *OCC.gov* (March 31). www.occ.gov.

Olson, Mancur. 1971. *The Logic of Collective Action: Public Goods and the Theory of Groups*. Cambridge, MA: Harvard University Press.

O'Toole, James. 2012. "Explaining the Libor Interest Rate Mess." *CNN/Money* (July 10). http://money.cnn.com.

Paltrow, Scot. 1988. "Drexel Seeks a Settlement to Avoid Charge of Racketeering." *Los Angeles Times* (November 24). http://articles.latimes.com.

———. 2012. "Insight: Top Justice Officials Connected to Mortgage Banks." Reuters (January 20). www.reuters.com.

Paltrow, Scot & Brown, Tom. 2011. "Special Report: Banks Continue Robo-Signing." Reuters (July 18). www.reuters.com.

Patterson, Scott, Lucchetti, Aaron, & Trindle, Jamila. 2013. "Corzine, O'Brien Charged in MF Global Collapse." *Wall Street Journal* (June 28). http://online.wsj.com.

PBS. 2013a. "Lanny Breuer: Financial Fraud Has Not Gone Unpunished." *Frontline* (January 22). www.pbs.org.

———. 2013b. "The Untouchables." *Frontline* (January 22). www.pbs.org.

People v. Ernst & Young, LLP. 2010. No. 451586 (NY Supreme Court, December 21) (Complaint).

Picketty, Thomas. 2014. *Capital in the Twenty-First Century*. Cambridge, MA: Belknap.

Pleven, Liam & Efreti, Amir. 2008. "Documents Show AIG Knew of Problems with Valuations." *Wall Street Journal* (October 11). www.wsj.com.

Podgor, Ellen, Henning, Peter, Israel, Jerold, & King, Nancy. 2013. *White Collar Crime*. St. Paul, MN: West.

Preston, Julia. 2013. "Huge Amount Spent on Immigration, Study Finds." *New York Times* (January 7). www.nytimes.com.

Protess, Ben. 2014. "MF Global Customers to Be Paid Back in Full." *New York Times DealBook* (April 3). http://dealbook.nytimes.com.

Protess, Ben & Corkery, Michael. 2015. "5 Big Banks Expected to Plead Guilty to Felony Charges, but Punishments May Be Tempered." *New York Times* (May 13). www.nytimes.com.

Protess, Ben & Craig, Susanne. 2013. "Inside the End of the U.S. Bid to Punish Lehman Executives." *New York Times DealBook* (September 8). http://dealbook.nytimes.com.

Pulliam, Susan & Solomon, Deborah. 2002. "How Three Unlikely Sleuths Exposed Fraud at WorldCom." *Wall Street Journal* (October 30). www.wsj.com.

Puzzanghera, Jim. 2013. "Ten Banks to Pay $8.5 Billion to Settle Foreclosure Abuse Review." *Los Angeles Times* (January 7). http://articles.latimes.com.

Raghaven, Anita. 2002. "How a Bright Star at Andersen Burned Out along with Enron." *Wall Street Journal* (May 15). www.wsj.com.

Ramirez, Mary Kreiner. 2003. "Just in Crime: Guiding Economic Crime Reform after the Sarbanes-Oxley Act of 2002." *Loyola University Chicago Law Journal* 34:359–427.

———. 2005. "The Science-Fiction of Corporate Criminal Liability: Containing the Machine through the Corporate Death Penalty." *Arizona Law Review* 47:933–1002.

———. 2010. "Prioritizing Justice: Combating Corporate Crime from Task Force to Top Priority." *Marquette Law Review* 93:971–1017.

———. 2013. "Criminal Affirmance: Going Beyond the Deterrence Paradigm to Examine the Social Meaning of Declining Prosecution of Elite Crime." *Connecticut Law Review* 45:865–930.

Ramirez, Steven A. 2003. "The Law and Macroeconomics of the New Deal at 70." *Maryland Law Review* 62:515–572.

———. 2009. "Lessons from the Subprime Debacle: Stress Testing CEO Autonomy." *Saint Louis University Law Journal* 54:1–54.

———. 2012. "Why President Obama Must Deal with the Megabanks." *Corporate Justice Blog* (November 21). http://corporatejusticeblog.blogspot.com.

———. 2013a. *Lawless Capitalism: The Subprime Crisis and the Case for an Economic Rule of Law.* New York: New York University Press.

———. 2013b. "Megabankers Face a 10 Year Statute of Limitations." *Corporate Justice Blog* (July 26). http://corporatejusticeblog.blogspot.com.

———. 2014. "The Virtues of Private Securities Litigation: An Historic and Macroeconomic Perspective." *Loyola University Chicago Law Journal* 45:669–737.

Rapaport, Michael. 2013. "Ernst & Young Agrees to Pay $99 Million in Lehman Settlement." *Wall Street Journal* (October 18). www.wsj.com/articles/SB10001424052702304384104579143811517891526.

Rappaport, Liz & Mullins, Brody. 2012. "Goldman Turns Tables on Obama Campaign." *Wall Street Journal* (October 10). www.wsj.com.

Raymond, Nate & Pierson, Brendan. 2015. "UPDATE 2-AIG Investors' $970.5 Mln Settlement Wins US Court Approval." *Reuters* (March 20). www.reuters.com.

Raymond, Nate & Stempel, Jonathan. 2013. "Moody's, S&P Settle Lawsuits over Debt Vehicle Ratings." *Reuters* (April 27). www.reuters.com.

Reckard, Scott & Rosenzweig, David. 1999. "Keating Pleads Guilty to Fraud: Legal Saga Ends." *Los Angeles Times* (April 7). http://articles.latimes.com.

Rexrode, Christina & Martin, Timothy. 2014. "Whistleblowers Score a Big Payday." *Wall Street Journal* (December 19). www.wsj.com.

Roe, John & Koutoulas, James. 2011. "White Paper: Background, Impacts & Solutions to MF Global's Demise." Commodity Customer Coalition (December 1). www.btrtrading.com.

Rucker, Philip, Hamburger, Tom, & Becker, Alexander. 2014. "How the Clintons Went from 'Dead Broke' to Rich: Bill Earned $104.9 Million for Speeches." *Washington Post* (June 26). www.washingtonpost.com.

Saez, Emmanuel. 2016. "Striking It Richer: The Evolution of Top Incomes in the United States (Updated with 2015 Preliminary Estimates)." Working paper (June 30). http://eml.berkeley.edu.

Scheck, Howard. 2010. "Speech by SEC Staff: Remarks before the 2010 AICPA National Conference on Current SEC and PCAOB Developments." *SEC.gov* (December 6). www.sec.gov.

Schoenberg, Tom & Farrell, Greg. 2014. "Enron Buster Is Back at Justice Taking Aim at Bankers Now." *Bloomberg* (September 12). www.bloomberg.com.

Schwartz, Nelson & Dash, Eric. 2008. "Where Was the Wise Man?" *New York Times* (April 27). www.nytimes.com.

SDNY. 2013. "Final Consent Order of Restitution, Civil Monetary Penalty, and Ancillary Relief, CFTC v. MF Global Inc., No. 11-CIV-7866" (November 8). www.cftc.gov.

———. 2014. "SEC v. Fabrice Tourre, 10 Civ. 3229 (KBF), Opinion and Order." *SDNY-blog.com* (January 7). http://sdnyblog.com.

SEC. 2002. "Certification of Disclosure in Companies' Quarterly and Annual Reports." *SEC.gov* (August 28). www.sec.gov.

———. 2009. "Securities and Exchange Commission v. Angelo Mozilo, David Sambol and Eric Sieracki: Complaint for Violations of the Federal Securities Laws." *SEC.gov* (June 4). www.sec.gov.

———. 2010a. "Former Countrywide CEO Angelo Mozilo to Pay SEC's Largest-Ever Financial Penalty Against a Public Company's Senior Executive." *SEC.gov* (October 15). www.sec.gov.

———. 2010b. "Goldman Sachs to Pay Record $550 Million to Settle SEC Charges Related to Subprime Mortgage CDO." *SEC.gov* (July 15). www.sec.gov.

———. 2010c. "SEC Charges Citigroup and Two Executives for Misleading Investors about Exposure to Subprime Mortgage Assets." *SEC.gov* (July 29). www.sec.gov.

———. 2010d. "SEC v. Goldman Sachs & Co. and Fabrice Tourre, 10 Civ. 3229 (S.D.N.Y.) (Complaint)." *SEC.gov* (April 16). www.sec.gov.

———. 2011a. "Citigroup to Pay $285 Million to Settle SEC Charges for Misleading Investors about CDO Tied to Housing Market." *SEC.gov* (October 19). www.sec.gov.

———. 2011b. "J.P. Morgan to Pay $153.6 Million to Settle SEC Charges of Misleading Investors in CDO Tied to U.S. Housing Market." *SEC.gov* (June 21). www.sec.gov.

———. 2012. "SEC Charges J.P. Morgan and Credit Suisse with Misleading Investors in RMBS Offerings." *SEC.gov* (November 16). www.sec.gov.

———. 2013a. "SEC Charges Royal Bank of Scotland Subsidiary with Misleading Investors in Subprime RMBS Offering." *SEC.gov* (November 7). www.sec.gov.

———. 2013b. "SEC Charges Bank of America with Fraud in RMBS Offering." *SEC.gov* (August 6). www.sec.gov.

———. 2013c. "SEC Charges Merrill Lynch with Misleading Investors in CDOs." *SEC. gov* (December 12). www.sec.gov.

———. 2013d. "Statement on the Tourre Verdict." *SEC.gov* (August 1). www.sec.gov.

———. 2014. "Bank of America Admits Disclosure Failures to Settle SEC Charges: Bank Also Resolves Separate SEC Case in $245 Million Settlement." *SEC.gov* (August 21). www.sec.gov.

———. 2015a. "Dissenting Statement Regarding Certain Waivers Granted by the Commission for Certain Entities Pleading Guilty to Criminal Charges Involving Manipulation of Foreign Exchange Rates." *SEC.gov* (May 21). www.sec.gov.

———. 2015b. "In the Matter of Harding Advisory LLC and Wing F. Chau, Initial Decision January 12, 2015." *SEC.gov* (January 12). www.sec.gov.

Sidney L. Gold & Associates. 2012. "Philadelphia Qui Tam Attorneys Report on Whistleblower Case Netting Largest False Claim Suit Settlement" (August 6). www. discrimlaw.net.

Siemaszko, Corky. 2008. "Lehman Brothers Big Shots Hit with Subpoenas: CEO Richard Fuld Reportedly Targeted." *New York Daily News* (October 17). www.nydaily-news.com.

Smith, Adam. 1776. *An Inquiry into the Nature and Causes of the Wealth of Nations.* London: Methuen.

Smith, Yves. 2010. "Rahm Emanuel and Magnetar Capital: The Definition of Compromised." *Huffington Post* (June 13). www.huffingtonpost.com.

Staff Report, US House of Representatives. 2012. "How Countrywide Used Its VIP Loan Program to Influence Washington Policymakers." *House.gov* (July 5). http://oversight.house.gov.

———. 2016. "Too Big to Jail: Inside the Obama Justice Department's Decision Not to Hold Wall Street Accountable." *House.gov* (July 11). http://oversight.house.gov.

Stein, Kara. 2015. "Dissenting Statement Regarding Certain Waivers Granted by the Commission for Certain Entities Pleading Guilty to Criminal Charges Involving Manipulation of Foreign Exchange Rates." *SEC.gov* (May 21). www.sec.gov.

Stemple, Jonathan. 2010. "Judge OKs Countrywide, KPMG $624 Mln Settlement." Reuters (August 2). www.reuters.com.

Stendahl, Max. 2014. "Magnetar Case Puts New Spin on SEC Revolving Door." *Law360* (January 8). www.law360.com.

Sterngold, James. 2010. "How Much Did Lehman CEO Dick Fuld Really Make?" *Bloomberg* (April 29). www.bloomberg.com.

Stiglitz, Joseph E. 2012. *The Price of Inequality: How Today's Divided Society Endangers Our Future.* New York: Norton.

———. 2015. *The Great Divide: Unequal Societies and What We Can Do about Them.* New York: Norton.

Story, Louise. 2009. "Cuomo Details Million-Dollar Bonuses at A.I.G." *New York Times* (March 17). www.nytimes.com.

Suskind, Ronald. 2011. *Confidence Men.* New York: Harper.

Tadena, Nathalie. 2012. "Gramm Retires as UBS Investment-Bank Officer." *Wall Street Journal* (February 12). www.wsj.com.

Taibbi, Matt. 2015a. "Eric Holder, Wall Street Double Agent, Comes in from the Cold." *Rolling Stone* (July 8). www.rollingstone.com.

———. 2015b. "A Whistleblower's Horror Story." *Rolling Stone* (February 18). www.rollingstone.com.

Teitelbaum, Richard. 2010. "Secret AIG Document Shows Goldman Sachs Minted Most Toxic CDOs." *Bloomberg* (February 23). www.bloomberg.com

Tor, Maria & Sarfaz, Saad. 2013. "Largest 100 Banks in the World." *SNL Financial* (December 23). www.snl.com.

Torres, Alec. 2013. "Hillary Clinton's Lucrative Goldman Sachs Speaking Gigs." *National Review* (October 30). www.nationalreview.com.

United States ex rel. Edwards v. JP Morgan Chase Bank, N.A., 13-CV-0220, First Amended Complaint, SDNY (2013).

United States ex rel. Hunt v. CitiMortgage (SDNY 2012).

United States ex rel. O'Donnell v. Countrywide Home Loans, Inc., Complaint-in-Intervention of the United States of America. 2012.

United States ex rel. O'Donnell v. Countrywide Home Loans, Inc., 33 F.Supp.3d 494 (SDNY 2014).

United States ex rel. O'Donnell v. Countrywide Home Loans, Inc., 822 F.3d 650 (2nd Cir. 2016).

United States v. Bank of New England, 821 F.2d 844 (1st Cir. 1987).

United States v. Clay, 618 F.3d 946 (8th Cir. 2010).

United States v. Dotterweich, 320 U.S. 277, 280–81 (1943).

United States v. Ebbers, 458 F.3d 110 (2nd Cir. 2006).

United States v. Gruenberg, 989 F.2d 971 (8th Cir. 1993).

United States v. Heinz, 790 F.3d 365 (2d Cir. 2015) (per curiam), cert. denied 2016 WL 100384 (January 11, 2016).

United States v. Park, 421 U.S. 658, 674 (1973).

US Senate. 2011. "Wall Street and the Financial Crisis: Anatomy of a Financial Crisis" (April 13). www.hsgac.senate.gov.

Valukas, Anton. 2010. "Report of Anton R. Valukas, Examiner, In re Lehman Brothers Holdings Inc., et al. Debtors." Southern District of New York, Bankruptcy Court (March 11). https://jenner.com.

———. 2012. "Interview of Anton Valukas: The Case Against Lehman Brothers." *60 Minutes, CBS News* (April 23). www.cbsnews.com.

vanden Heuvel, Katrina. 2014. "Eric Schneiderman Is Still Seeking Justice for the Financial Crisis." *Washington Post* (October 7). www.washingtonpost.com.

Van Voris, Bob. 2014. "Rajat Gupta Agrees to Surrender to Prison on June 17." *Bloomberg* (April 17). www.bloomberg.com.

Van Voris, Bob & Hurtado, Patricia. 2013. "Tourre's Junior Staff Defense Seen Leading to Trial Loss." *Bloomberg* (August 2). www.bloomberg.com.

Viswanatha, Aruna. 2015. "Banks to Pay $5.6 Billion in Probes." *Wall Street Journal* (May 20). www.wsj.com.

Viswanatha, Aruna & Tracy, Ryan. 2016. "Financial-Crisis Panel Suggested Criminal Cases Against Stan O'Neal, Charles Prince, AIG Bosses." *Wall Street Journal* (March 30).

Viswanatha, Aruna & Wolf, Brett. 2012. "HSBC to Pay $1.9 billion U.S. Fine in Money-Laundering Case." Reuters (December 11). www.reuters.com.

Wall Street Journal. 2009. "The Secret 'Friends of Angelo'" (June 25). www.wsj.com.

———. 2013. "Jack Lew's Golden Parachute: His Citigroup Contract Paid Him a Bonus for Returning to Government" (February 26). www.wsj.com.

Weil, Jonathon & Barrionuevo, Alexei. 2002. "Arthur Andersen Is Convicted on Obstruction-of-Justice Count." *Wall Street Journal* (June 16). www.wsj.com.

Weise, Karen. 2013. "Mortgage Fraud Whistle-Blower Lynn Szymoniak Exposed Robo-signing's Sins." *Bloomberg* (September 12). www.bloomberg.com.

Weissmann, Jordan. 2011. "Countrywide's Racist Lending Practices Were Fueled by Greed." *Atlantic* (December). www.theatlantic.com.

White House, Office of the Press Secretary. 2011. "News Conference by the President." *WhiteHouse.gov* (October 6). www.whitehouse.gov.

Wong, Grace. 2005. "Kozlowski Gets up to 25 Years." *CNN/Money* (September 19). http://money.cnn.com.

Yates, Sally Quillian. 2015. "Individual Accountability for Corporate Wrongdoing." Office of the Deputy Attorney General (September 9). www.justice.gov.

Zardkoohi, Asghar, Kang, Eugene, Fraser, Donald, & Cannella, Albert A. 2016. "Managerial Risk-Taking Behavior: A Too-Big-to-Fail Story." *Journal of Business Ethics*. http://link.springer.com.

Zuill, Lilla & Somerville, Glenn. 2009. "AIG Enters Record Books with $61.7 Billion Loss." Reuters (March 2). www.reuters.com.

INDEX

Abacus, 155–158, 169, 172, 175; jury finding of civil securities fraud, 160–167

Abacus 2004-1, 167–168

ABN Bank, 167

Abu Dhabi Commercial Bank, 104–105

ACA Management LLC, 155, 163, 164–167

adversarial criminal trials, xi–xiii, 26–27, 198, 204–205, 207, 211–212, 226

AIG, 25, 133–154, 161; AIG Financial Products (AIGFP), 134–152; audit committee, 142, 147; Cassano, Joseph, 135, 138–139, 143–145, 147, 149–154; civil fraud settlements, 136–137, 145–149, 154; credit rating, 134, 136, 139, 145, 151; deferred prosecution agreements, 148; Enterprise Risk Management, 141; Goldman Sachs, 168–169, 174, 176; negative basis adjustment, 142; SEC disclosures, 142–145; shareholder losses, 133–134, 145; subprime mortgages, 133–142

AIG Financial Products (AIGFP), 134–152

American Express, 214

Angelides, Phil, 178

apathy, 225–226, 228

Arthur Andersen: Enron, 34, 42, 44; Sunbeam Corporation, 43; Waste Management, 43

Ashcroft, John, 55

AT&T, 44

Ayers, David, 55

bailout, 93, 135, 139, 150, 168–169, 174, 176, 180, 215

Bank Holding Company Act, 12–13

Bank of America Corporation, 100–103, 108, 183, 206, 214; AIG, 134; civil fraud settlements, 2, 25, 59, 66, 71, 100–102, 181; Covington & Burling, 55; successor to Countrywide, 63, 72

Bank of America, NA, 102, 182

Bank Secrecy Act, 195; money laundering, 50, 195

Barclays: LIBOR guilty plea, 191–192; money laundering, 198

Bear Stearns, 54, 56, 97, 106, 110, 111, 127, 211

Belden, Timothy, 35

Bensinger, Steven, 138

Berardino, Joseph, 34

Bernanke, Ben, 133; individual responsibility for crisis, 1

bid rigging, 5

Bilderberg Group, 186

Black, Bill, 17, 29, 56

Blankfein, Lloyd, 168, 169, 175

Boesky, Ivan, 39, 207, 211

Boland, John, 64

bonus compensation, 62, 92, 93, 96, 123, 135, 138–139, 148, 152, 183, 194, 199

Bowen, Richard, 91–92, 94–96, 206

break up megabanks, 10, 14–16, 95, 157–159, 179, 223–225

Breuer, Lanny, 205–206; appearance of impropriety, 55–57; collateral consequences, 196–199; Covington & Burling, 214; too-big-to-jail, 200

bribery, 80–81

ABOUT THE AUTHORS

Mary Kreiner Ramirez is Professor of Law at Washburn University School of Law. She is a former Prosecutor for the Department of Justice Antitrust Division, where she prosecuted white-collar criminals, and a former Assistant US Attorney for the District of Kansas. She has published numerous articles addressing the challenges in combating white-collar crime.

Steven A. Ramirez is Professor of Law and Associate Dean at Loyola University of Chicago, where he also serves as Director of the Business Law Center. This is the second book he has authored relating to the subprime mortgage crisis and its meaning in terms of the rule of law. He previously served as an Enforcement Attorney for the Securities and Exchange Commission and a Senior Attorney for the Federal Deposit Insurance Corporation.